D1059006

BIG CHIEF ELIZABETH

ALSO BY GILES MILTON

The Riddle and the Knight: In Search of Sir John Mandeville

Nathaniel's Nutmeg: or The True and Incredible Adventures of the
Spice Trader Who Changed the Course of History

BIG CHIEF ELIZABETH

The Adventures and

Fate of the First

English Colonists

in America

GILES MILTON

FARRAR, STRAUS AND GIROUX

NEW YORK

12/00

$74.00

Farrar, Straus and Giroux
19 Union Square West, New York 10003

Copyright © 2000 by Giles Milton
All rights reserved
Printed in the United States of America
Originally published in 2000 by Hodder & Stoughton, Great Britain
Published in the United States by Farrar, Straus and Giroux
First American edition, 2000

Library of Congress Cataloging-in-Publication Data
Milton, Giles.
    Big Chief Elizabeth : the adventures and fate of the first English colonists
in America / Giles Milton.
        p.   cm.
    Includes index.
    ISBN 0-374-26501-1
    1. Indians of North America—First contact with Europeans.   2. Indians,
Treatment of—North America.   3. Indians of North America—Govern-
ment relations.   4. Elizabeth I, Queen of England, 1533–1603.   5. Great
Britain—Colonies—America.   6. Great Britain—Foreign relations—
United States.   7. America—Discovery and exploration—English.

E98.F39 M55   2000
970'.00497—dc21

                                                                00-031522

The publisher is grateful for permission to use the following illustrations: Walter
Ralegh and son; Sir Richard Grenville: National Portrait Gallery, London.
Thomas Harriot: The President and Fellows of Trinity College, Oxford. Pocahon-
tas: The British Museum.

FOR MY FATHER

CONTENTS

ACKNOWLEDGEMENTS   x

1. SAVAGES AMONG THE ICEBERGS   5

2. SIR HUMFREY AND THE CANNIBALS   16

3. THE JOLLY TRIBESMAN   37

4. HARRIOT'S DEVILS   62

5. STORMS, SPRITES, AND GOBLINS   74

6. GOVERNOR LANE'S SANDCASTLE   100

7. ENTER SIR FRANCIS   129

8. SMOKE INTO GOLD   152

9. THE UNFORTUNATE MASTER COFFIN   173

10. ARISE, LORD MANTEO   198

11. SOUNDING A TRUMPET   219

12. ONE BESS FOR ANOTHER   238

13. A MIRACLE AMONG SAVAGES   250

14. THE KING'S DEAREST DAUGHTER   273

15. MR. AND MRS. ROLFE GO TO ENGLAND   300

EPILOGUE   331

BIBLIOGRAPHY   345

INDEX   351

ACKNOWLEDGEMENTS

Sir Walter Ralegh's adventurers were instructed to keep journals of their exploits in the New World. Many of these priceless manuscripts were lost or mislaid over time, and have only been rediscovered and printed in recent years.

I owe a debt of gratitude to Professor David Beers Quinn, who has devoted a lifetime's study to Ralegh's colonies. Without his magnificent *Roanoke Voyages*—a collection of almost every surviving manuscript—this book could not have been written. I am also grateful to him for kindly inviting me to his Liverpool home to share his encyclopaedic knowledge.

I received much help from experts in America. I am particularly grateful to Tom Shields, editor of the *Roanoke Colonies Research Newsletter*, for generously sparing time to show me Roanoke Island. Thank you also to John Gillikin and Steve Harrison of the Fort Raleigh National Historic Site, to the staff at the Outer Banks History Center, and to librarians at the University of North Carolina at Chapel Hill.

Thank you to William Kelso, chief archaeologist of the Jamestown Rediscovery Project, for guiding me around the recent excavations, and to curator Beverly Straube for allowing me access to the remarkable artefacts that have been unearthed.

In London, I am deeply grateful to Paul Whyles for poring over the manuscript at short notice and suggesting many much-needed changes. Thank you also to Frank Barrett, Wendy Driver, Simon Heptinstall, Roland Philipps, Maggie Noach, Jill Hughes, and John Glusman; to Mrs. Angela Down, owner of Hayes Barton, Ralegh's childhood home; and to the staffs of the British Library and the Institute of Historical Research. A particular thank you to the ever helpful librarians of the London Library.

Lastly, I wish to thank Alexandra for her support and encouragement, and Madeleine and Héloïse for their tea-break entertainments.

BIG CHIEF ELIZABETH

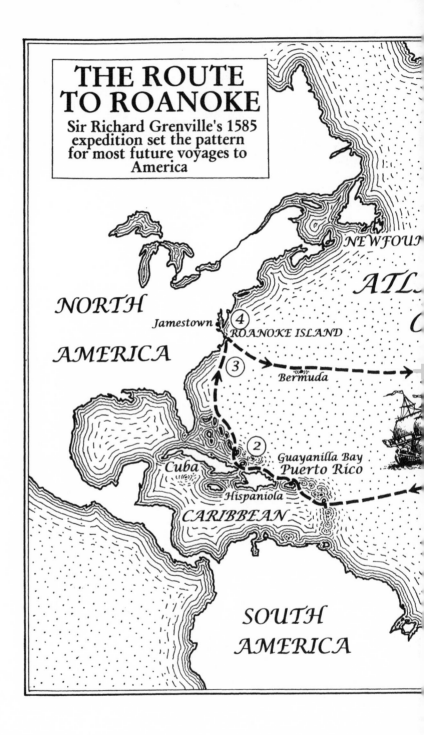

THE ROUTE TO ROANOKE

Sir Richard Grenville's 1585 expedition set the pattern for most future voyages to America

NORTH

AMERICA

NEWFOU

ATL

Jamestown ④ ROANOKE ISLAND

③ Bermuda

Cuba

② Guayanilla Bay Puerto Rico

Hispaniola

CARIBBEAN

SOUTH

AMERICA

Plymouth

EUROPE

ENGLAND

FRANCE

SPAIN

PORTUGAL

Azores
⑤

Madeira

Canaries
①

AFRICA

PITSTOPS & HAZARDS

1 The Canaries: to buy wine and water
2 The Caribbean: to acquire salt, fruit and livestock
3 The American coastline: treacherous shoals and rip-tides
4 Roanoke Island
5 The Azores: the fresh water and fruit saved many lives

Savages Among the Icebergs

The half-timbered mansion disappeared long ago, and the paved thoroughfare lies buried beneath the dust of centuries. The Great Fire tore the heart out of this corner of Elizabethan London, devouring books, buildings, and streets. One of the few things to survive is a small, insignificant-looking map—crinkled, faded, but still bearing the proud mark of its owner.

This was once the treasured possession of Sir Humfrey Gilbert, a flamboyant adventurer, who suffered such adversity in the aftermath of his disastrous 1578 expedition to North America that even Queen Elizabeth I noted drily that he was a man "of not good hap." But in the summer of 1582, after four years of virtual bankruptcy, Gilbert's misfortunes appeared to be over. As he unrolled his newly acquired map, he allowed himself a rare and self-satisfied smile. It provided the most detailed record to date of America's wild, barbarous shores, and contained a treasure trove of priceless and hitherto unknown information. Such was Sir Humfrey's pride in adding it to his collection that he reached for his quill and inscribed it with the words "Humfray Gylbert, knight, his charte."

This circular sheet of parchment depicted the entirety of North America as if viewed from high above the mid-Atlantic, and its inky squiggles confirmed what Gilbert had believed all along: that America was cut in two by a wide channel, and that the interior of the continent was not land at all, but a vast inland sea.

More discerning observers might have expressed concern that the map's provenance was uncertain and that it contained glaring errors. One of the few parts of America that was well charted, the triangular island of Newfoundland, was shown as four separate lumps of rock, while the eastern seaboard appeared to be little more than a topographical flight of fancy. But to Sir Humfrey, any such objection would have been a mere trifle. This map was to be the key to the crowning achievement of his life: a voyage to America, with the audacious goal of founding the first English colony on the shores of this mighty continent.

Gilbert had not been the first Englishman to be fascinated by the North American continent. After its discovery by John Cabot in 1497—just five years after Christopher Columbus had made his historic landfall in the Bahamas—England claimed possession of the whole of North America by virtue of the fact that her flag was the first to be planted on American soil. Ever since, a handful of dreamers and adventurers had toyed with the idea of visiting those distant shores across the ocean. A few of Bristol's more enterprising merchants had quickly launched expeditions in the wake of Cabot's voyage, hoping to make their fortunes in trade with the "savages." John Thomas, Hugh Elyot, and Thomas Assehurst all sailed into the sunset with high hopes, only to return in bitter disappointment. The scantily clad Indians had showed no interest in English woollens and broadcloths—the country's most important export—and even less desire to truss themselves up in slashed doublets and taffeta bonnets. Nor did they have anything of substance to offer the merchants. Their bows and arrows fetched a reasonable price as collectors' items; hawks were in some demand among Tudor courtiers, and "cattes of the montaign"—lynx—made fanciful pets for their noble lordships. But a trade based solely on exotica was never going to be profitable; after five or six years of failure, the Bristol merchants abandoned their enterprise.

In 1517 there had been a brief flurry of enthusiasm when a London bookseller named John Rastell startled his customers by announcing his intention of founding a colony in America. It was an eccentric idea, even by his own standards, yet he was so confident of success that he refused to allow anyone to deflect him from heading off into the sunset. He gathered "thirty or forty soldiers" and bought "tools for masons and carpenters," but his dream of building a dwelling in America was not to be. The mission ended in farce when two captains refused to set sail and Rastell's expedition got no further than Falmouth harbour. He ended his days lamenting his failure in verse:

> *O what a thynge had be than*
> *Yf they that be Englysshe men*
> *Myght have be the furst of all*
> *That there shulde have take possessyon*
> *And made furst buyldynge and habytacion*
> *A memory perpetuall.*

Most of these early expeditions had suffered from poor leadership, and all had been jeopardised by a lack of resources. But in 1536—exactly forty years before Sir Humfrey first began toying with his colonial project—an expedition to America got under way that seemed to overcome both of these hurdles. It was the brainchild of Richard Hore, a wealthy London leather seller who had grown weary of his endless trading voyages to and from the Canary Islands. To his friends he was "a man of goodly stature and of great courage, and given to the studie of cosmographie," but his business contacts knew a less savoury side to his character. Hore wanted to be rich and was forever dreaming up schemes which combined money making with adventure.

In 1535 he had been struck by an idea of such sparkling originality that he knew it could not fail to make him wealthy. In that year, the Plymouth adventurer William Hawkins had successfully returned from his voyage to South America, carrying with him "one of the savage kings of the countrey of Brasill." This unfortunate captive caused a sensation in Tudor London, especially when he was ushered into the commanding presence of King Henry VIII. At the sight of him, "the king and all the nobilitie did not a little marveile, and not without cause: for in his cheekes were holes made accordinge to their savage manner, and therein small bones were planted, standing an inche out from the said holes, which in his own countrey was reputed for a great braverie." As the king and courtiers prodded the chieftain, they discovered that "he had also another hole in his nether lippe, wherein was set a precious stone about the bignesse of a pease: all his apparell, behaviour and gesture were very strange to the beholders."

The sight of this savage astonished the court and was a cause of such excitement in the capital that Hore realised it presented a fine opportunity to make money. He decided to launch an expedition to North America with the intention of capturing one of King Henry VIII's more primitive subjects. He could then be paraded around the capital and displayed—for a fee, of course—to curious Londoners.

The dangers of such a voyage were considerable. Tudor vessels, not built to withstand the powerful Atlantic swells, were fearsomely top-heavy, and there was a very real danger of them foundering in the vastness of the ocean. Only a few English ships had ever crossed the Atlantic, and the land on the far side was as mysterious and barbarous as the fabled Orient. But Hore remained optimistic about the chances of success; a brilliant self-publicist, he realised that hunting for savages was certain to excite London's gentlemen adventurers.

No sooner had word of his expedition been leaked to the court than dozens of courtiers began to approach him, begging that they might have a place on his voyage. When news reached the ears of King Henry, who was still enthralled by his South American captive, he thought it such a splendid project that he gave it his unconditional blessing and support. Hore was "assisted by the king's favour and good countenance," and began to sign up men for the greatest adventure of their lives. "His perswasions tooke such effect that within a short space, many gentlemen of the Innes of Court, and of the Chancerie, and divers others of good worship, desirous to see the strange things of the world, very willingly entred into the action with him." Thirty "gentlemen" signed up for the voyage, many of them from rich and distinguished families. Armigil Wade was a close acquaintance of the king; Thomas Buts was a son of the wealthy Sir William Buts; William Wade was Clerk of the Counsel, and Master Weekes was "a gentleman of the West Countrey of five hundred markes by the yeere." All of these men, the cream of Tudor society, were delighted to be taking part in such an historical adventure. Reckless, fearless, and foolhardy, they eschewed the comfort of their gabled manors for a place on a unique expedition whose purpose was as swashbuckling as it was daring: to capture one of the "savages" of North America. They willingly poured money into the venture; by February 1536, Richard Hore had raised enough capital to begin negotiations to hire two small ships, the *William* and the *Trinity*.

If Hore had given as much attention to the voyage as he had to publicising the venture, he might have realised that he was placing himself and his companions in the gravest danger. He did not think to carry out even a cursory check on the seaworthiness of the vessels, nor did he have the foresight to calculate the quantity of dried victuals needed to feed 120 sailors for an expedition that was certain to last three months and possibly many more. Relying on the trusty formula of good wind and good luck, he took his men to receive the sacrament in Gravesend Church and, with the breezes urging them to get under way, "they embarked themselves in the ende of Aprill, 1536."

The two vessels made a splendid sight as they cruised majestically down the Thames estuary, their foremasts decked with bunting and their mainmasts flying the George. The adventurers were dressed in such finery that onlookers could have been forgiven for supposing them to be en route to a royal wedding: some wore silk-brimmed hats adorned with ostrich plumes, gaudy popinjay waistcoats, and square-toed shoes slashed with velvet. But scarcely had the men entered the turbulent waters of the English Channel than they realised that their cosseted backgrounds had done little to prepare them for the hardships of life at sea.

"From the time of their setting out from Gravesend, they were very long at sea . . . above two moneths, and never touched any land." So reads the account of Thomas Buts, one of the two men who would later tell their stories to Richard Hakluyt, author of *The Principall Navigations*. Both accounts are full of inconsistencies, for by the time the men were quizzed about their suffering their minds were addled with old age. But they allow a partial reconstruction of an audacious voyage that would later inspire the champion of American colonisation, Sir Walter Ralegh.*

The men caught their first glimpse of land in the first week of July, by which time food supplies were perilously low. Believing themselves to have reached Cape Breton, the northeastern tip of Nova Scotia, they steered their ship north to "the Island of Penguin"—the outlying Funk Island—which was a landmark for the few mariners who fished these lonely waters. It was "full of great foules, white and grey, as big as geese, and they saw infinite numbers of their egges." This strange bird was the flightless great auk, which was unafraid of man and proved easy to catch. "They drave a great number of the foules into their boates upon their sayles," and began to pluck them, a tiresome business, for "their skinnes were very like honycombes [and] full of holes." The men were so hungry that they declared them "very good and nourishing meat."

*Ralegh's name was spelled by both himself and his contemporaries in dozens of different ways, including Rawleyghe, Ralle, and Raulie. From the age of thirty until his death, Sir Walter consistently signed himself Ralegh, the form adopted throughout *Big Chief Elizabeth*. The spelling most commonly used today—Raleigh—was never once used by Sir Walter.

After resting up at Penguin Island, the two ships went their separate ways. The *William*, manned by seadogs and fisherfolk, headed to the Newfoundland Banks, where cod was plentiful. The *Trinity*, meanwhile, was to carry the gentlemen adventurers into unknown and uncharted waters in the hope of capturing a savage. The men were poorly equipped for such latitudes and totally unprepared for the rigours of exploration. "They were so farre northwards that they sawe mighty islands of yce in the sommer season, on which were haukes and other foules to rest themselves, being weary of flying over farre from the maine." They shot at polar bears that had drifted south on icebergs and caught brown bears on the mainland; in this way they supplemented their meagre diet.

It was as they coasted the remote and bleak shores of Labrador that they first sighted the "savages." One of the adventurers, Master Oliver Dawbeny, was standing on the foredeck of the *William* when he noticed a strange object far off in the water. He strained his eyes in staring at the horizon and realised with a start that he had certainly not been deceived. It was "a boat with savages of those partes, rowing downe the bay toward them, to gaze upon the ship and our people."

He called to the mariners below decks and "willed them to come up if they would see the natural people of the countrey that they had so long and so much desired to see." The men on deck "tooke viewe of the savages rowing toward them and their shipp, and upon the viewe they manned out a shipp boat to meet them and to take them." There was not a moment to be lost, for they might never be presented with this opportunity again. They pushed off their boat and set out in hot pursuit.

The "savages," dressed from top to toe in skins and carrying spears, were paddling a hollowed-out tree trunk. The Tudor gentlemen were determined to capture one of these primitive and exotic creatures and carry him back to London. But scarcely had the English boat set off in pursuit than the "savages" spun their canoe around and headed in the opposite direction, handling their blunt-nosed craft with considerable dexterity. "Spying our ship-boat making towards them, [they] returned with maine force and fled into an island that lay up in the bay or river there; and our men pursued them into the island and the savages fledde and escaped." Despite a lengthy search, the English party could find no sign of their quarry. All they saw was "a fire, and the side of a beare on a wooden spit, left at the same by the savages that were fled." In normal circumstances they would have at least taken the bear, but a mixture of disappointment and aching bellies caused them to leave even this. Their only consolation was a strange souvenir that was certain to have curiosity value in England. "They found a boote of leather garnished on the outward side of the calfe with certaine brave trailes, as it were rawe silke, and also found a certaine great warme mitten. And these caryed with them, they returned to their shippe, not finding the savages." It was a bitter disappointment.

When the men prepared to set sail, they realised their ship had been fatally weakened by storms and ice and needed substantial repairs before it could rejoin the *William*. When Hore delved into the hold of his vessel, he discovered to his horror that all the barrels and casks were empty and that all of their fishing equipment had been transferred onto the other vessel. "[The men] grew into great want of victuals . . . [and] found small relief." They did have one stroke of good fortune. An osprey made its nest in a nearby tree and "brought hourely to her yong great plentie of divers sorts of fishes"—fish that the men eagerly took from the fledglings. But when the osprey grew wise to their tricks, it moved the nest and the men began to starve.

"Such was the famine," Dawbeny later recalled, "that they were forced to seeke to relieve themselves of raw herbes and rootes that they sought on the maine." He now found himself longing for polar bear or roasted auk, but the Labrador wilderness proved to be almost devoid of life. Small parties of men were sent into the forest to search for food, but they returned empty-handed. As each day

Richard Hore's 1536 expedition to America hoped to return to England with "savages" in tow. But the Indians escaped in their dugout canoes, leaving Hore with debts and disappointments

passed the men grew weaker and weaker. It was not long before they grew so crazed from hunger that the dark lust for food affected their reason.

"[With] the famine increasing, and the reliefe of herbes being to little purpose to satisfie their insatiable hunger . . . [a] fellowe killed his mate while he stooped to take up a roote for his reliefe." He hauled the body into the forest and, "cutting out pieces of his bodie whom he had murthered, broyled the same on the coles and greedily devoured them." It soon transpired that he was not the only one to turn in desperation to cannibalism. A head count revealed that several men had gone missing, and Hore began to grow suspicious. He had at first assumed that they had been "devoured with wilde beastes" or "destroyed with savages," but he soon learned that there was a far more sinister explanation. "It fortuned that one of the company, driven with hunger to seeke abroad for reliefe, found out in the fieldes the savour of broyled flesh." The man went to investigate the smell and spotted one of his shipmates grilling juicy gobbets of what looked like human flesh over a fire. A heated conversation ensued, and tempers flared into "cruell speaches" until the culprit confessed. "If thou wouldest needes know," he said, "the broyled meate that I had was a piece of such a man's buttocke."

When this news reached Richard Hore, he sank to his knees in horror. He immediately summoned the men and launched into "a notable oration," telling them "how much these dealings offended the Almightie; and vouched the Scriptures from first to last." He added that "it had bene better to have perished in body and to have lived everlastingly . . . [than] bee condemned everlastingly both body and soule to the unquenchable fire of hell." As he ended his speech he "besought all the company to prey that it might please God to looke upon their miserable present state and for his owne mercie to relieve the same."

Their prayers for food went unanswered and, as the famine grew ever more desperate, even their Christian resolve failed them. "They agreed amongst themselves rather then all should perish, to cast lots who should be killed." But no sooner had the first unfortunate victim been selected than they spied a French ship on the horizon—a stray fishing vessel—which was "well furnished with vittaile." It did not take the men long to decide on a course of action. "Such was the policie [trickery] of the English, that they became master of the

same and, changing ships [abandoning the damaged *Trinity*] . . .
they set sayle to come into England."

These proud Tudor gentlemen, who had set out with such high
hopes of adventure, were utterly broken by their experiences. They
were so heartily sick of the sea that they put into the first port they
came to—St. Ives—and elected to travel overland to London, resting at "a certaine castle belonging to Sir John Luttrell." All of the
men were dejected, and one of their number, Thomas Buts, "was so
changed in the voyage with hunger and miserie, that Sir William his
father and my Lady his mother knew him not to be their sonne untill
they found a secret marke, which was a wart upon one of his knees."

The men fully expected to be punished for their cannibalism, but
to their surprise their plight was met not with shame and stigma but
with sympathy. King Henry was untroubled by their desperate
recourse to cannibalism and declared himself "so moved with pitie
that he punished not his subjects." When the French authorities
complained about the English theft of their ship, he "of his owne
purse, made full and royall recompence."

The voyage that had set sail with such confidence and expectation
had failed in every respect. Hore had hoped to return home with a
primitive "savage" in tow—a seminaked chieftain decked in skins
and headdress. Instead, he arrived with a band of sick and emaciated
men who had experienced an adventure they would try hard to forget. Hore himself was saddled with debt and, worse still, the owner
of the *Trinity* was demanding compensation for the loss of his ship.
Far from exciting public enthusiasm for America, Hore's expedition
killed off all interest in the land over the water. The king, too, had
lost his enthusiasm. For the next quarter of a century, there were no
officially sanctioned voyages of discovery to America.

The "new founde lande" had been abandoned to its "savages."

2

Sir Humfrey and the Cannibals

On a brilliant summer's evening in 1582, Maurice Browne and Thomas Smythe could be seen strolling down Red Crosse Street, a prosperous quarter of London that lay just a stone's throw from the River Thames. Browne was a close friend of Queen Elizabeth's secretary of state, Sir Francis Walsingham. Smythe was the son of Customer Smythe, who had amassed an immense fortune from farming customs duties. Although both men were still in their twenties, they had already made an impression at court.

They were dressed in considerable splendour, sporting foppish doublets and jaunty hats, yet their presence passed almost unnoticed by the hawkers who were accustomed to loiter in the neighbourhood. Courtiers were among Red Crosse Street's most regular visitors, for this gabled thoroughfare was home to a number of important merchants and adventurers.

These two men were to be the guests of Sir Humfrey Gilbert. He had invited them to his imposing dwelling to show them his "charte" of America in the hope that it would convince them to accompany him on his greatest adventure. They had scarcely reached the porch of one of the grander houses when the door was flung open by a striking gentleman, a dozen or so years older than his visitors. Gilbert was a familiar figure in the Elizabethan court and a man of such dynamic energy that he was doomed never to be content in the parochial atmosphere of Elizabethan England. "He is not worthy to live at all," he once wrote to his brother, "that for fear or danger of death shunneth his country's danger or his own honour."

Ever since he was a child, Gilbert had thirsted for adventure, dreaming up overseas schemes and projects—many of them fantastical—which he nonetheless tried to put into practice with a foolhardy determination. He was so reckless and boastful that his contemporaries were unable to decide whether to stand in awe of him or to be repulsed. To his friends he had a "verie pregnant wit" and "excellent vertues," but his enemies at court saw a darker and less savoury aspect to his character: "unsound and brimful of fickleness, and bragging and overflowing with vanity."

If his portrait is at all honest, Sir Humfrey carried himself with a suitably buccaneering swagger, his pranked ruff forcing him to walk with his head bolt upright. He had jet-black hair and a cold, calculating expression that would have been sinister were it not for his flamboyant moustache, clipped, frounced, and brushed back in such a way that it looked as if he had two doormice stuck to his face. In later portraits he is shown caressing a globe, a suitable pose for one of the leading spirits in that group of intrepid Elizabethans, the gentlemen of the West, who looked towards the horizon—the Americas—for glory, riches, and adventure.

Sir Humfrey had already attempted to land men in America in 1578, the first Atlantic voyage of exploration for many a year. He had persuaded the queen to grant him a licence to discover "such remote, heathen and barbarous landes, countries and territories not actually possessed of any Christian prince." He had then furnished a little flotilla and set sail across the ocean with a motley crew of pirates and criminals, trusting to fair winds and good luck. He was blessed with neither. Most of his vessels limped home without ever losing sight of England. Only one ship, the *Falcon*, actually left English waters; it was captained by Gilbert's youthful half-brother, who

Sir Humfrey Gilbert had long thirsted for adventure. Ignoring the queen's warning that he was a man noted "of not good hap," he sailed for America in pursuit of riches and glory

set his course for the West Indies with the intention of pillaging Spanish treasure ships. But this vessel also returned to England "sore battered and disabled," and its captain was roundly condemned for his behaviour. His name—then entered into the official records for the first time—was Walter Ralegh.

Gilbert's two visitors knew all about his abortive 1578 expedition, for they shared his fascination with the land across the sea. Gilbert hoped that his newly found chart would fire their enthusiasm for his proposed voyage. "Within a whyle after our cominge to hym," recalled Browne, "he shewed us the card of the whole country where he ment to settill hymselfe." Gilbert spoke with such gusto about his voyage that he almost persuaded his two guests to accompany him. "We fell to discoursing with Sir Humfrey of his [planned] voyage," wrote Browne, "and in that discourse kept on so longe that he wolde have us staye to supper." The men continued to chat as they munched their broiled capons, and "had no other talke but of the fruitfullness and great riches that was in that country." After much discussion, Gilbert's friends reluctantly informed him that they "were sory that we had not knowledge of these matters in tyme, for if we had, we wold have made provysion to have accompanied hym."

Gilbert was disappointed but not disheartened, for as he led the two men out of his study he played his trump card. With a theatrical flourish, he announced that he had in his possession another unique

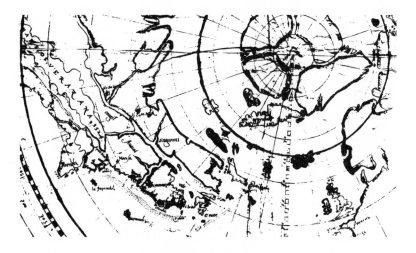

Sir Humfrey Gilbert believed his map of America to be the most accurate in existence. The British Isles (far right) were well charted, but the American coastline was guesswork. The interior of the continent was optimistically depicted as a series of broad waterways

document that he knew would cause them to change their minds. This document was to remain a secret until the next evening, but he promised them that it contained some truly astonishing news about America. This, he felt sure, would dispel their reluctance to join him on a new adventure—and besides, both men were in possession of vast fortunes that he could put to good use.

Before dusk had descended on the following day, the two men were once again seated in Gilbert's study, and they soon discovered that they were not to be disappointed. Sir Humfrey informed them that a humble Englishman called Davy Ingrams—known to him personally—had walked the entire Atlantic coastline of America and brought back the first eyewitness account of the interior of the country, as well as an account of its "beastly" natives. This information was priceless and highly secret, but Gilbert was prepared to share it with his visitors on the condition that they would reconsider their earlier decision not to accompany his expedition.

The story that he recounted had the ring of truth. Davy Ingrams was a common sailor who had left England in 1567 on a slave-trading mission under the command of Sir John Hawkins. The mission had ended in disaster after a battle with the Spanish and Hawkins had been forced to abandon half his men on the shores of Mexico. One of these castaways was Ingrams, a man of Herculean strength who was not prepared to wait the two or three years it would take for Hawkins to return for the men. Aware that English fishing vessels were regular visitors to Newfoundland—and ignorant of the fact that it lay more than three thousand miles away—he selected a band of his more adventurous colleagues and set off on what was to prove a very long march.

What happened on that marathon hike was anyone's guess. Ingrams claimed that after twelve months of extreme hardship, he and two other haggard survivors emerged from the wilderness in Nova Scotia. Half-starved and clothed in skins, they were approached by natives who told them "that they had seene shippes on that coast, and did draw upon the ground the shape and figure of shippes." The men dashed to the clifftop and saw a French ship lying at anchor. They secured a passage to Le Havre, crossed the English Channel in a fishing vessel, and paid a call on Hawkins before touting their story around Devon taverns. When Ingrams finally made it back to his home in Barking, Essex, his family nearly fainted in astonishment.

Sir Humfrey realised that Ingram's story was, if true, of immense importance. Virtually nothing was known about the natives of North America, nor was there any information about the lay of the land, and he decided to grill the sailor for more information. His experience of interrogation—learned in Ireland—was limited to torture and mutilation, but he had the foresight to realise that such methods were not necessarily the best way to extract information from Ingrams. He turned for help to the queen's secretary of state, Sir Francis Walsingham, who was famed for his skill in extracting men's secrets. He was "one who knew excellently well how to win men's affections to him," wrote William Camden, "and make use of them for his own purpose." He was to find himself tested to the limits when confronted with this humble sailor from Barking.

Davy was "abowt the age of fortye yeeres" when he was summoned to be interrogated, and more than a dozen years had passed since the events he was about to describe. Yet he claimed to remember every detail of his trip. Not wishing to disappoint his distinguished interrogators, he peppered his account with tales of fearsome cannibals and ghoulish monsters. He did so safe in the knowledge that his tale could not be cross-checked for accuracy, since both of his fellow travellers were dead: Richard Browne "was slaine about five yeeres past," and Richard Twide had died in 1579.

He gave a remarkable description of the cannibalistic "savages" of America, "brutish" tribesmen who wore skins more colourful than the queen's most extravagantly dressed jester. From afar, they resembled patchwork eiderdowns, their naked bellies "painted with divers colours" and their heads "shaven in sundry spots." Some even decked their gleaming brows with red and russet feathers. In hot weather many of the men stripped off their feathers and skins and wandered around stark naked, although Ingrams recalled that "the noble men's privities are covered with the necke of a goorde."

Their comely wives displayed rather less flesh and a great deal more modesty. They covered their private parts "with the hayre or leafe of the palme tree" and in winter they trussed themselves up in skins, "the hayrie side being next to their bodies." Ingrams displayed such a keen interest in "privities" that it was one of the first Indian words he learned — *carmugnar*.

He soon found his own *carmugnar* an object of curiosity. On arriving at one village, he and his men were summoned to a meeting of tribal elders who "caused them to be stripped naked." The Indians then prodded them, poked their bellies, and, "wondring greatly at the whitenes of their skins, let them depart without further harme."

The more Ingrams embellished his story, the more he realised that Gilbert and Walsingham were spellbound. Hoping to be richly rewarded at the end of his interview, he told them he had watched adulterers being knifed to death, and even observed a bizarre form of euthanasia. With a twinkle in his eye, he said that he met one tribe which, "when any of them is sicke and like to dye, [the] nexte of his kinne doe cutt his throte and all his kinne must drinke up his bloude." He even watched them carve the corpse into juicy gobbets and munch the pieces raw, licking the bones with relish, "for they make a religion to have none of his bloudde lost." Domestic disputes invariably ended in mutilation and torture. Unfaithful husbands and wives were pinned to a stone slab, "flatt on their backes, and their handes and legges being holde or tyed, the executioner commeth and kneeleth on their breastes and, with a crooked knife cutteth both their throtes." It made for a gruesome spectacle, yet Ingrams assured Sir Humfrey that no harm was done to him or his companions. He added that although the tribesmen had "teeth like dogs," they were quite charming, "a curteous people, and no meneaters," at least where Englishmen were concerned.

A far greater threat was posed by the monstrous beasts that stalked America's forests. Ingrams claimed that the sheep were bright red, as were the rabbits, while the birds of prey had heads "as big as a man's." Gilbert could have justifiably asked how such a top-heavy bird could fly, but Ingrams never gave his interrogators time to respond. He was already telling them about the hideous creature that had "nether heade nor necke, his eyes and mouthe weare in his brest." This, added Ingrams, "is very ugly to beholde, and cowardly."

The bad news about the wild animals was tempered by a glowing report of the land's rocks and minerals. Ingrams assured Sir Humfrey that America's Indians were exceedingly rich in treasure, and that he saw with his own eyes buckets made of "massie silver," lumps of gold "as bigge as his fyst," and "great rockes of chrystal." Women that were not stark naked tended to wear "plates of gold over there body." That was not the only good news. The countryside, he said, was more fertile than England: "good and most delycate [and] havinge greate playnes as large and as fayer in many places as maye be sene."

Impressed with Ingrams's observant eye, Gilbert noted every detail of the interrogation. Now, in the company of Browne and Smythe, he relayed all that he had been told, and soon realised that his words were making a deep impression. When he had finished, Browne declared that he wished to accompany Gilbert to America. "Whereuppon Sir Humfry presently wrote unto my master requestinge my master's lawfull favore if he thought me sufficient to such a matter." Browne's master wrote back giving his consent and, without further ado, Browne began equipping himself for the biggest adventure of his life. Smythe was more hesitant; although he spoke enthusiastically about the expedition, he expressed his regret at being unable to accompany the voyage.

Gilbert launched himself into planning his voyage with his customary gusto. He was pleased to learn that his half-brother, Walter Ralegh, had decided to accompany him. Young Walter had been making something of a name for himself at court. Finding himself

Castaway Davy Ingrams spent a year with America's savages and brought back stories of their cannibalistic rituals. "When any of them is sicke, they cutt his throte and drinke up his bloude."

with cash to spare, he decided to invest it in Gilbert's expedition. "[He] hath at his owne cost and charges bought a newe ship . . . she is of bourden twelfe-score tones, redy furnyshed of all thinges belonginge to her and victuled for 60 men." This was extremely good news, for Gilbert's biggest problems were financial. His disastrous 1578 expedition had swallowed his fortune and left him with so many debts that three years later he was still a virtual bankrupt. In a begging letter to Walsingham, he described himself as being "subjecte to daylye arestes, executions and owtlawreis; yea, and forside to gadge and sell my wyffes clothes from her back." He was well aware that it was not ideal for the man spearheading American colonisation to be bankrupt, but he had rich and influential friends. With land in England at a premium, he hit upon the rather brilliant idea—permitted under the terms of his charter—of selling estates in America. These would be of a size and scale that were guaranteed to excite even the most miserly of courtiers. They would cover limitless tracts of wilderness, millions of acres, and would be sold to the highest bidder, complete with semifeudal powers.

It was only when Gilbert began publicising his scheme that he realised he had produced a winning formula. Lords and merchants alike beat a path to Red Crosse Street and begged him to sell them land. Gilbert was in his element; he distributed huge estates to his investors, carving up America with a few strokes of his quill. Philip Sidney was granted three million acres, others took a million or more, while Sir Thomas Gerard stood to gain "two fifte partes of all the gold, sylver, perle and precyous stones there found." Between June 1582 and February 1583 he managed to dispose of a staggering 8,500,000 acres.

Excitement spread through the capital as courtiers began planning how they would manage their estates. One adventurer, Sir George Peckham, was quite bowled over by his new responsibilities and vowed to treat his tenants—the native Americans—with great generosity. He promised to present each and every one with "looking glasses, bells, beades, braceletts [and] chaines," explaining that "though to us of small value, yet [they are] accounted by them of high price and estimation." He even intended to kit them out in fashionable clothing "[such] as a shirt, a blewe, yellow, redde or greene cotton cassocke [and] a cappe or such like." They were to be the smartest Indians on the far side of the Atlantic.

Gilbert himself had given little thought to the native population. He intended to govern his own men "as nere as convenyently may be agreable to the forme of the lawes and pollicie of England" and granted himself full "power and aucthority to correcte, punyshe, pardone, governe and rule." But he also promised to show "good discretions" when it came to capital punishment.

There was to be one law for the English and quite another for the

natives, and the Indians would have been quaking in their moc-
casins had they known of Gilbert's track record in Ireland, where he
had quashed riot and rebellion with a savagery that approached barbarism. He had learned to treat the native population with ruthless
contempt, severing the heads of his enemies and using them to line
the path to his tent. So contemptuous was he of the Irish that he was
heard to say that "he thought his dogges ears too good to heare the
speeche of the greateste noble manne emongst them." He had concluded that colonisation was certain to lead to conflict, and that "no
conquered nation will ever yield willingly obedience for love, but
rather for fear."

Since clashes with the natives were likely to lead to deaths on
both sides, he deemed it pointless to send men of quality with the
first wave of settlers. Rather, he proposed dispatching "such needie
people of our countrie which now trouble the commonwelth." As a
first step, thieves, murderers, and wastrels could be transported
across the Atlantic, the jetsam of society that had committed "outragious offences whereby they are dayly consumed with the gallowes."

Gilbert was on the point of setting sail when Queen Elizabeth
unexpectedly withdrew her permission, fearing that Gilbert would
die at sea. It was only after numerous petitions that she unexpectedly
changed her mind and "used Sir Humfrey with very great favore,"
promising him that "he shall not want anythinge that may be for his
assistaunce." On the eve of his departure, she sent as a token of her
favour a "very excellent jewell." It was a priceless piece of craftman-
ship; "an anchor of gold set with 29 diamondes with the portracture
of a queene holding the ringe of the ancor in one hand."

Sir Humfrey Gilbert's little fleet of five ships, led by the *Delight*,
eventually slipped out of Causand Bay near Plymouth on June 11,
1583. It was a quiet departure for such an historic voyage: Gilbert
had said his farewells on leaving Southampton some two weeks previously, and he now left England with not so much as a fanfare to
send him on his way.

There were already murmurings among the mariners and colonists about the meagre quantity of victuals on board. There were 260 men in total—"shipwrights, masons, carpenters and smithes"—but scarcely food for half that number. The fleet had departed in haste, for Gilbert had "resolved to put unto the sea [before] our store yet remaining . . . were too far spent." He placed his trust in the Almighty, hoping that the winds would blow him swiftly across the Atlantic.

After a few days at sea, Gilbert and his subordinates suddenly realised that they had neglected to plan a route across the ocean. "It seemed first very doubtfull by what way to shape our course and to begin our intended discovery," writes Edward Hayes, the on-board chronicler, "either from the south, northward; or from the north, southward." There was a hastily convened conference in Gilbert's cabin at which various captains gave suggestions and advice. Those favouring a southerly route soon won the day, arguing that they did not wish "to be surprised with timely winter." But no sooner had this route been chosen than others renewed their call for the northern route, claiming that if they reached the waters of Newfoundland before the onset of winter, they would find "a multitude of ships repairing thither for fish, [and] we should be relieved abundantly with many necessaries." Sir Humfrey agreed and, although fearful of "continuall fogge and thicke mists, tempest and rage of weather," he set his course for Newfoundland.

Life on board ship turned out to be more comfortable than anyone had dared imagine. Gilbert had hired a troupe of entertainers to amuse the "savages" they would meet on their arrival, and these kept the sailors occupied during the long Atlantic crossing. "For the solace of our men," writes Hayes, "and allurement of the savages, we were provided of musicke in good variety: not omitting the least toyes, as morris dancers, hobby horsse, and maylike conceits to delight the savage people, whom we intended to winne by all faire meanes possible."

There was the occasional setback. Ralegh's ship was forced to return to England when her crew was "infected with a contagious sickness," probably dysentery, a reversal that sent Gilbert into a brief rage. There was also bad weather, with so much mist and fog that the ships almost crashed into "mountaines of yce driven upon the sea." At one point the *Swallow* disappeared from view and was not seen for some weeks, but as the fleet neared the American coastline, they caught sight of her on the horizon and hurriedly gave chase. As they neared the vessel, Sir Humfrey's men were amazed to see the crew dressed in fancy waistcoats and hear them singing at the tops of their voices. "For joy and congratulation of our meeting they spared not to cast up into the aire and overboord their caps and hats in good plenty." They soon learned why. The *Swallow*'s captain, who was none other than the "vertuous, honest and discrete" Maurice Browne, had been indulging in a spot of piracy. He had captured two French vessels—one of which was laden with wine and gar-ments—after which the voyage resumed with the utmost merriment.

Seven weeks after leaving England, Gilbert at last caught a glimpse of the land he had spent the greater part of his life dreaming about. It was not quite the paradise that he had come to expect—it was nothing but "hideous rockes and mountaines, bare of trees and voide of any greene herbe"—but Gilbert put a brave face on his dis-appointment and turned his ship south towards Newfoundland, where he expected to find a few English fishing vessels. To his sur-prise, he arrived at St. John's to find "boats of all nations, to the num-ber of thirty-six sailes." Anxious to make an impressive entrance, he sent messages to inform the various captains that he was here to claim the land for Her Majesty, Queen Elizabeth of England. He then prepared to sail into the natural harbour with as much pomp and ceremony as he could muster. It was unfortunate that he "fell upon a rocke" at the mouth of the bay—much to the amusement of the foreign captains—and suffered the ignominy of being towed off by a flotilla of small boats.

Once Gilbert had recovered his composure, he ordered the En-glish fisherfolk to his vessel and grandiloquently announced "his purpose to take possession of those lands to the behalfe of the crowne of England, and the advancement of Christian religion in those pagan-ish regions." The fishermen seemed delighted and celebrated the occasion by firing their biggest guns, but the Spanish and Por-tuguese anchored in the harbour had watched Gilbert's arrival with considerable alarm. Outnumbered and outgunned, they realised that they had no option but to join in the festivities. On learning that Sir Humfrey was preparing a great feast, "they did most willingly and liberally contribute," bringing "wines, marmalads, most fine ruske or bisket, sweet oyles and sundry delicacies." Afraid that this might not satisfy Gilbert, they hurriedly returned to their ships and pre-pared vast platters of "fresh salmons, trouts, lobsters and other fresh fish." When all the food was assembled, Sir Humfrey prepared to step ashore.

"On Munday, being the fift of August, the Generall caused his tent to be set upon the side of an hill, in the viewe of all the flete of Englishmen and straungers." Accompanied by his captains, officers, and soldiers, he marched with great solemnity towards his tent and invited the Spanish and Portuguese to join him. When all were assembled, he brushed down his doublet and, after pinning the queen's brooch to his jerkin, formally "tooke possession of the sayde land in the right of the crowne of England by digging of a turfe and receiving the same . . . delivered unto him after the manner of the lawe and custome of England." He decreed that the country's reli-gion should be in accordance with the Church of England and that high treason would be punishable by death, and added that "if any person should utter words to the dishonour of her majestie, he should lose his eares." His speech was enthusiastically received by the fishermen, who promised to obey his command. Satisfied, Sir Humfrey granted plots of land to the various fisherfolk and erected "the armes of England ingraven in lead and infixed upon a pillar of wood."

Gilbert had never intended to settle his colony in Newfoundland,

and his brief survey of the land had done nothing to alter his opinion. There was "extreme cold"—far colder, even, than an English summer—and he was informed by fishermen that in winter the land was covered with a thick blanket of snow. Although the skies were filled with partridges and "beastes of sundry kindes" roamed the forests, this was no country to choose as a new homeland.

Many of the prospective colonists were dismayed by the barren wasteland and felt they had been duped into signing up for a future that looked even bleaker than that from which they had fled. One group tried to steal a fishing vessel and return to England, while "a great many more of our people stole into the woods to hide themselves, attending time and meanes to returne home by such shipping as daily there departed from the coast. Some were sicke of fluxes, and many dead: and in briefe, by one meanes or another our company was diminished."

Edward Hayes was contemptuous of such men, noting that the ships were still laden with marmalades and lemons and enough supplies to last for many months. Sir Humfrey agreed and had no intention of abandoning his colonial project. With the wind billowing his sails, he ordered his ships southwards to more temperate climes. It proved a fateful decision, for swirling mists obscured the coastline, making the voyage extremely treacherous. As the "fowle wether increased, with fogges and mysts," the crew on the *Delight* began to be afflicted with a collective psychosis. Weird creatures were plucked from the sea with a harpoon, the wind moaned "like the swanne that singeth before her death," and when the on-board musicians attempted to jolly the crew by striking up a tune, it sounded "like dolefull knells." Worse still, the *Delight* began to echo with "strange voyces" like those of ghosts, "which scared some from the helm."

To the superstitious crew, such mysterious happenings could only portend doom. That night their very worst fears were realised. "The wind rose and blew vehemently at south and by east, bringing withal raine, and thicke mist, so that we could not see a cable length

Experienced explorers wore fur hats and jerkins. Richard Hore's adventurers lacked the proper clothes and equipment, and when food ran out, they ate each other

before us." The vessels soon found themselves in treacherous waters and in grave danger of running aground.

"Master Cox, looking out, discerned (in his judgement) white cliffes, crying, 'land withall!' " Observing from an adjacent ship, Gilbert saw to his horror that the *Delight*, which was carrying all the supplies for his colony, was being driven inexorably towards the shallows. He shouted to its helmsman, urging him into deeper waters, but his words were snatched by the wind. The *Delight*, pride of the fleet, was now so close to the sandbank that her destruction was all but assured. Just a few minutes after Gilbert's warning, "the admirall strooke aground, and had soone after her sterne and hinder partes beaten in pieces." Stuck fast and unable to free herself, she was torn apart by the waves. Her timbers were plucked one by one from the hull and tossed into the sea. The crew clung to the wreckage, hoping that the storm would abate and allow them to swim for safety, but as the wind increased in intensity, the *Delight*'s captain—Maurice Browne—realised the end was nigh and composed himself with stoic dignity. He refused to leave the ship, telling his men that "he would not give example with the first to leave . . . choosing rather to die then to incurre infamie by forsaking his charge." He had determined to die heroically and, "with this mind, hee mounted upon the highest decke where hee attended imminent death, and unavoidable. How long, I leave it to God, who withdraweth not his comfort from his servants at such times."

Sir Humfrey, observing the unfolding tragedy from afar, was in a state of shock, not only at losing his flagship but also at witnessing the death of Browne, a dear friend whom he himself had persuaded to accompany him to America. "This was a heavy and grievous event, to lose at one blow our chiefe shippe fraighted with great provision, gathered together with much travell, care, long time and difficultie." He searched desperately for survivors in the turbulent seas, "but all in vaine, sith God had determined their ruine: yet all that day, and part of the next, we beat up and downe as neere unto the wracke as was possible."

As the storm continued to batter his fleet, Sir Humfrey flickered between melancholy and despair, lamenting "the losse of his great ship, more of the men, but most of all his bookes and notes." "The remembrance touched him so deepe, as not able to containe himselfe he beat his boy in great rage." His punishment for this act of wanton violence was to step on a nail and tear open his foot.

Heartily sick of their misadventures, the surviving colonists begged Sir Humfrey to let them return to England. Gilbert realised that he had no option but to agree. Genuinely moved by the pleas of his captains, he stood on deck and announced his intentions in the following words: "Be content," he said, "we have seene enough and take no care of expence past: I will set you foorth royally the next spring, if God send us safe home. Therefore, I pray you; let us no longer strive here, where we fight against the elements."

If he was downhearted, he was certainly not prepared to show it in front of his men. He spoke at length of how he would set sail again in the spring and assured everyone on board that the queen would lend him ten thousand pounds to finance this new expedition. The speech was Gilbert at his most optimistic. Whenever he was struck by adversity, he sought strength in the demonic energy that coursed though his Devonshire bones. Even the chronicler of the voyage, Edward Hayes, was impressed. It was, he wrote, "a demonstration of great fervencie of mind, being himself very confident."

But not all the colonists cared for his bullish talk; a vociferous few began to make sarcastic jibes about Gilbert, mocking him for being scared of the sea and taunting him for a lack of will and resolution. Sir Humfrey was incensed. He was particularly wounded by the jest that he was afraid. To prove it nonsense, he insisted on making the homeward voyage on the diminutive *Squirrel*, which was already dangerously overloaded with firearms and fishing gear. His friends begged him to reconsider, using "vehement perswasion and intreatie," but Gilbert refused to listen: "I will not forsake my little company going homeward," he roared, "with whom I have passed so many stormes and perils." Hayes, who was growing tired of Gilbert's insufferable pride, commented that it was typically poor judgement "to prefer the wind of a vaine report to the weight of his own life."

The ingredients for tragedy were now in place: all that was needed was a thundering tempest, and it came soon enough. As the ships neared the Azores, "we met with very foule weather, and terrible seas, breaking short and high, pyramid wise." As the skies darkened and the wind screamed through the rigging, the waves grew so huge that they swept over the decks. "Men which all their lifetime had occupied the sea never saw more outragious seas." Several had terrifying visions of fire "which they take an evill signe of more tempest."

Those on the *Squirrel* were in serious danger. She was hopelessly overloaded and sat so low in the water that the sea gushed into her hold. On the afternoon of Monday, September 9, as the storm reached its climax, the crew feared the worst. The frigate was filling with water faster than they could bail her out; it was only a matter of time before she would slip beneath the waves. The other ships realised her peril, yet when they came alongside they were astonished by what they saw. Sir Humfrey Gilbert had risen to new heights of eccentricity. With a deranged grimace on his face, he "was sitting abaft with a booke in his hand." Every time the other ships came near, he would roar to them, "We are as neere to heaven by sea as by land."

His end was not long in coming. "The same Monday night," wrote Hayes, "about twelve of the clocke, or not long after, the frigat being ahead of us . . . suddenly her lights were out." The lookout raised the alarm but it was too late. "For in that moment, the frigat was devoured and swallowed up of the sea." Sir Humfrey Gilbert was never seen again.

The other ships limped back to England, arriving battered but safe some two weeks after the loss of the *Squirrel*. The men disembarked at Dartmouth and, after collecting their belongings, returned to homes they thought they would never see again. It fell to Hayes to take stock of the expedition and question why it failed. Poor leader-

Davy Ingrams claimed to have watched in horror as the natives hacked corpses into juicy gobbets and munched ravenously on arms and legs

ship and bad planning had dogged the expedition from the outset. So little was known about America that Sir Humfrey had set sail without any idea where he should plant his colony. He had proved a poor commander, for his wild fluctuations of temper had affected his ability to lead. "He both was too prodigall of his owne patrimony and too careles of other men's expences, to imploy both his and their substance upon a ground imagined good." He was "enfeebled of abilitie and credit," "impatient," and, in a word, "unfit."

It was a bitter conclusion to an expedition that had set out with such high hopes. But Hayes was a realist. He knew that if England was to colonise "those north-west lands," it would require men of a far higher calibre than Sir Humfrey Gilbert.

3

The Jolly Tribesman

Sir Humfrey's death sparked off a fierce debate as to who would inherit his American project. The most obvious person to pick up the baton was his brother, Sir John, who had not sailed with the 1583 expedition; but he had been dissuaded by the scale of the disaster and showed even less enthusiasm to get involved when he learned that America was a land of "hideous rockes and mountaines." He preferred the rolling pastures of south Devon, and he headed to the family home of Compton Castle near Dartmouth, where he devoted himself to recouping the losses sustained by the sinking of the *Delight*.

The adventurer Sir George Peckham showed a great deal more enthusiasm, even though he, too, had lost his investment. Eager to meet his Indian tenants, he began planning an expedition on a truly epic scale. He expressed his intention of teaming up with England's greatest mariners, and espoused grand dreams of leading an armada of ships across the Atlantic. But Peckham's ideas proved rather too ambitious. When he staged a public meeting for prospective merchants and investors, only seven men bothered to turn up. They offered him a mere £12 10s., and even the plucky Peckham was forced to admit that they were "adventurers in the second degree."

For a time, it seemed as if Gilbert's proposed colony was doomed.

No one had the adventurous spirit—backed by the requisite fortune—that was necessary to embark on a voyage across the Atlantic. But in the spring of 1584, the young Walter Ralegh stepped forward and boldly announced his intention of taking over the leadership of his half-brother's abortive project.

That he was in a position to do so was due to his dazzling rise through the ranks of Queen Elizabeth's court: a progress so meteoric that the lords of the realm felt they had been caught off guard. Soon after Walter was introduced to the court he was an intimate of the queen, and their noble lordships were so taken aback that their initial response was to mock him as a vulgar parvenu.

There was, on the surface, plenty to joke about in young Walter. He "spake broad Devonshire" and came from such straitened circumstances that his family did not even own their own dwelling. But although the Raleghs were a family in decline, they came from good stock. Previous centuries had produced a distinguished bishop and a judge, and a Ralegh had helped England to victory on the battlefield of Agincourt.

The fighting spirit had been broken by misfortune and, by the time young Walter came into the world, in about 1554, much of the family's ancestral land had been sold. The only reminder of their illustrious pedigree was to be found in the names of south Devon villages—Combe Ralegh, Withycombe Ralegh, and Colaton Ralegh.

Despite their fall in the world, the Raleghs still married into powerful Devon families—the Carews, Grenvilles, and Champernownes—and Walter's father retained the privilege of occupying the front pew in East Budleigh Church, where his coat of arms was (and still is) carved into the polished oak. Old Walter had been twice married when, in 1548, he found himself in a position to make a most advantageous match. Katherine Champernowne came from a prosperous Devon family that could count among their immediate relations the vice-admiral of the county and a tutor to the future Queen Elizabeth. Her first marriage, to Otho Gilbert, had produced three brilliant sons—John, Humfrey, and Adrian—

while her second, to the older Ralegh, would give her two more boys, Carew and Walter.

Young Walter displayed all the arrogance and ruthlessness of his half-brothers, but he combined it with such cavalier gallantry that it was clear from an early age that he was destined for greatness. He was still in his teens when he joined a band of hot-blooded Devon adventurers in a swashbuckling crusade against French Catholics. Fighting under the black standard of the Compte de Montgomerie, they adopted his motto as their rallying cry: "Let valour end my life." Walter next headed to Ireland, where he fought the native warlords with a gritty determination. In his spare time he lambasted his commanders with such withering contempt that they would have dismissed him from service had he not been related to Sir Humfrey Gilbert. "I like neither his carriage nor his company," wrote Lord Grey, his commanding officer, "and, therefore—other than by direction or commandment—he is not to expect [promotion] at my hands."

Grey had made a mistake that was to be repeated by many of the queen's courtiers: misjudging Ralegh's single-mindedness and underestimating his attraction. His first meeting with the queen—recorded by the antiquarian Thomas Fuller—is vintage Ralegh, even though the account may be apocryphal: "[He] found the queen walking till, meeting with a plashy place, she seemed to scruple going therein. Presently Ralegh cast and spread his new plush cloak on the ground; whereon the queen trod gently, rewarding him afterwards with many suits, for his so free and seasonable tender of so fair a foot cloth." Such chivalry was not uncommon in the courts of Spain and France, but it was unheard of in England. Elizabeth's doting courtiers were stunned by the theatricality of the gesture.

Having gained the queen's attention, Ralegh wooed her with honeyed words. "He had gotten the Queen's ear in a trice, and she began to be taken with his elocution, and loved to hear his reasons to her demands. And the truth is, she took him for a kind of oracle, which nettled them all." At this first meeting Ralegh was just twenty-six years old. His behavior was outlandish—sheer coquetry—but he knew that he had to strike while he had the chance.

He was fortunate to have arrived in London at a time when the leading courtiers were losing their sparkle. Elizabeth's favourite in earlier years had been the swaggering Robert Dudley, her "sweet Robin," who had come within a codpiece of depriving the Virgin Queen of her much-vaunted epithet. But their flirtatious antics had come to nothing. The crude chattermongers of London had concluded that although the queen might open her legs to Robin, she had "a membrane on her which made her incapable of men." Anything but sweet, Robin was a portly and ruddy individual whose saccharine charm had been transferred to his new love, Lettice Knollys.

The harmless love games were still eagerly pursued by young blades like Sir Philip Sidney and Sir Christopher Hatton, men who doted on the queen even though she was no longer the fragile maiden of her youth. At the time of Ralegh's first meeting, she was already in her late forties and was betraying the first signs of the wizened harridan she would become in her later years. She was "well-favoured but high-nosed" and her skin was rather pale, but her eyes were still "lively and sweet" and flashed with a mischievous sense of fun. When dignity was required, she was "of such state in her carriage as every motion of her seemed to bear majesty," but when she was among friends at Hampton Court, Richmond, or Nonesuch, her more playful nature emerged. She swore like a trooper, picked her teeth with a gold toothpick, and delighted in coarse jokes. She was playful, theatrical even, and was never one to fight shy of melodrama. When she learned that her physician was involved in a plot to take her life, she "tore open her garment, exposing her breasts, exclaiming that she had no weapon to defend herself, but was only a weak female." But while she could scream abuse at the Spanish ambassador and duff her groom of the Chamber about the ears, she was dutifully conscientious about matters of state, and read even the small print of official documents. She was cultivated as well. She spoke French and Italian, read Greek tolerably well, and was confi-

Walter Ralegh spent vast sums on clothes and accessories. At his first meeting with Queen Elizabeth, he cast his cloak over a puddle to save her shoes. Ralegh's son Wat (right) was killed in Guiana in 1617

dent in Latin. In her later years, she astonished her court by berating the Polish ambassador with a torrent of Latin, after which she chuckled with laughter. "God's death, my Lords! I have been forced this day to scour up my old Latin!"

Into Elizabeth's magnificent court walked the youthful Walter Ralegh. He cut an imposing figure, especially among the older generation, who paid scant regard to their dress and even less to their hair. Some still sported the old "Christ cut" or pudding basin, which gave them the look of "an old Holland cheese." Ralegh, by contrast, wore his locks "long at the ears and curled" and perfumed them with civit, musk, or camphor. His customary cartwheel ruff was his most extravagant gesture to foppishness, spreading peacocklike from his neck in dentilated lace. It was a perfect complement to his satin pinked vest and gauche doublet cut from finely flowered velvet and embroidered with pearls. The most shocking element of his dress was the accessories: he wore a dagger with a jewelled pommel, a black feather hat held at a jaunty angle by a ruby-and-pearl drop, and buff shoes tied with white ribbons. The expense of such attire was truly staggering. In 1584, a certain Hugh Pugh was charged with stealing items from Ralegh's wardrobe which included a jewel worth £80, a hatband of pearls worth £30, and five yards of silk worth £3. The total was more than the yearly cost of a household, including servants.

Queen Elizabeth was enchanted by Ralegh and his risqué flirtatiousness. At one of his earliest audiences, he had removed his diamond ring and scratched a half-finished couplet into one of the palace's latticed windows: "Fain would I climb, yet I fear to fall." Quick as a trice, the queen took the ring and rejoined: "If thy heart fail thee, climb not at all."

But Ralegh had no intention of halting his climb. An accomplished poet, he began writing sonnets to his queen, creating a whole new language of devotion as he struggled to describe his feelings towards her. She was Gloriana, emanating light and beauty; Diana, the chaste goddess of the moon; and Venus, "her pure cheek like a nymph."

Elizabeth's less eloquent courtiers despised this West Country genius with his *faux* airs and graces. They found him so "damnable proud" that they hit back with their own rhyming couplets that contained puns on his name: "The enemie of the stomach [i.e., raw] and the word of disgrace [i.e., lie] / Is the name of the gentleman with the bold face [i.e., Ralegh]." It was a poor attempt at a jest and the queen was not amused. She preferred to tease him about his West Country accent, jestingly calling him "Water." When she was at her most coquettish, she would joke that she was thirsting for "Water."

She soon began showering her young favourite with gifts, beginning, in 1583, with the lease of two estates belonging to All Souls, Oxford. She also granted him the right to charge every vintner in the country one pound a year for the privilege of selling wine. This was the foundation of Ralegh's enormous fortune, gaining him a huge income that was further augmented when he was given a lucrative licence to export woollen broadcloth. It was not long before the gifts came with titles. Ralegh was made vice-admiral of the West and then given the additional posts of lord-lieutenant of Cornwall and lord warden of the Stanneries, the latter giving him command of the Cornish tin mines. A man with such powers needed a suitably magnificent home, and even here the queen did not fail Ralegh. She offered him the use of Durham House, a rambling edifice that sprawled along the northern bank of the Thames. At the age of thirty, Walter had a London mansion of his own.

Like so many gifts bestowed by Elizabeth, Durham House was something of a white elephant. It was an ancient building whose crumbling charm held little appeal in stormy weather when the leaded gutters flooded and the towers moaned in the wind. It looked picturesque enough from the exterior: it rested on bulky Norman foundations and was adorned with crenellated battlements that rose sheer from the Thames. But this waterside hulk was a mildewed place whose medieval charm was not appreciated by the army of servants who found themselves living there. In the rain, it looked as if it had risen dripping from the subaqueous depths.

Yet it retained the vestiges of its former splendour. It had once been an ecclesiastical palace belonging to the bishops of Durham and it occupied one of the finest positions in the capital—downstream from the Palace of Westminster, close to Whitehall, and just a stone's throw from Leicester House, Arundel House, and York House. It had a watergate with steps leading down to the river and a huge, steep-roofed hall which was "stately and high [and] supported with lofty marble pillars." Indeed, the roof of the great hall was one of the landmarks of London, with a panorama that encompassed the entire capital.

Ralegh went to considerable expense to make Durham House habitable. Tapestries were hung from stone corbels and braziers were kept burning in the principal chambers. Visitors were impressed with the speed with which he had converted the palace into a home befitting the queen's suitor. "His lodging is very bravely furnyshed with arrace," wrote one, "the chamber wherein hymself doth lye hath a feild-bed, all covered with greine velvett . . . [and] set with plumes of whit feathers with spangles." It was furnished in the very latest Elizabethan fashion, and there had been no concessions to cost. Bolsters and hassocks cut the chill of the flagstone floors and damask hung from the embrasures. It was as comfortable as it could be.

Visitors were staggered by Walter's extravagance. "I have harde it credibly reported that Master Rawley hath spent within this halfe yeere above 3,000*l*," wrote one shocked courtier. "He is very soumptous in his aparell . . . [and] all the vessell with which he is served at his table is silver with his owne armes on the same." Ralegh's newfound status had also encouraged him to hire servants, and once again he saw no reason to compromise. "He hath attendinge on hym at lest 30 men who[se] lyveryes are chargable, of which number half be gentillmen, very brave felloes, divers havinge cheynes of gold."

After all the gifts that had already been bestowed upon young Walter, the transferral of Sir Humfrey Gilbert's American grant into his name passed unnoticed by the courtiers and diarists. But to Walter himself, it was the most welcome present of all, for he had already vowed to go down in history as the man who established the first English colony in America. Durham House had provided him with the ideal building from which he could plan and execute this bold adventure.

Ralegh spent much of his time in his private study at the top of one of the towers, from where he could watch the Thames wherries and lightermen. It was here that he kept his library and his sea charts, and it was from this room that he would sift through the details of his enterprise. "I remember well his study," wrote John Aubrey, who visited the palace some ninety years later, "which was a little turret that looked into and over the Thames and had the prospect which is pleasant, perhaps, as any in the world." There was a well-beaten path to this room. Scientists and artists, metallurgists, draughtsmen, and botanists—anyone, in fact, who might have knowledge to contribute—were summoned to Ralegh's study. Jews from Prague and mineral experts from Holland: all were welcome at Durham House, and there were often as many as forty experts living under the one roof.

On one particularly wet afternoon in late 1584, Ralegh had left his tower early and adjourned to the hall where his household had gathered to dine. Most of the men knew each other well—Michael Butler, Laurence Keymes, Philip Amadas, and Arthur Barlowe were old friends—but there was one figure missing from the familiar crowd. Thomas Harriot, a friend of Ralegh's since their Oxford days, had yet to be drawn downstairs. He was still in his chamber, lost in his thoughts, idling away the rainy twilight hours.

Harriot was a young man, still in his early twenties, yet he was already on intimate terms with the highest echelons of Elizabethan society—no small achievement for someone of such humble background that no record exists of his parentage. That he should find himself in this position was due to his algebraic gift. He was a math-

Ralegh invested a fortune in turning Durham House into the nerve centre of
his American enterprise. "I have harde it credibly reported that Master Rawley hath spent within this halfe yeere above 3,000*l*," wrote a courtier

ematical conjurer, a wizard, who was also blessed with an imagination that spawned such side shoots that he had already solved some
of the most impenetrable scientific conundrums of his day.

Harriot was the antithesis of Ralegh in looks, dress, and temperament. If the surviving portrait of him is to be believed, he cared little
for his appearance. He had a high forehead and thin hair and had
allowed his wispy beard to grow to a point, accentuating his elfish
chin. His skin was sallow and his face gaunt, yet his bold nose and
almond eyes rescued him from ugliness. He had long extolled the
virtues of a sober, monkish diet; he abhorred the debauched habits
of his contemporaries at Oxford, who spent so much of their time
engaged in wassailing that the university had been forced to clamp
down on their antics with a series of draconian decrees. Even dress
had been subjected to restrictions, and louche student bachelors
were forbidden to wear jerkins "of blew, green, redd, white, or any

other lite coller." Such decrees had made no difference to Thomas Harriot. He bought an ankle-length black robe on the day he arrived in Oxford, and wore it until the day of his death.

Walter had been quick to spot Harriot's genius and soon managed to enlist him in the cause of American colonisation. There were many hurdles to be overcome, not least of which was the challenge presented by the long ocean voyage. Few English mariners possessed sufficient skill to sail safely across the Atlantic, and Ralegh believed that navigation would never be reliable until "the aid of the mathematical sciences were enlisted." Harriot, an expert in applied mathematics, was clearly the right man to train his captains. Ralegh offered him "a most liberal salary" if he would give instruction on the theory and practice of navigation. Harriot launched himself into this task with enthusiasm, and soon had his first breakthrough, solving the perennial problem of determining compass variation by a single observation of the sun. The solution was complex, innovative, and extremely important. First, he taught Ralegh's navigators to use their compass to obtain a reading for the apparent direction of the sun at sunrise. He then instructed them to compare this with a theoretical reading for the latitude of the ship, which they could find in Harriot's own tables of the sun's declination at different positions of the globe. When these two figures were placed in a mathematical formula—also devised by Harriot—the mariners could calculate the variation of the compass. This in turn enabled Ralegh's mariners to determine their true direction of sailing with considerable accuracy.

Harriot was given a small chamber underneath the eaves of Durham House. Soon after moving in, he erected a huge *radius astronomicus*—a primitive telescope—on the roof above his room, enabling him to take the most accurate celestial observations of his day. Even in his brief moments of relaxation, when the London drizzle brought to a halt his rooftop experiments, Harriot was unable to tear himself away from his beloved mathematics. On one wet afternoon he was listening to the rain beating on the roof with monotonous regularity when he found himself calculating how much water

Thomas Harriot had a towering intellect and was destined to become the leading light in Ralegh's colonial enterprise

would enter his room were it not for the lead sheets over his head. "Over my chamber at Durham House," he recorded, "the measured levell square (accountinge half the thickness of the wall which casteth in the rayne) . . . is 268¾ foote square." He did not have a clock to help him solve his puzzle, so he used his pulse, assuming that each beat represented a second. By measuring the cubic volume gushing from the downspout, he was able to calculate that his room would collect eight and a half inches of water in every twenty-four-hour period.

While Harriot taught Walter's mariners how to sail across the Atlantic, Ralegh devoted his time to reading everything he could about America. He was particularly fascinated by the paint-daubed savages, and keen to ensure that his own colonists did not behave with the same murderous efficiency as had Spain's New World governors. Terrible tales of the conquistadors had leaked back to Europe in dribs and drabs, and it was not until 1583 that a sensational new book, *The Spanishe Colonie*, blew the whistle on exactly how the native Americans were being wiped off the face of the earth. The author, Bartolomé de Las Casas, had written his account to correct the misdeeds of Spain's governors, but he also shed considerable light on the sort of natives that Ralegh's colonists were likely to meet. Far from depicting them as savages, as had Davy Ingrams, he had been charmed by the innocence of their lives. "[They are] very simple," he wrote, "without suteltie or craft, without malice, very obedient and very faithfull." They lived such frugal lives that he would have happily compared them with "the holy fathers of the desert," were it not for the fact that they insisted on exposing their "shamefast partes"—a lack of modesty that even the sympathetic friar was unable to condone.

Las Casas also warned of the dangers of colonising a land peopled with such "simple" folk. He recounted in graphic detail the methods by which these tribesmen had been systematically slaughtered by the Spanish. His descriptions are written with such grisly relish that it is hard not to conclude that he took a voyeuristic pleasure in watching the butchery. He showed an unhealthy interest in torture by fire, and admitted that he had looked on as many an innocent victim was burned alive. On one occasion, he "sawe four or five of the principall lordes roasted and broyled uppon these gradeirons . . . they cryed out pitiously, which thing troubled the captayne that hee could not then sleepe; he commaunded to strangle them." But the hangman refused to dispatch them so quickly. He filled their mouths with bullets "to the ende that they should not crie, [then] put [them] to the fire until they were softly rosted after his desire." The Spaniards later refined their cruelty, choosing to roast only a part of their victim so as to cause maximum suffering. With one Indian, they "bent his feete agaynst the fyre untill that the very marrowe sprange out and trylled downe the soules of his feete."

Las Casas wrote his account in 1542, yet it was not until 1583— when anti-Spanish feeling was running high in England—that it was finally translated. Much of it is exaggerated, but the English publishers did not care a jot. They knew they had laid their hands on dynamite: their preface virtually admitted that they were printing it because it contained all the necessary ingredients—violence, torture, and adventure—to make it an Elizabethan best-seller.

Ralegh, a more discerning reader than most, found himself fascinated by its detailing of the first encounters between the New World and the Old. He later admitted his debt to Las Casas for setting him thinking about the issue that was to become the greatest problem of colonisation—the treatment and status of the native peoples of America.

He had long been aware that to send colonists across the Atlantic without knowing a great deal more about the country would be both dangerous and foolhardy, but it was only when he sat down with his old friend and colonial enthusiast, Richard Hakluyt, that he was struck by an ingenious idea. Hakluyt had in his possession the account of Richard Hore's disastrous 1536 expedition to America, and had also been gathering information about one of the earliest French forays across the Atlantic. Both of these voyages had stumbled upon the same plan for discovering more about America, but whereas Hore had failed miserably, the French party had achieved a certain success. They had set sail with the intention of capturing a native American who, "having once atchieved the French tongue . . . mighte declare more substantially their minde and knowledge." The hostage they selected was none other than the local "king," a deliberate choice since it was believed that he would be "best infourmed of such partes as were somewhat remote from his owne countrey." He proved stubbornly reluctant to play ball and had to be coaxed aboard the French vessel by devious means. He was invited onto the ship, "being required thither to a banquet," but instead of being offered fine food and wines, he found himself "traiterously caryed away into France, where hee lived foure yeeres . . . and then dyed." Whether the French learned anything of use from their captive is not recorded, but Walter quickly realised that here, in a nutshell, was the only surefire way to discover more about America. He immediately decided to send a small reconnaissance vessel across the ocean with orders to bring back a native American—one who could be taught to speak English.

It was preferable that this Indian should be accompanied by other members of his tribe, and imperative that he come dressed in his native attire. Ralegh was a tireless publicist who was only too aware of the value of a tattooed Indian wandering through the Elizabethan court. Such an exotic creature was guaranteed to please the queen, and was also certain to help him raise money for his projected colony.

In the spring of 1584, Ralegh was at last presented with the queen's patent that transferred Sir Humfrey's American rights into his own name. They were every bit as extensive as those of his half-brother and gave him absolute authority over all "cittyes, castles, townes, villages and places." With his team of enthusiasts now hard at work in Durham House, he knew the time was right to send his first expedition.

Two of the regulars at Harriot's navigation classes had been

Ralegh believed his ships would only reach America if "the aid of the mathematical sciences were enlisted." He employed Harriot to instruct his captains

Philip Amadas and Arthur Barlowe, both of whom were members of Ralegh's household. They had acquitted themselves well in his study group and, when Ralegh began selecting men for his reconnaissance mission, he chose them as expedition leaders.

Plymouth-born Amadas was tiny—his nickname was "little Amadas"—and fiery in temperament. On one occasion, he was rowing up the Thames when his double-wherry ploughed into another river boat. He immediately attacked the master of the other boat, but was forced to beat a hasty retreat when one of his oarsmen was struck with such violence "that his heade was grevouslye broken and blede abundantlye."

Arthur Barlowe, captain of the second ship, was a more inspired choice. A colleague of Ralegh's since their days together in Ireland, he was calm, well-travelled, and quick-witted. What particularly impressed Ralegh was his observant eye, for which he was given the important task of recording his impressions of America and its native population. He was ordered to keep his account as upbeat as possible. There was little widespread interest in America and nothing, so far, to encourage prospective colonists. The land across the sea was widely believed to be barren and inhospitable, and Ralegh knew that positive propaganda would do his cause no end of good.

Barlowe excelled himself from the outset, scoring the remarkable achievement of making the always dreadful ocean crossing sound more pleasurable than a day's boating on the Thames. There was none of the usual griping about putrid victuals and atrocious weather. The ships were "wel furnished," their orders were "perfect," and no sooner had the prevailing trade winds wafted them to a Caribbean landfall—the quickest, but by no means the shortest route to America—than they found "sweete water" gushing out of the ground.

After a brief rest the men pointed their vessels due north—towards Florida—and picked their way through notoriously treacherous waters until they sighted the sandy banks of Cape Hatteras in what is now North Carolina.

Barlowe did not panic when he discovered they were in "shole water": he was far too busy sniffing the air, "which smelt so sweetly, and was so strong a smell, as if we had bene in the midst of some delicate garden, abounding with all kind of odoriferous flowers."

It was not long before the men sighted the long, low sand dunes of the Outer Banks. They had now entered the region which Ralegh had thought might be suitable for the colony: far enough away from the prying eyes of the Spaniards yet close enough to launch privateering raids against their treasure ships. Barlowe liked what he found. He rightly assumed that the sand banks enclosed a vast lagoon and thought that this could be a perfect location for a colony, offering a safe anchorage yet hidden from the sea. He sailed along the Outer Banks for 120 miles before finding an entry into the shallow waters of Pamlico Sound. "After thankes given to God for our safe arrival thither, we manned our boates and went to viewe the lande."

Barlowe was enraptured by the landscape. The shores of the lagoon were lined with lofty cedars and grapevines and the abundant wildlife obligingly frolicked in his line of fire. He waxed lyrical in his journal, pausing only to pluck juicy grapes from trailing vines: "I think in all the world," he declared, "the like aboundance is not to be founde: and myselfe, having seene those partes of Europe that most abound, find such difference as were incredible to be written."

The men landed at the island of Hatarask and took possession "in the right of the Queene's most excellent majestie"; they then set off to explore more fully. Barlowe was convinced that he had arrived in paradise. As he crashed through the undergrowth, he was amazed at the "incredible aboundance" of deer, hares, and game birds, all of which sought shade under the "highest and reddest cedars of the world." When he blasted his musket into the undergrowth, the result was little short of spectacular: "such a flocke of cranes—for the most part white—arose under us, with such a crye redoubled by many ecchoes as if an armie of men had showted all together."

It was not until the men had been on the island for several days that they realised they were being watched. At first they saw no one, but they slowly became aware of shadowy figures lurking in the undergrowth. The men kept their muskets loaded in case of trouble, but the Indians kept their distance. On the third day Barlowe and his men made contact. "We espied one small boate rowing towards

us," he wrote, "having in it three persons." The Indians appeared
unfazed by the English ships and headed directly for the shore,
where one of them leaped gaily onto the beach and "walked up and
downe uppon the point of the lande next unto us."

Barlowe and his men cautiously approached the Indian, who
made no "shewe of feare or doubt." Conversation proved impossible
since neither side could understand the other, but by using a mixture of sign language and pictures, Barlowe managed to coax the
tribesman on board ship. The captain then had to consider what to
offer as a token of friendship. Sir George Peckham had suggested
gifts of clothing for the Indians, recommending caps and cassocks.
Barlowe had absentmindedly forgotten to pack any of these, but he
did have other items of clothing. "[We] gave him a shirt, a hatte, and
some other things, and made him taste of our wine and our meate,
which he liked very well." The Indian left after thanking his hosts,
and the Englishmen congratulated themselves on their skill in handling their first meeting with a savage.

That, at any rate, was the official account. Thomas Harriot gave
an altogether different story in his record of the voyage, suggesting
that the first meeting with the Indians was altogether more dramatic.
"As soone as they saw us, [they] began to make a great and horrible
crye, as people which never befoer had seene men apparelled like
us, and camme away makinge out crys like wild-beasts or men out of
their wyts. But, beeinge gentlye called backe, wee offred them of our
wares, as glasses, knives, babies [dolls] and other trifles which wee
thougt they delighted in." Harriot adds that once the men had overcome their fear, they invited the Englishmen to their village and
"entertained us with reasonable curtesie," although they continued
to be "amased at the first sight of us."

Whatever the truth about their first encounter, the English did
manage to behave with uncharacteristic courtesy. Even the hot-
headed Amadas kept his cool, and the Indians were encouraged to
return the following morning. This time they were accompanied by
a tribal elder—the brother of the "king"—along with forty retainers.

Barlowe was impressed by this merry band. He found them "very handsome and goodly people," "their behaviour as mannerly and civill as any of Europe." Their grinning leader cut an extraordinary figure. His skin was a startling "colour yellowish" and his hair was shaved at the sides, leaving a floppy cock's comb on top. He had a sheet of beaten metal tied to his head and in each ear he wore six copper rings. Even more disconcerting to the starched and buttoned Barlowe was the fact that, apart from a skimpy loincloth, he was completely naked.

The English had great difficulty in communicating with the Indians: Barlowe managed to discover that this tribal elder was called Granganimeo and was more than a little proud of himself when he learned the name of the surrounding countryside, Wingandacoa. This was put into all the official paperwork; it was some months before the English realised that this unpronounceable word—which the Indians kept repeating to Barlowe—actually meant "you've got nice clothes."

The English had initially feared that the elder's arrival heralded an attack, but such fears were soon proved to be misplaced and they laid down their muskets and culverins. The Indian elder, a jolly fellow, proposed a picnic on the beach. After issuing a command in his native tongue, "his servants spread a long matte upon the grounde, on which he sate down." Barlowe and Amadas joined him, gingerly seating themselves next to this seminaked warrior.

Davy Ingrams had recommended kissing the Indians to show friendship. Barlowe baulked at such a suggestion, preferring to wear a continuous smile in order to make his pleasure known. All was going well when suddenly, and quite without warning, Granganimeo began "striking on his head and his breast, and afterwards on ours." He rained down blows on his guests, and the two men might have fought back had they not surmised—in the nick of time—that this one-sided boxing match was a traditional Indian greeting "to shewe we were all one, smiling, and making shewe the best hee could, of all love and familiaritie."

Amadas and Barlowe decided it was time to distribute presents. They had brought with them numerous trinkets, but the tribal elder was most taken by a hand-crafted serving platter made of "bright tinne." He eagerly grabbed it from Amadas and shouted something to his men, but any hopes that he was about to fill it with food were quickly dashed. "[He] clapt it before his breast and after made a hole in the brimme thereof and hung it about his necke, making signes that it would defende him against his enemies' arrows."

The English were astonished by this primitive yet intelligent people who had no knowledge of the wheel and still lit their fires by laboriously rubbing together two sticks. They looked every inch the "devill," yet they were generous and amiable and showed no signs of hostility.

To the Indians, the arrival of the English was a cause of great wonder. "[They] wondred mervelously when we were amongest them," wrote Barlowe, "at the whitenes of our skinnes, ever coveting to touch our breastes and to view the same." They were no less impressed by the two English vessels which towered over their dugout canoes. "They had our shippes in marvelous admiration, and all things els was so strange unto them as it appeared that none had ever seene the like before."

But what really took their breath away was the English weaponry. They fought with bows and arrows, clubs, and wooden swords, and were terrified by the noise and power of the guns carried by Barlowe and his men. "When we discharged any peece, were it but a harquebush, they would tremble thereat for very feare and for the strangenes of the same."

Soon the English sailors were bartering for animal skins. They could scarcely believe how little the Indians valued their merchandise. A cheap tin dish bought twenty skins, a copper kettle bought fifty, and when they produced hatchets and knives the Indians were willing to offer almost anything. "The king's brother had a great liking of our armour, a sworde, and divers other things," wrote Barlowe, "and offered to lay a great boxe of pearl in gage of them." Barlowe was tempted but refused. He wanted to be absolutely sure that he could rely upon these tribesmen before he set about arming them.

The hospitality had so far been one-sided. Every day the Indians brought a wicker hamper filled with "fatte buckes, conies, hares, fishe, the best of the worlde." When Barlowe hinted at their need for vegetables, he found himself inundated with "divers kindes of fruites, melons, walnuts, cucumbers, gourdes, pease and divers rootes, and fruites very excellent good."

The English realised it would be diplomatic to return the hospitality. This was no easy matter, for they had few provisions on board, and those they did have were scarcely appetizing: rancid pork, salted herring, and dried peas so alive with weevils that they were in danger of jumping out of the cooking pot. But they did still have wine—lots of it—and they hoped that this would help to jolly along the meal.

"The king's brother came aboord the shippes," wrote Barlowe, "and dranke wine and ate of oure meate and of our bread, and liked exceedingly thereof." To their surprise, he seemed to relish the rancid meat and asked if he could return within a few days, together with his family. This he duly did. "[He] brought his wife with him to the shippes, his daughter, and two or three little children."

Barlowe took an instant fancy to Granganimeo's wife. "[She] was very well favoured, of meane stature, and very bashfull." Unlike most of the women, who left much of their breasts exposed, she had covered herself with "a long cloke of leather"; to Barlowe's immense disappointment, she left it on throughout the meal. She was adorned with little clusters of pearls. The Englishmen, knowing of Ralegh's penchant for jewellery, bought a bracelet to present to him on their return.

It did not take the English long to realise that they had stumbled across the perfect location for Ralegh's colony. The natives—Algonquins—were friendly and the land was fertile; all they needed now was a good strategic site for a settlement. In this they were unwittingly aided by Granganimeo, who suggested they row across Pamlico Sound to the little island of Roanoke, where he himself had a house. Barlowe jumped at this suggestion and immediately set off to the northern end of this small wooded island, where he found "a village of nine houses, built of cedar and fortified round about with sharpe trees." No sooner had his boat been spotted by the villagers than Granganimeo's wife—still fully clothed—"came running out to meete us very cheerfully and friendly." She ordered the villagers to haul the pinnace onto the sand and had the men carried to her longhouse, where a "great fire" was crackling in the hearth.

Her first task was to scrub down these stinking, sweat-stained mariners, who had not washed since leaving London. "[She] tooke off our clothes, and washed them, and dried them againe. Some of the women pulled off our stockings and washed them. Some washed our feete in warme water, and she herselfe tooke great paines to see all thinges ordered in the best manner she coulde, making great haste to dresse some meate for us to eate."

She proved an attentive hostess. Once the men had been bathed and warmed, the food began to appear. "[She] brought us into the innere roome where she set on the boord . . . some wheat like furmentie [wheat boiled in milk], sodden [stewed] venison and roasted, fishe sodden, boyled, and roasted, melons rawe and sodden, rootes of divers kindes, and divers fruites."

There was a brief moment of panic when three armed hunters appeared in the twilight, but when the villagers noticed Barlowe's alarm they "beate the poore fellowes out of the gate againe." Nevertheless, the incident reminded the men that they were alone in an alien land. As soon as they had finished their meal, they insisted on returning to their boat, much to the chagrin of Granganimeo's wife.

"[She] was much grieved, and sent divers men and thirtie women to sitte all night on the bankes-side by us, and sent us into our boates fine mattes to cover us from the rayne, using very many wordes to intreate us to rest in their houses: but because we were fewe men, and if we had miscarried, the voyage had been in very greate daunger, we durst not adventure anything."

Barlowe remained anchored off Roanoke Island for some five

America's lush shores delighted Ralegh's men. "I think in all the world the like aboundance is not to be founde," wrote one. Roanoke Island (middle left) was sheltered from the sea by the Outer Banks

weeks, exploring the area and searching for the most suitable place in which to plant a colony. He and his men surveyed "about a hundreth islands," but none could match Roanoke. It was fertile, richly stocked with wildlife, and sheltered from the Atlantic storms by the sand dunes of the Outer Banks. Better still, it was well hidden from any Spanish captain who happened to be sailing along the coastline. The one drawback—its dense population—was not given a moment's thought.

Barlowe and Amadas still had one important matter to attend to before they could return to England. Ralegh's last instruction before they had set sail was to bring back a native American so that he could be taught English and reveal the secrets of his land. He had not offered any advice on how the men were to coax this tribesman on board, nor did Barlowe see fit to explain how they achieved their goal. But when the two vessels set sail for England, they had on board "two of the savages, being lustie men, whose names were Wanchese and Manteo."

It is unlikely that the two men knew each other. Wanchese came from Roanoke while Manteo lived on Croatoan, a long sandy spit that formed part of the Outer Banks. It was not long before the two Indians found they had little in common. While Manteo saw the English as his hosts, Wanchese came to view them as captors.

The ships arrived in England in the middle of September 1584. Barlowe dashed straight to Durham House to inform Ralegh of his exciting news. The content of their discussions was secret and will never be known, but by the time Barlowe's account was published, America was being promoted as a second Eden. "We found the people most gentle, loving and faithfull," he wrote, "void of all guile and treason, and such as lived after the manner of the golden age." He added that "the earth bringeth foorth all things in aboundance, as in the first creation, without toile or labour."

The myth of the noble savage was born, but it remained to be seen if Manteo and Wanchese would live up to expectations.

4

Harriot's Devils

Arthur Barlowe brought Manteo and Wanchese to London, where the Indians were given chambers in Durham House. There are no surviving records of their first days in the city, nor of the reaction of curious Londoners, but they must have made an extraordinary sight as they wandered through the capital's alleys and markets clothed in deerskin breechcloths, their hair decked with feather mantles. They were probably given the standard tour of the city's sights—the Tower of London, the markets of Cheapside, and the rotting heads of traitors impaled on London Bridge. London did not impress all of its visitors, but its sheer size and noise must have left a deep mark on the two Indians.

The bridge was one of the most magnificent sights—its twenty arches of squared stone supporting such a hodgepodge of gabled houses that "it seemeth rather a continual street than a bridge." It led to Southwark, where the stews, bear pits, and fighting dogs drew many curious visitors. But the most impressive vista extended along the northern bank of the Thames. The grandiose edifices that lined the Strand must have astonished Manteo and Wanchese, who had never before seen a building larger than a wood-framed shelter covered with wicker mats. Further downstream, the Tower, which was already an ancient monument in Elizabethan times, also made a fine sight. Those fortunate enough to be granted access to its cavernous interior were left rubbing their eyes at the treasury, which housed "objects of silver gilt and also of pure gold"; regal beds "of red velvet embroidered with gold and numerous little pearls," and gold and agate chalices "set with large pearls, emeralds, diamond and rubies."

In the third week of October, Manteo and Wanchese accompanied Ralegh to Hampton Court, where the queen was in residence. Their visit coincided with that of a Pomeranian traveller, Lupold von Wedel, who had spent much of the year at the court and was most impressed by what he had seen. Here, in the palace's formal gardens, the Elizabethan court made a magnificent spectacle, especially on Sundays when the queen and her retinue proceeded to church with all the pomp and ceremony they could muster.

They were led by her lifeguard, "strong and tall," who were dressed to the nines. "They bore gilt halberts, red coats faced with black velvet [and] in front and on the back they wore the queen's arms." Next came the "gentlemen of rank"—her privy councillors— "two of them bearing the royal sceptre each, a third with the royal sword in a red velvet scabbard, embroidered with gold and set with precious stones and large pearls." There were ladies of noble birth, children of lords, and the yeoman of the guard, who carried "small gilt hunting spears." The queen's heralds made the greatest concession to flamboyant dress. They wore bright blue mantles with extraordinary wings made of beaten gold. As the queen passed, eight trumpeters blew their brass, two drummers gave a dramatic roll, and a piper whistled a merry tune.

No one was allowed to outshine Her Majesty, the focus of all attention. Von Wedel had met her on several occasions and each time she looked more splendid than the last. She wore a long velvet mantle, "lined with ermin, white with little black dots," and liked to travel in her ornate sedan chair borne by "two cream-coloured horses with yellow manes and tails."

It was not easy to talk with the queen, for it was she who decided who had something of interest to say. When gentlemen were called to her side, a strict protocol had to be observed. The chosen courtier had to squat on his knees and continue in this pose "until she orders him to rise." Leaving the queen involved a more elaborate charade. Courtiers had to walk backwards and "bow down deeply, and when they have reached the middle of the room, they must bow down a second time."

One courtier who was frequently called to the queen's side, according to Von Wedel, was Ralegh. She chatted with him in "a very friendly manner, making jokes," and liked to tease him in front of others. "She pointed with her finger in his face, saying he had some uncleanness there, which she even intended to wipe off with her handkerchief." Ralegh was embarrassed and "took it away himself." Von Wedel noticed that "she loved this gentleman now in preference to all others" and added that "two years ago he was scarcely able to keep a single servant, and now she had bestowed so much upon him that he is able to keep five hundred servants."

Ralegh kept a careful eye on the Indians during his time at Hampton Court, anxious not to overawe them. There were many who wished to meet these curious individuals, but he kept a tight control over who was introduced into their company. He even made them dress in dowdy taffeta blouses, in the English fashion, to detract from the attention they received. His protective veil worked well, and explains the lack of written records about the two Indian tribesmen.

One visitor who was given access was Von Wedel, who met them after church on October 18, 1584, and excitedly recorded the event in his journal. "Their faces as well as their whole bodies were very similar to those of the white Moors at home," he wrote. "They wear no shirts, only a piece of fur to cover the pudenda and the skins of wild animals to cover their shoulders. Here they are clad in brown taffeta." Von Wedel thought "they had a very childish and wild appearance" and added that "nobody could understand their language."

Queen Elizabeth liked to joke with Ralegh. "She loved this gentleman in preference to all others," a court visitor noted

The attempt to decipher their native tongue was indeed proving extremely difficult. Several visitors had tried to ask them simple questions in sign language, but it proved impossible to understand their answers. The strange nuances and weird inflections of their speech stumped even gifted linguists, and it soon became apparent that a superior intellect would be required to crack the cryptic riddle of this language.

There was never any doubt as to who this genius might be. Thomas Harriot was immediately set to work on Manteo and Wanchese, employed not only to learn their language but to compile a detailed phrasebook and dictionary. Harriot jumped at the opportunity to work on a project that had stumped everyone else. He was convinced that the language of the Indians conformed to some sort of logical system and that complete mastery of grammar and pronunciation was possible, given time. He quickly learned a few basic words and phrases, but when he came to writing them down, he found himself up against an intractable problem: the English alphabet could not accurately represent the Indians' speech. Many of their words contained sounds that had no corresponding letters in English, and even when the letters did exist, the written word gave no clue as to how they should be pronounced. The English words *wall* and *man* both contained an *a*, yet that one letter was pronounced in different ways. Harriot knew that without giving some clue as to how Indian words should be pronounced, any phrasebook would be as good as useless.

He was not a linguist, so he turned to the experts for advice. One of these, John Hart, had spent considerable effort devising a phonetic alphabet for Welsh so that any man wishing to speak the language could do so perfectly, "when and wheresoever he may see it . . . though he understoode no worde thereof." It had worked well. Hart had written down long sentences of Welsh in his alphabet— though he did not understand a word—and read them back to complete strangers, who affirmed "that I coulde speake Welsh."

The language of the Indians, known as Algonkian, was altogether more complicated than Welsh, and Hart's system was too simplistic for the perfectionist Harriot. The mathematician took the bold step of devising a new and highly complex alphabet that precisely represented every Algonkian speech sound. This was no easy matter. He worked obsessively, often studying late into the autumn evenings, long after the great gates of Durham House had been bolted for the night. He wanted his alphabet to be a work of perfection. To this end, he studied the Indians' vocal chords, noting the position of their lips and tongues, and, where necessary, created new symbols to record strange sounds. It was a laborious process, for there were literally hundreds of nuances to be recorded, but over the course of a few months his alphabet slowly took shape. Harriot left no notes as to how he carried out his research, but he probably adapted Hart's work on the inflexions of speech and how words were formed. Hart had written at length about the "dumb and dul sounds in our speech" and categorised sounds by the manner in which they were made—"eyther by touching of the lippes togither, or of the under lippe to the upper teeth, or of the tongue to the palet."

Harriot's resultant alphabet had thirty-six characters in total and looked extraordinary—a hodgepodge of algebraic symbols, Greek and Roman letters, invented characters. One scholar described the letters as looking "like devills," perhaps because some ended in forked tridents. The shape of the letters provided a clue as to how they should be pronounced. English equivalents were recorded alongside where applicable, while sounds that were unfamiliar were categorised as "barbarouse wordes" and placed in a separate column. Harriot tested his alphabet on English phrases, putting passages of the Lord's Prayer into his new script to see whether they were readable. The alphabet was a work of unparalleled creativity—one that had required the logic of a scientist and the imagination of an artist. It successfully represented every sound of this complex language. He planned at a later date to expand his work into an English-Algonkian dictionary—and may well have done so—but the work is long since lost. Even his short vocabulary was destroyed in the Great Fire of London in 1666. Only the alphabet itself now survives.

Harriot had not devoted all his time to the dry science of phonetics. He had also invested considerable energy in learning conversational Algonkian and in teaching the Indians some basic English. It soon became apparent that Manteo was far more compliant than Wanchese, who evinced no interest in learning English and showed even less desire to stay in London.

By Christmas 1584, Harriot and Manteo were able to engage in simple conversations. Harriot managed to coax a small amount of information from the Indian and was able to inform Ralegh, directly from Manteo, about "the goodnesse of the soile and of great commodities that would arise to the realme of England, by traffique, if that the English had anie habitation and were planted to live there." This news was deemed to be of sufficient interest to be discussed in Parliament and cited in the bill that confirmed Ralegh's American patent.

It was not long before Harriot had attained considerable fluency in Algonkian. This enabled him to quiz Manteo about his land and people, amassing information that was to prove of the greatest importance. The two men spent whole days in each other's company in their Durham House chambers—the scientist in his customary black gown and Manteo in his taffeta blouse. Harriot noted down everything that he learned, to be written up in greater detail later in his book about America, *A Briefe and True Report*. He managed to capture something of the sense of wonder and bewilderment felt by the Indians when they first came into contact with Elizabethan England. "Many things they sawe with us," he wrote, "as mathematicall instruments, sea compasses . . . [and] spring clocks that seemed to goe of themselves—and many other things that we had—were so strange unto them, and so farre exceeded their capacities to comprehend the reason and meanes how they should be made and done, that they thought they were rather the workes of gods then men."

Manteo's revelations about his land and people quickly enabled Harriot to add a great deal of flesh to the bones of Barlowe's discoveries. He learned that the region around Roanoke Island was ruled by competing tribal chieftains whose power was dependent upon the number of fighting men they could field. Roanoke itself had fallen under the rule of Wingina, a devious chief whose authority extended for some distance up and down the coast. Combative and fiercely ambitious, Wingina had recently overreached himself in an attack on a neighbouring tribe and had almost been killed. He was "shott in two places through the bodye and once cleane through the thigh." This was why Barlowe's men "sawe him not at all."

Manteo also revealed to Harriot something of the tactics of intertribal warfare. The most successful chieftains were wily and deceitful and thought nothing of using subterfuge to destroy their enemies. He described how one tribe had invited all the leading families of a nearby village to a feast, and "when they were altogether merrie and praying before their idoll . . . the captaine or lorde of the towne came suddenly upon them and slewe them every one." Such "cruell and bloodie" violence had drastically reduced the population and "the people are marvelously wasted, and in some places the country left desolate."

Day after day, Manteo fed Harriot with priceless information about battle strategy and weaponry. "Their maner of warres amongst themselves is either by sudden surprising one another," recorded Harriot, "most commonly about the dawning of the day, or moone light, or els by ambush—or some suttle devises."

Weapons were extremely primitive. Harriot was assured that they had "no edge tooles or weapons of yron or steele to offend us withall, neither knowe they how to make any." Most Indians possessed only "bowes made of witch-hazle and arrowes of reeds," although a few warriors carried "flat-edged truncheons, also of wood about a yard long" and some had shields made of bark. Their armour was laughably ineffectual when compared to the helmets and breastplates still worn by England's knights. It was made of "stickes wickered together with thread" and fell apart at the mere tap of a halberd. All in all, the

Harriot quizzed Manteo about Indian battle tactics. They usually attacked "about the dawning of the day, or moone light," but were armed with primitive weapons

Indian tribesmen made for a derisory fighting force. Harriot was able to assure Ralegh that the result of any clash between the English and Indians was a foregone conclusion, since the English would have the "advantages against them [in] so many maner of waies, as by our discipline, our strange weapons, and devises else, especially by ordinance great and small." He added that it was most unlikely that the Indians would fight back, and that "the turning up of their heels against us in running away was their best defence."

Walter Ralegh had amassed a considerable fortune by the winter of 1584. His expenses were immense—his shoes alone were later rumoured "to be worth six thousand gold pieces"—but he was in receipt of rich gifts from the queen. "When will you cease to be a beggar?" she once asked him. "When your majesty ceases to be a benefactor," he nonchalantly replied.

For all his flamboyance, there was a cautious individual lurking within the ostentatious shell. Prattling courtiers constantly reminded Ralegh of his humble roots, and, as his poetry reveals, he was keenly aware that fate could quickly plunge him straight back to his rented farmhouse in Devon.

When he came to planning his colony in America, his first preference was that the state should carry the costs. Sir Humfrey had sunk a fortune into equipping a fleet that had failed to make a successful landfall. Ralegh's expenses—if and when he landed his colonists—were going to be far greater. It was for this reason that he asked his gifted friend Richard Hakluyt to pen a treatise for the queen, explaining why Her Majesty should finance the establishment of his colony. The treatise was entitled A Discourse of Western Planting; just in case the queen never got beyond the cover, it was given the unambiguous subtitle Certain reasons to induce her majesty and the state to take in hand the western voyage and the planting therein.

Hakluyt's treatise was a cogent argument for state-financed colonial expansion. Many of his arguments were well rehearsed, particularly those that dealt with the growing power of Spain. He argued that Ralegh's colony could be a base from which "we may arreste at our pleasure . . . every yere, one or twoo hundred saile of [Spanish] shippes." It could also serve as a training ground for native Indians, tribes who rejected "the proude and bluddy governemente of the Spaniarde" and were desperate to "shake of their moste intollerable yoke."

Mindful of the queen's spendthrift nature, Hakluyt also stressed the economic benefits of a colony. "The savages," he wrote, "are greatly delighted with any cappe or garment made of coarse wollen clothe, their contrie beinge colde and sharpe in the winter." He assured Her Majesty that they would like nothing better than to wrap themselves up in English cloaks, and begged the queen to consider the employment that a colony would bring to "cappers, knitters, clothiers, wollmen, corders, spynners, weavers, fullers, sheremen, dyers, drapers, hatters and such like." Hakluyt was not a gambling man, but even he was prepared to hazard that the savages would be so delighted with English clothes that they would bring to the country an annual revenue that would run into hundreds of thousands of pounds.

Hakluyt presented his treatise on bended knee. His humble mien so enchanted the queen that she rewarded him with the canonry of Holy Trinity in Bristol. But Elizabeth had already made up her mind on the issue of investing in Ralegh's colony and no amount of persuasion was going to change it. She demurred from the suggestion that she should spend her own money on the project, arguing that the costs would be enormous, and said that the results of any clash with the Spanish would have serious repercussions if she was involved. Worse still, if the colony failed, she herself would become an object of ridicule.

The queen had her own proposal, one that was more in tune with her imperial aspirations. Instead of pouring money into a bottomless pit, she decided to donate something that was less costly yet at the same time infinitely more precious—her name. The country across the ocean could not continue to be called Wingandacoa, a word that no one except Harriot could pronounce. Henceforth it was to be known as Virginia, in honour of Elizabeth, the Virgin Queen.

Only she could have turned the tables with quite such panache. And only she could have dreamed up something that was clever, politic, and wildly egotistical. It was coquettish and romantic, yet it also sent an unambiguous political message to King Philip II of Spain. The queen had staked her honour on the New World and was personally entrusting its future to her chosen favourite, the young Walter Ralegh.

She realised, of course, that this was not a task to be undertaken by a mere commoner. Queenly honour needed to be defended by a knight—one who displayed all the chivalrous gallantry of his medieval forebears. And so at the Twelfth Day celebrations in 1585, at the palace of Greenwich, Queen Elizabeth called her favourite to her side. Ralegh fell to his knees a commoner, but when he arose he found himself a knight. The future champion of Virginia was now Sir Walter Ralegh.

5

Storms, Sprites, and Goblins

It was not a good year to be travelling. No sooner had the bells of London tolled in New Year's Day, 1585, than the quacks and soothsayers of the capital were prophesying doom on a scale not seen since the death of old King Henry. Catastrophe was written in the heavens. The planets showed malevolent conjunctions and the moon revealed disturbing signs. Worse still, there was to be an eclipse on April 19—only a partial one in England, but warning enough of impending disaster.

The writings of the soothsayers were taken extremely seriously by Elizabethan Londoners, especially those about to attempt a long sea voyage. To such men, the prophecies of experts like Thomas Porter made for grim reading. "Yf any man hath many journeys to take by land or by water," warned Porter, "let hym have an eye rounde about hym, for force is lykely to exceede in all places, and violence already shaketh its head and frowneth upon travaylers." He added that "warinesse and courage are the best spelles agaynst such sprites and goblins." The only consolation for those leaving England was that "pestilence and pestilent fevers . . . wyll sweepe cities and scoure townes."

Others were scarcely more encouraging. Astronomer Euan Lloyd confirmed Porter's gloomy prognostication and added that "discov-

London's astrologers predicted doom for Ralegh's fleet. "Discoveries this yeere are like to prove but badly," wrote one

eries this yeere attempted are like to prove but badly." He predicted that travellers would "sustaine great labour and trouble therein" and promised a particularly awful year for "effeminate persons" and those with venereal disease. Nor was he overly optimistic about the weather, forecasting "many tempests, fogges and mysts at the sea; also many stormes, muche foule weather and shipwracke by occasion thereof."

Ralegh was neither effeminate nor suffering from venereal disease. He dismissed such talk as gibberish and began to sketch out rough plans for his colony. He quickly became aware of the ambitious nature of his undertaking. An operation on this scale had never before been attempted by Elizabethan England and no one had the faintest idea whether it would succeed. It was going to be hard enough to ship some 300 colonists across the ocean and plant them on a little-known coastline. But that was the easy part. Even if they arrived in spring—when they could sow their crops—they would still need food supplies to last them five months until harvest time.

There was also the daunting logistical problem of transporting to America the immense quantity of equipment and hardware needed to construct a fortified settlement. A fort required masonry and iron-work; that, in turn, required a foundry and a smithy as well as masons, tilers, and carpenters. And, since Manteo had revealed that the area around Roanoke lacked even the most basic raw materials, including stone, everything would have to be shipped from England.

The first and greatest hurdle to be overcome was raising enough money to buy ships and supplies. The queen had graciously offered one of her vessels, the *Tiger*, and given Ralegh £400 of gunpowder from the Tower. But an expedition on the scale planned by Sir Walter required far greater resources than even the queen could afford. He was forced to turn elsewhere for sponsors. The usual method of harnessing finance was to raise subscriptions as a joint-stock com-pany, to be repaid with profit (or loss) at the end of the voyage. But the astronomical cost of equipping a colony was never going to be covered by a trading expedition to North America; Ralegh had to offer merchants a more attractive incentive. There was never any question as to what this might be. With tensions between England and Spain growing by the day, Ralegh promised them a summer sea-son of piracy on the high seas—smash-and-grab raids on any Span-ish ship that was foolish enough to sail into his line of fire. Such attacks had already been given the unofficial blessing of the queen, whose patience with King Philip II was wearing thin. Indeed, her "payment" for the loan of the *Tiger* was almost certainly a share in any Spanish plunder that Ralegh's captains were able to seize.

Ralegh had dangled an alluring bait before England's merchants and they were soon offering their financial support. Sir Francis Walsingham and Sir Richard Grenville both ventured capital, the West Country gentry provided supplies, while the wealthy London entrepreneur William Sanderson introduced him to some of the city's richest merchants. Ralegh was so exultant that he struck a seal bearing his new arms and title: "Sir Walter Ralegh, Lord and Governor of Virginia." Money quickly flowed into his coffers. By early spring he had raised enough hard cash to begin detailed planning of the prospective colony.

He sought expert advice from the two Richard Hakluyts—uncle and nephew—who had amassed a considerable amount of knowledge about previous overseas expeditions. They considered every aspect of Ralegh's project and reached a conclusion that would have dampened the enthusiasm of all but the most optimistic of adventurers. The younger Hakluyt believed that construction of the settlement alone was going to require "brickmakers, tilemakers, lymemakers, bricklayers, tilers, thackers (with reede, russhes, broome or strawe), synkers of welles and finders of springes, quarrellers to digge tile, rough masons, carpinters and lathmakers." And, since the colonists would have no access to supplies from England, they would require blacksmiths "to forge the yrons of shovels" and spade makers "that may, out of the woods there, make spades like those of Devonshire."

Neither of the Hakluyts was able to predict the exact number of skilled craftsmen that would be needed to build the colony, but the construction of any reasonably sized settlement was certain to require perhaps fifty or sixty men. All of these would have to be kept fed and watered, a logistical nightmare that would require crops to be grown on a scale that few Elizabethan farmers could contemplate. The younger Hakluyt prepared a second list of farming specialists whose task would be to hunt, fish, and produce a bumper harvest in soil that had never been manured. He proposed sending marksmen "skilfull to kill wilde beasts" and warreners to breed rabbits, and added that to maintain the supply of meat during the winter it would be necessary to ship greyhounds to kill deer, bloodhounds to recover the kill, and mastiffs "to kill heavie beastes." The colony would also require both "sea-fisshers" and "freshwater-

Ralegh sought advice on what equipment and specialists would be needed by his colony. No settlement could survive without a village blacksmith

fisshers," while the cultivation of vegetables and pulses would call for specialists with a proven track record.

Health was a prime concern. The young Hakluyt was well aware that the colony could not afford to lose men to sickness and proposed employing a team of men to care for their physical welfare. These included a surgeon "to lett bloude," an apothecary to concoct potions, and "a phisition . . . to kepe and to cure such [as] fall into disease and destemperature." Mindful of the men's spiritual welfare, he urged that "there be appointed one or twoo preachers . . . that God may be honoured." This last suggestion was studiously ignored, to the probable relief of most of the men.

Though Hakluyt's list was by no means comprehensive, it did at least cover the basic skills required to establish a colony. But if the community was to achieve anything more than mere subsistence, it would also require artisans, craftsmen, and experts such as cobblers and tanners, coopers and "tallowchanders," bottlemakers, tailors, and fletchers.

Ralegh was advised that mastiffs would be required "to kill heavie beastes."

When Ralegh read this advice he was struck by the immensity of his undertaking. What he was attempting to do—in effect—was transplant a large English village such as Stratford-on-Avon into a little-known wilderness whose most fertile land was already being farmed by native inhabitants. As if that was not daunting enough, there was a very real possibility that the fledgling colony would come under attack from the Spanish, who were most unlikely to allow the English to settle on land that they claimed by virtue of Columbus's 1492 discovery.

Despite the dangers and difficulties, Ralegh had little trouble finding a commander for his expedition. Sir Richard Grenville—a Devonshire kinsman—had the two qualities that were deemed essential: a yearning for adventure and a hatred of Spain. Grenville had swashed his buckle from a very early age, riding into Hungary to serve the Emperor Maximilian in his fight against the Turkish sultan's janissaries. As he grew into adolescence, his hotheadedness got the better of him; his first mention in the official records is for stabbing a London gentleman in an affray, "giving him a mortal wound six inches in depth and one and a half in breadth." Grenville was most fortunate to have been pardoned by the queen.

With his ruddy cheeks and lapis-blue eyes he looked very much the West Country sea captain. His character, too, was not untypical of that class of Devon adventurers whom he could count among his close relatives. He was restless, loyal, intensely proud, and he had no time for self-doubt or introspection. But he was also plagued by a disturbingly fickle temper that revealed itself in his erratic and impulsive behaviour. Grenville's father having been drowned in the *Mary Rose* disaster when young Richard was still a toddler, the lad had grown up without a steadying paternal hand to curb his excesses.

Age did not temper his fiery outbursts; indeed, he became increasingly unhinged as he grew older, fired by the same demonic energy that had cost Sir Humfrey Gilbert his life. "He was of so hard a complection," wrote one, "[that] he would carouse three or foure glasses of wine, and in a braverie take the glasses betweene his teeth and crash them in peeces and swallow them downe, so that oftentimes the blood ran out of his mouth." On the American expedition he was rarely loved by his men, more often feared, and his impetuous behaviour frequently caused his subordinates to despair. He was forever being accused of carelessness in command of his ship, although the numerous scrapes he got into were perhaps a result of inexperience. Apart from a short hop across the English Channel, Grenville's maiden voyage to America was also his first attempt at seamanship.

He saw no earthly reason why a long sea voyage should necessitate discomfort. Even when the ship's food was at its most putrid and stinking, he insisted on dining off "plate of silver and gold," and he was accustomed to listening to music as he dined—a trait that must have delighted his gentlemen colleagues until they learned that his favourite instrument was the "chirimia" or clarion, a shrill trumpet that had a sound not dissimilar to a cockerel being strangled. Most commanders used it to signal the beginning of a battle: Grenville used it to announce the entrée. Everyone knew when he was at his table, for the hellish cacophony of "chirimias, organs and others" penetrated the thickest of the ship's timbers.

Grenville's task was to ferry Ralegh's colonists across the Atlantic. Once they were safely ashore, his orders were to bring the rest of the ships safely back to England, leaving the fledgling settlement under the command of Master Ralph Lane, a battle-hardened soldier who was serving in Ireland when he found himself unexpectedly recalled by the queen.

Lane was an expert on fortification and had worked hard to defend Ireland's coastline from a possible Spanish invasion. His gritty determination to succeed had clearly impressed Ralegh, for he won the coveted position of governor of England's first colony in America. He was tough as old jerkins and only truly happy when his food supplies had run out and he was forced to live off his wits. He later boasted that he far preferred a life of hardship and endurance "to ye greateste plenty yt ye courte coolde give me." He felt most at home in the company of his two trusty mastiffs, which he decided to take to America. They might not have showed such loyalty to their master had they seen him pack a cooking pot that almost exactly matched their size.

All the key posts were soon filled by Sir Walter's men. Philip Amadas, commander of the 1584 reconnaissance mission, was named as "admiral" in charge of the colony's boats and pinnaces, while the important job of expedition pilot fell to Simon Fernandez, a renegade Portuguese mariner whom Ralegh had known for years. He liked to boast of being "at war with the king of Spain," which endeared him to Sir Walter, but he soon found himself at war with Grenville as well, creating a damaging rift at the highest level.

Hakluyt had urged Ralegh to hire "a skifull painter . . . to bring the descriptions of all beasts, birds, fishes, trees, townes." This he duly did, appointing a brilliant draughtsman by the name of John White to work in tandem with Thomas Harriot. Harriot, of course, was the lynchpin of the entire expedition. As the only member who could communicate with Manteo—who was returning to America to establish liaison with the Indian tribes—his role was critical. He was "specially imploied" to deal with the native inhabitants, as well as being responsible for producing an account of the early days of the colony. He was also charged with mapping the new territories, studying natural curiosities, and recording all materials and resources that could prove useful to the colony.

The assembling of the fleet was conducted rapidly and efficiently, in striking contrast to Sir Humfrey's expedition two years previously. The flagship was the *Tiger*, the queen's vessel, commanded by Sir Richard Grenville, while the *Lion* was captained by George Raymond. The *Roebuck* was under the command of John Clarke, a good friend of Ralegh; the *Dorothy*'s captain was probably Arthur Barlowe. Thomas Cavendish, who would later emulate Sir Francis Drake's feat of circumnavigating the globe, was in charge of the fifth vessel, the *Elizabeth*.

None of the ships was large—even the *Tiger*, a "great ship," was just 200 tons—and much of the available deck space was cluttered with the heavy weaponry necessary to deter a Spanish attack as they passed through the Caribbean.

The smaller ships were made ready in Plymouth, but the *Tiger*, the pride of the fleet, was fitted out in the Thames shipyards. She was to carry virtually all the perishables, a strange decision, for although it enabled Grenville to keep an eye on the supplies, it also meant that the entire mission would be placed in jeopardy if disaster struck the flagship.

By the end of March, the London quaysides were stacked high with casks and barrels, crates, tubs, chests, and trunks. Hakluyt's list gives a dockside perspective of the kind of equipment needed by the colonists. Supplies were divided into "dead victuall" and "victuall by rootes and herbes." The dead victuall was the most susceptible to putrification and was packed with great care. There was "hoggs fleshe barrelled and salted in greate quantitie" and "befe barrelled in lesse quantitie." "Stockfishe" and "oatmeale" were also barrelled, as were butter, honey, and olives. There were butts and hogsheads for ale, firkins for oil, and cumbersome puncheons containing canary sack. Hessian bags were filled with seed, grain, currants, and prunes; dried and salt fish were loaded into wicker creels.

Great attention was given to the alcohol being stowed on board. There were "syders" from France, Spain, and England; wines, sacks, and hollocks—a clear red wine—and pitchers of aqua vitae for the higher ranks. The beer was "brewed specially in speciall tyme" to ensure it did not turn sour. All of these provisions were expected to last not only for the duration of the voyage but also for the first few months on Roanoke.

The most important of the stores—the seeds—were packed in dry-lined chests, and some, mainly the beans and peas, were "dryed on the kiln" to enhance their preservation. These were the lifeblood of the colony and would prove critical to the success or failure of the entire mission. Little was known about the soil on Roanoke, and no one could be sure which plants would flourish. Hakluyt advised taking a large selection of seeds in the hope that some would germinate soon after arrival. There was "turnep seede and passeneape seede"—good winter vegetables—and quick-growing radishes and "cariotts." Garlic and onions could be relied upon to thrive in most soils, while "cowcombers" and "cabage cole" were heavy croppers. Hakluyt also recommended taking a large selection of herbs, including "parseley, orege, tyme, rosemary, mustard seede [and] fennell." Many of these were considered to have medicinal properties and could be turned into pomanders and elixirs by the colony's apothecary.

Although the quantity of supplies impressed the common mariners, the *Tiger* could carry only a fraction of what was required

Sir Richard Grenville had a violent temperament. After drinking bouts, he would "take the glasses betweene his teeth and crash them in peeces and swallow them."

to sustain the colony. It was soon realised that Grenville would have to stop en route to stock up on salt, fruit, and, most importantly, livestock. There was simply not enough space on deck to carry cattle and swine, and the only opportunity of supplying the colony with farm animals would be to acquire them from settlements in the Caribbean. This was not going to be easy, since every port and harbour was controlled by the Spanish, who were under strict orders not to sell anything to the English. Grenville would have to use his considerable charm—or his ten cannon—to persuade the Spanish to change their minds.

Spain had been keeping a close eye on Ralegh's preparations, but her attempts to monitor the assembling of his fleet had been dealt a serious blow when her ambassador, Bernadino de Mendoza, was expelled from England after being informed "that Her Majesty was much displeased with me on account of the efforts I had made to disturb her country." He was told that "it was the queen's will that I should leave the country without fail in fifteen days." This was unwelcome news to the Spanish: Mendoza had built up an efficient network of spies in England—several of whom had infiltrated Ralegh's project—and had hoped to keep a close eye on developments. Now, it seemed, his spy ring would be leaderless.

The ex-ambassador realised his predicament and gave full vent to his Castilian temper, informing the queen's council that "I was not fond of staying in another person's house as an unwelcome guest." He made a secret vow to work against the queen, recording that "as I have apparently failed to please the queen as a minister of peace, she would in future force me to try to satisfy her in war." He meant every word, and from now on he became one of Elizabeth's bitterest enemies, directing his network of spies and informers from his new base in France.

The information he received was not always accurate, but by February he was able to scribble a coded letter to King Philip informing him that the queen had given Ralegh the *Tiger* "with five guns on each side of the ship and two demi-culverins in the bows." Six weeks later, he scored a notable success when one of his secret agents, Pedro de Cubiaur, managed to smuggle a man into Plymouth harbour and infiltrate the dock workers and suppliers. He produced a detailed report on "the number of the ships and men, and quantity of stores," and the information he sent to Mendoza caused sufficient alarm for a Spanish frigate to be dispatched to America—the first of many—to determine whether or not an advance party had already established a base.

Mendoza overestimated the strength of Ralegh's fleet, but almost certainly underestimated the number of men. Sir Walter probably intended the total complement to be about 600, of whom perhaps half would settle in America. But when he began recruiting in the West Country ports, he suddenly found himself up against an intractable problem that had been more than eighteen years in the making. For at the very time he was trying to persuade men to settle in America, the haggard survivors of Sir John Hawkins's 1567 expedition—colleagues of Davy Ingrams—finally returned to England, bringing with them stories of such unspeakable brutality that even the hardiest of mariners began to think twice about setting sail for a land still claimed by Spain.

One of these survivors was Miles Philips, who had foolishly chosen to throw himself on the mercy of the Spanish rather than join Ingrams on his year-long walk across America. He soon regretted his decision, for it began a sixteen-year ordeal in which he and his companions suffered terrible atrocities. Their reception at a Spanish settlement in Mexico had been ominous enough: they were locked in "a hogstie" and given pigswill to eat. When they asked for a surgeon to dress their wounds, they were thrown in prison and told "that we should have none other surgeon but the hangman, which should sufficiently heale us of all our griefes."

In 1571, they learned some disturbing news that was to haunt English mariners for years to come. King Philip II had become increasingly concerned that the purity of the Catholic faith was under threat in his New World empire and ordered the dreaded henchmen of the Inquisition to begin their grisly work in the Americas, rooting out heretics and torturing them to death. "We were a very good booty and pray to the Inquisitors," Philips later recalled, "[and were] committed to prison in sundry darke dungeons where we could not see but by candle-light."

The unfortunate English mariners soon learned that they were to become the first victims of an auto-da-fé, or act of faith, a hideous yet compelling public torture ceremony that combined medieval barbarism with the theatricality of a real-life Day of Judgement. Philips and his men were dressed in yellow cloaks and, after being given cups of bitter wine, were marched to the marketplace where the local inhabitants had gathered to "heare the sentence of the Holy Inquisition against the English heretikes."

"Every man [was] alone in his yellow coat," recalled Philips, "and a rope about his necke, and a great greene waxe candle in his hand unlighted, having a Spaniard appointed to goe upon either side of every one of us." They were taken to the scaffold where "we found a great assembly of people" who had gathered to hear them receive their sentence for being heretics. Three of the men "had their judgement to be burnt to ashes," while others were tortured and flogged. After many hours of whippings and beatings, the battered survivors were led away "with their backes all gore blood, and swollen with great bumps."

Philips eventually escaped from captivity and arrived back in the West Country more than sixteen years after leaving England. Other survivors trickled home slowly, "carrying still about them (and shal to their graves) the marks and tokens of those inhumane and more then barbarous cruell dealings." Their horrific tales of suffering captivated both commoners and courtiers, and even the pious Richard Hakluyt could not stop himself from publishing them, with a cautionary note condemning "these superstitious Spaniards . . . that they thinke that they have done God good service when they have brought a Lutheran heretike to the fire to be burnt."

The West Country mariners that Ralegh hoped to employ on his ships were horrified when they heard such tales. They had never trusted the Spanish, but the auto-da-fé was an extremely sinister development. They knew that anyone who had the misfortune to be captured during their passage through the Caribbean could expect much the same fate as Miles Philips and his men. Their terror was so great that many refused to sign up for Ralegh's adventure, leaving him with a severe shortage of deckhands. His original patent had allowed him to take with him such men as gave their "assent and good-wylle," but such was the reluctance of mariners to join the expedition that in January 1585 Ralegh asked to be given sweeping new powers by the queen. Her draft commission now allowed her "trusty and welbilovid servant" to impress mariners into service "in any [of] our portz, havons, crekes or other places within our countries of Devon, Cornewall and at Bristowe." This was not all; he was also given full authority to impress "such shipping, maisters of ships, maryners, souldyours and all other provisions and munition whatsoever as he shall see to be mete and requisite for this service." How much Ralegh used these powers is unclear, but several members of the expedition claimed to have been forced to go against their will. Such unwilling participants were to prove a dangerous liability, and Ralegh later regretted having used impressed seamen, claiming that they were "so ignorant in sea-service as that they know not the name of a rope and [are] therefore insufficient for such labour."

Towards the end of March, Grenville sailed the *Tiger* from London to Plymouth, where the rest of the fleet was awaiting him. He hoped to set sail for America on April 9, for the sun would rise at 5:19 a.m. on that day, enabling the fleet to be well under way by mid-morning. The immediate forecast was for "fayre and April shewers," but the long-term outlook did not look so good. Within ten days, the weather was expected to worsen and there would be "dangerous tymes for all thynges, the ayre seditious and troublesome."

After a final check on supplies, the crews were brought on board, followed by the gentlemen adventurers and Manteo and Wanchese.

Tales of the Spanish Inquisition deterred England's mariners from signing up for voyages to America. Ralegh was forced to impress seamen, plucking them from prisons and taverns

At the crack of dawn the squadron raised its sails and put to sea. It was a low-key departure. A few curious onlookers had gathered on the quayside, but there was no music or fireworks, and even the city's cannons remained silent. Only the mayor of Plymouth realised that he was witnessing something of great historical significance, inscribing the fleet's departure in the city's official records.

Just ten days after leaving England, Grenville and his men noticed a peculiar darkening of the western sky, quite unlike anything they had previously experienced. It turned suddenly chill and the midday sun was reduced to a slim crescent. To Harriot, the explanation was obvious: it was a partial eclipse of the sun. But what no one realised—not even Harriot—was that on the east coast of America, where the eclipse was total, the natives saw it as an omen of some catastrophe which "unto them appeared very terrible." When a shooting comet added to the turmoil in the heavens, the Indians were convinced that some evil was soon to arrive at their shores.

The fleet was making good progress towards the Canary Islands when a storm blew up from nowhere. "By force and violence of fowle weather" the fleet was dispersed and the *Tiger*'s pinnace sank to the bottom. The superstitious crew saw this as vindication of the soothsayers' warnings, but Grenville took a more pragmatic approach. Aware that his ships were likely to get scattered on such a long voyage, he had previously arranged for them to reassemble in Guayanilla Bay on the uninhabited southern coast of Puerto Rico.

The *Tiger*'s Atlantic crossing was rapid and the warm waters of the Caribbean were reached in just twenty-one days. It was now so hot that several of the mariners plunged headlong into the surf, a bad mistake, for "a sharke cut off the legge of one of the companie." The unfortunate man faced the painful necessity of having his stump dipped into a vat of boiling pitch.

The *Tiger* passed safely through the palm-fringed chain of the Antilles, then veered northwest towards Puerto Rico. Grenville ordered his men to drop anchor at an uninhabited island, "where wee landed and refreshed our selves all that day." Life on board had been tough ever since they had entered tropical waters. The biscuits had long been infested with weevil; now the humid air caused a thick layer of furry mould to form on the surface. The dried cheese had turned rancid and the water was so full of worms that it was necessary for the sailors to clench their teeth to strain out the fauna. The Caribbean was infamous for sickness and disease—"burnyng agues . . . blysters, noysome sweates, aches in the body . . . byles, yellowe jaundyse [and] inflammations of the eyes." The stinking May heat dramatically increased the risk of infection, and none of the traditional cures was available to the men on board. The usual advice of physicians was to "refrayne from salt meates" during the summer—hardly possible on board ship—while many suggested eating cucumbers and keeping "cleane from fylthy sweate and from all noysome and stynking smelles, which are most dangerous and able to infect with contagious and pestilent diseases." Such advice was useless to the men on the *Tiger*; and the only injunction they could obey, "to refrayne from carnall lust," was the one they would have most liked to break.

Grenville pressed on to Guayanilla Bay, where he hoped to find the rest of his fleet at anchor. But as the *Tiger* passed the headland, he was disappointed to note that not a single vessel had arrived. This was a serious setback, for the expedition could not continue without at least one extra ship. He prepared himself for a long wait, dropping anchor "within a fawlcon-shot of the shoare" and landing most of his men.

Grenville was now in hostile Spanish territory and well aware that his presence was unlikely to be greeted with any enthusiasm by King Philip's belligerent governors. It would only be a matter of time before his vessel was spotted by lookouts, and there was a very real chance that he would come under attack. He now showed himself to be a capable commander, playing his hand with skill. He had on board governor-elect Ralph Lane, a man who had spent many years designing and building defensive earthworks in Ireland. Lane was immediately sent ashore and put to work constructing a fort on Guayanilla Bay that would be strong enough to deter any Spanish attack.

Although Lane resented being given orders by Grenville—viewing him as his equal in rank and status—he kept his silence and set to work. Within a week he had constructed a military encampment of such strength that when a troop of Spaniards unexpectedly stumbled across its ramparts they rubbed their eyes in disbelief. They described it as "a great breastwork . . . with a moat and a long stretch of beach enclosed with trenches, huts erected, and a smithy; and all in as great perfection as though they had proposed to remain there ten years." The fort was protected on one side by a freshwater river and on the other by a marshy lake. Huge earthworks were thrown up around the rest of the site—protecting the encampment from any ambush from the dense woodland—while a ditch and bank protected the exposed eastern flank.

Three days after the fort was finished, Grenville's sentinels raised the alarm. "There appeared unto us out of the woods, eight horse-men of the Spaniards, about a quarter of a myle from our fort, stay-ing about halfe and hower in viewing our forces." Grenville had been anticipating this moment and acted with characteristic ebul-lience, dispatching ten heavily armed musketeers to challenge the Spanish patrol. His bluff paid off, for "they presently retyred into the woodes."

There was no time to be complacent. After a two-day standoff, a ship was sighted on the horizon. Grenville was convinced it was "either a Spaniard or French man-of-warre [and] thought it good to waigh ankers." He gave chase and was about to blitz the vessel with cannonfire when a sharp-eyed lookout "discerned him at last to be one of our consorts." It was the *Elizabeth*, Thomas Cavendish's ves-sel, and her arrival was a cause of such joy that the *Tiger*'s crew "dis-charged their ordinance and saluted him, according to the manner of the seas."

The presence of the English, now in a position of considerable strength, alarmed the Spanish governor. He sent a party of twenty horsemen to the English fort to discover Grenville's intentions and assess their military strength. "They shewed to our men a flagge of truce, and made signes to have a parle with us, whereupon two of our men went halfe of the way upon the sands and two of theirs came and met them." The Spaniards appeared friendly enough and "offred very great salutations," but it was not long before they began, "according to their Spanish proud humors, to expostulate with them." Grenville's men haughtily informed them that "our princi-pal intention was onely to furnish ourselves with water, and victuals, and the necessaries whereof we stood in neede"; and added that if the Spanish so much as raised a gun in their direction, "our resolu-tion was to practise force and to releeve ourselves by the sworde." A tense standoff followed. The Spanish promised to return with food and provisions, but Grenville doubted their intentions. When they failed to show up at the appointed hour, "keeping their old custome for perjurie and breache of promise," he rather pointlessly "fired the woods thereabout." He then ordered the crews back on board and told them to be ready to sail at dawn.

The men passed an uncomfortable night. The weather was sultry and many had been bitten by ferocious "muskitoes." In the great cabin of the *Tiger*, the commanders of the expedition sat late into the night, deliberating on their next course of action and pondering over how they were going to acquire the pigs and chickens they so desperately needed. Manteo had warned that although food stocks on Roanoke were generally plentiful in autumn, there was always a shortage in winter and that it was imperative that livestock and seedlings be acquired in the Caribbean. Grenville decided that from now on he would pursue a more aggressive course of barter and plunder—buying from the Spanish what they would sell and stealing everything else.

The ships set sail at dawn. They were fortunate to cross the path of a Spanish frigate whose captain was so terrified of the *Tiger*'s guns that the vessel "was forsaken by the Spanyards upon the sight of us." Just a few hours later, Grenville repeated his success by capturing a second frigate, richly laden with cloth. He returned to Puerto Rico and attempted to exchange his prisoners for cattle, but when this failed he settled for "good round summes" of cash.

Grenville cut an impressive figure as he swaggered the decks of the *Tiger*. The Spanish prisoners were full of stories of how he dined off golden plates to the accompaniment of music. They also brought tales of the expedition's purpose, informing the Spanish governor that the ship was filled with men "skilled in all trades, and among them were about twenty who appeared to be persons of some importance." Of particular concern was the fact that "they were accompanied by two tall Indians whom they treated well and who spoke English." These Indians were said to share Grenville's passion for music, and one prisoner went so far as to suggest that it was they who had persuaded Grenville to bring clarions and organs on the voyage.

As the vessels left Puerto Rico for a second time—the *Tiger*, the *Elizabeth*, and the two prize ships—Grenville could reflect on what had so far proved a successful voyage. But the simmering discontent that had long existed between the gentlemen was about to break out into open warfare, with one side supporting Grenville and the other side Ralph Lane. The catalyst was a salt-collecting raid on the southwestern tip of Puerto Rico, which Lane believed to be unduly dangerous. But Grenville brushed aside his criticisms. Lane complained of "grete unkindnes afterwards on his parte towards me." Relations between the two men soon worsened; it was not long before Lane was openly accusing Grenville of "intollerable pride and insatiable ambition." Many of the gentlemen agreed; Captain Thomas Cavendish of the *Elizabeth* and Captain Clarke of the *Roebuck* would later be chastised by Grenville, much to their annoyance, and many of the crew were on the receiving end of his sharp tongue. When Fernandez the pilot was unfairly accused of navigational errors, Lane leaped to his defence. "[He] hath carryed himselfe both with greate skille and grete government all thys voyeage," he wrote, "notwithstandying thys grete crosse [Grenville] to us all."

On the first of June, 1585, Grenville's ship dropped anchor at the island of Hispaniola—his last hope of acquiring provisions before sailing for the North American mainland. There was by now a desperate need for fresh fruit and livestock, but Hispaniola was one of the worst places to be looking for such supplies. The island was reputed to have a strong garrison under the command of a military governor who was most unlikely to welcome Grenville's approach. But when Grenville landed his men he discovered that the Spaniard in charge of the island, Captain Rengifo de Angulo, was quite unlike his colleagues in the rest of the Caribbean. Not for him the military-style regime of a Spanish encampment. He enjoyed frivolity and fancy foods, and when he heard that the distinguished Sir Richard Grenville had pulled into port, Angulo prepared a right royal welcome. He was greatly excited at the thought of all the "brave and gallant gentlemen" on board and sent a missive to Grenville, joshingly addressing him as Verdo Campo (Spanish for Green Field) and sending his "gentle commendations." A few days later he appeared in person at the harbour, accompanied by "a lusty frier" and a few friends. Angulo was the very model of politeness, humouring Grenville and receiving him "very curteously." So amicable was this first meeting, and "the curtesies that passed on both sides were so great, that all feare and mistrust on the Spanyardes part was abandoned."

Grenville must have been taken aback by the enthusiastic reception. For years he had learned to hate the Spanish, having heard numerous tales of the racks and wrenches of the Inquisition's henchmen. Now he found himself whiling away the afternoon in a shady bower, chatting jovially with the Spanish governor and sipping fine rioja. He was delighted to have at last met someone not only whom he could treat as an equal, but who also shared his love for the finer things in life. As the two men relaxed in the languid heat, Grenville proposed staging a beach banquet that very evening. Captain Angulo thought this a splendid idea, and within minutes Grenville was barking orders to his men. Food and supplies were landed and the two commanders watched as the *Tiger*'s crew constructed "two banquetting houses covered with greene boughs, the one for the gentlemen and the other for the servants." The ship's cook, meanwhile, excelled himself in preparing a delicious feast.

At last everything was ready and the two commanders took their seats in the pleasure house, followed by the English and Spanish gentlemen. "A sumptuous banquet was brought in served by us all in plate," records the author of the *Tiger* journal, "with the sound of trumpets and consort of musick, wherewith the Spanyards were more than delighted." The gentlemen quaffed wines, beers and aqua vitae. Once they had finished eating, a tipsy Angulo leaned over to Grenville and proposed a great bullfight "in recompense of our curtesie." This was met with a roar of approval. The Spaniard immediately ordered a huge herd of bulls to be brought down from the mountains, "then singled out three of the best of them to be hunted." To Grenville's sea-weary crew, such entertainment was a rare treat. "The pastime grew very pleasant for the space of three houres, wherein all three of the beasts were killed, whereof one tooke to the sea and there was slaine with a musket." The day ended with much good humour on all sides. "Many rare presents and gifts were given and bestowed on both partes, and the next day we plaied the merchants in bargaining." In one stroke, Grenville was able to acquire everything he needed to put the colony on a sound footing, including horses, donkeys, goats, sheep, and pigs. He also bought bulls for breeding as well as a variety of root plants, and purchased large quantities of sugar, ginger, and pearls which were guaranteed to reap him a handsome profit when he eventually returned to England. His last act was to inform the Spanish that he was founding his colony in Newfoundland, more than one thousand miles from his real destination, just in case their "harty goodwill" should ever turn sour.

On June 7, the *Tiger* and the *Elizabeth* set a northwesterly course from Hispaniola. A fortnight later Grenville was so convinced he was nearing mainland America that he sent men aloft to keep a watch for land. For hours they saw nothing but sea, then slowly an inky smudge could be discerned on the horizon. Their voyage was nearing its end.

The elation came to an abrupt halt when the *Tiger* was caught in a ferocious tidal rip that pushed her towards the beach. Not for nothing was this promontory known as Cape Fear, and it took all Fernandez's skill to keep her from being washed ashore. It was a lucky escape, for if the vessel had grounded, there would have been nothing to prevent the waves from pouring into the hold, destroying all the supplies. When the ship was finally brought to anchor, the men dropped lines over the bows and "caught in one tyde so much fishe as woulde have yelded us twenty pounds in London."

Grenville proceeded up the coastline with extreme caution, plotting inlets and shoals and noting the limits of high and low tide. Two days after catching the fish, he ordered the anchors to be dropped at Wococon Island at the southern end of the Outer Banks, known to all who had sailed on Amadas and Barlowe's reconnaissance mission. The coastline here was extremely treacherous. The line of sandbanks stretched far to the north—further than the eye could see—and there were numerous uncharted shoals that lay offshore. Fernandez had accompanied the 1584 mission so he knew that the Atlantic was unforgiving and could whip up a storm at a moment's notice, washing the *Tiger* and the *Elizabeth* to certain destruction. His immediate concern was to edge the *Tiger* over the sandbar and into the safe waters of Pamlico Sound, yet he must have been aware that the channel through the so-called Wococon Inlet was extremely shallow and that the deeper Port Ferdinando—named by him—lay just eighty miles to the north.

Fernandez decided to chance his luck. After taking soundings, he edged the *Tiger* towards the inlet, followed by the *Elizabeth* and the two Spanish prize ships. It was now that disaster struck. The depth soundings had been wildly inaccurate; as the *Tiger* neared the gap in the sandbanks, she grounded on a bar and stuck fast. The other captains, sensing danger, wrestled with their vessels and tried to come about, but to no avail. They, too, were grounded on the bar.

The storm that had been threatening to break now unleashed its fury on the disabled fleet. With the wind rapidly increasing in ferocity and large breakers crashing in from the Atlantic, the *Tiger*—side-on to the waves—was in danger of breaking up. For more than two hours she lay "beatynge uppon ye shoale," the surf pounding against her weakened timbers and tearing away the sea-weathered planks. "We were all in extreeme hasarde of beyng casteawaye," wrote Ralph Lane, adding that "all the marryners aborde thoughte [she] coolde not possybelly but have beene brooken in sunder." He was aware that only the arrival of high tide offered any hope of refloating the vessels, and after a few hours of nail-biting suspense, the *Eliza-beth* and the Spanish prize vessels were indeed released from the sand. But the *Tiger* had a deeper draught and would not budge. She "beat so manie strokes upon the ground" that she was almost given

The flagship of the 1585 expedition, the *Tiger*, made history by landing the first English colonists in the New World. She survived storms and shipwreck, and capped her triumphant voyage by returning to England with a Spanish prize ship in tow

up as lost, but finally an enormous surge of water lifted her clear of the bar and she "ranne agrounde, harde to ye shoare." She had been battered by eighty-nine "strockes" or breaking waves, and her lower timbers were smashed to pieces.

The exhausted mariners were thankful for their own salvation and that of "ye noble shippe," but there was a high price to be paid for Fernandez's error. Grenville's ship "was so brused that the salt-water came so aboundantlie into him that the most part of his corne, salt, meale, rice, bisket and other provisions, that he should have left with them that remained behind him in the countrie, was spoiled." This was the worst possible news for the colonists. It was already late in the year to be planting, but now most of their seed had been ruined by the seawater. Since the *Tiger* had been carrying virtually all the supplies—a reckless error of judgement that stemmed from

Grenville's fear that they would be safer from pilfering on his flagship—the colonists would be totally reliant upon the Indians for food and provisions until a harvest could be gathered.

Since that was almost a year away, they all knew that they were now dependent for their very survival upon Manteo and Wanchese.

6

Governor Lane's Sandcastle

Sir Richard Grenville's most pressing concern was to haul the *Tiger* onto the beach at Wococon and repair her shattered hull. As high tide approached, he arranged for teams of men to pull on ropes; after much effort, the vessel was hauled above the high-water mark. She was then emptied of supplies and, by fixing a series of ropes and pulleys to her mainmast, dragged onto her side to be careened.

The vessel was not as badly damaged as Grenville had feared. Parts of her outer shell had been "brused" and "broken," but the frame itself was still in good condition. As soon as he had satisfied himself that the vessel could be made seaworthy, he set his carpenters to work, replacing timbers and plugging gaps with rope and pitch. The beach was transformed into a dry dock as his mariners felled trees, cut planks, and scraped tropical marine growth off the timbers that were to be reused.

The damage to supplies was a far more serious concern. Almost all of the expedition's perishables had been carried on the *Tiger*, and most of these had been ruined by seawater. As the vessel was unloaded, the colonists watched in dismay as sack after sodden sack of food was laid out on the beach for Grenville to inspect. The wheat was "musty and had taken salt water," the oatmeal was damp and virtually all of the beer and cider was ruined. As Grenville divided the supplies into two piles—damaged and undamaged—he saw his worst fears confirmed: the greater part of his provisions was spoiled.

The small pile of dry goods was dwarfed by a much larger pyramid from which flowed a small stream of saltwater. Even the salvaged victuals were not entirely undamaged. The cheeses had crumbled, the prunes had swollen, and although the dried peas and beans were still edible, they could no longer be expected to germinate if planted.

The lack of food was not Grenville's only worry. He was also concerned by the fact that he still had no news of the other ships—the Lion, the Dorothy, and the Roebuck—which had not been sighted since the storm off the coast of Portugal. But he did not have to wait long to learn that they had safely crossed the Atlantic. A small reconnaissance party sent to explore the southern end of the Outer Banks returned after a few days with thirty-two colonists, the contingent carried on the Lion, who had been unceremoniously set ashore by their captain, George Raymond. Grenville was not pleased to learn that Raymond had already departed for Newfoundland's cod-rich waters, for he would have welcomed the opportunity to confer with him and, if possible, borrow some supplies. But his anger was assuaged when, a few days later, he sighted the Dorothy and the Roebuck on the horizon—a great boost to his men's morale. At last his scattered fleet was reunited or accounted for.

Grenville intended to settle Ralegh's colonists on Roanoke Island, some sixty miles to the north of his present position, but since this was impossible while the Tiger was being careened, he proposed that the newly arrived ships ride at anchor while he lead a small expedition through the shallow waters of Pamlico Sound. This was a mission of the greatest importance. It was essential to make friendly contact with the scattered tribes that lived along the banks of this vast lagoon, since there was every likelihood that the colonists would be forced to rely upon them for food and supplies. It would also enable Grenville to assess the pros and cons of the colony's geographical position.

He chose with care the men who were to accompany him. It was likely to be a gruelling and dangerous expedition that would lead the party into uncharted waters. The shores of the lagoon were a tangled wilderness that had never before been trodden by Englishmen, and, in the stinking heat of midday, the humidity was insufferable and made considerably worse by the clouds of mosquitoes that swarmed in the shadows. There were also the Indians to consider; Grenville had no idea how they would react when they first caught sight of his heavily armed men.

He decided to take a sizeable party—sixty in total—and included many of the gentlemen adventurers. Ralph Lane, Thomas Harriot, and Thomas Cavendish were selected, while John White, the artist, was also enlisted so he could provide Grenville with sketches to take back to Ralegh. Manteo's presence was of paramount importance, for he alone could guide the boats through the reed-choked backwaters of the sound. He had been born on Croatoan Island, close to its southern end, and was familiar with many of the neighbouring tribes. It would be his task to persuade them that these wild and unkempt strangers, clothed in fetid burlap, should be given a warm welcome. Wanchese, who came from Roanoke, was not invited to accompany Grenville, probably because he had already made clear that his patience with the English was fast running out.

The party was divided among four small craft. Most of the men were crammed into the pinnace and smaller boats, while Grenville and his chosen favourites sat in his tiltboat, a four-oared wherry that had been built for use on the Thames. It was quite small—it "could not carry above fifteene men with their furniture, baggage and victual"—but provided some degree of comfort. As commander, he allowed himself the luxury of a canvas awning to provide some respite from the torrid midday heat. Then, when everything was loaded aboard, the men "passed over the water from Wococon to the mayne land, victualled for eight dayes." If they were away for any longer, they were likely to go hungry.

Grenville was wise to have taken Manteo in the lead boat, for the passage through the sound proved extremely treacherous and was "full of flats and shoales." The tiltboat was ideally suited to such waters, but the pinnace—which had been hastily knocked together in Puerto Rico—"drewe too deepe water for that shalow sound [and] would not stirre for an oare." It kept grounding on the bottom and the men had to slip into the sluggish waters and heave her off the mud. Despite the difficulties, Manteo safely guided the little flotilla through the swampy sound to the settlement of Pomeioc, some thirty miles distant from the *Tiger*, which was reached after a hard day's rowing.

Once the boats had been pulled ashore, Grenville's musket-wielding platoon set off along a well-worn trail from the marshy shoreline, with Manteo leading. In spite of their weaponry, the English party was filled with trepidation, unsure how the natives would react to their unexpected arrival. Only a few of the men had accompanied the previous year's expedition or had ever seen a native American—except for Manteo and Wanchese. There was a feeling of tense excitement as they neared the palisaded settlement.

Ralegh had prepared for this moment long before his men had set sail, commissioning one of his military friends to write a strict code of conduct to be observed by all sailors and colonists. This ordered "that no souldier do violat any woman; thet no Indian be forced to labour unwillingly . . . that non shall stryke or mysuse any Indian; that non shall enter any Indian's howse without his leve." The punishments for offences were severe: death for rape, twenty "blows with a cuggell" for striking an Indian (to be carried out in the presence of the victim), and imprisonment or slavery for entering an Indian's property.

As the men reached the village, they were shocked that it looked so primitive. There were eighteen longhouses built from rough poles, and most were "covered with boughes of trees as every man lusteth or liketh best." Others were draped with rush mats that were thrown aside at daybreak to admit the light.

The party was almost inside the settlement when they spotted a group of Indians seated around a campfire. The first thing that struck them was their extraordinary attire. The old men looked so bizarre that even Harriot could scarcely conceal his sniggers. They wore off-the-shoulder furry petticoats "which hangeth downe beneath their knees," and their heads were shaven into a pointed coxcomb. "They weare their heare cutt like a creste," he added, "on the toppes of their heads as others doe, but the rest are cutt shorte, savinge those which growe above their foreheads in the manner of a perriwigge."

The women looked even more extraordinary. They were strongly boned and had partially exposed breasts, and might have been considered attractive had it not been for their razored heads and tattooed cheeks.

"They tye deers' skinne doubled about them," wrote a bemused Harriot, "hygher about their breasts, which hange downe before, almost to their knees." When they turned around, the men were somewhat surprised to notice that they were "altogither naked."

John White was unabashed by their nudity and immediately set to work on a watercolour of a young woman and child, but the toddler was unsettled by the bearded stranger; it was only when she was handed a doll—complete with Elizabethan bonnet and buskin—that she would stand still. "They are greatlye delighted with puppetts and babes [dolls]," wrote Harriot, "which wear brought oute of England."

Surviving records of the men's brief stay reveal little of relations between the English and the Indians, but they were cordial enough to enable White to produce detailed watercolours of the villagers. Harriot declared himself to be charmed by his hosts, and was so impressed with the settlement that he was moved to write that "the contrye abowt this plase is soe fruitfull and good that England is not to bee compared to yt."

When the English reached Pomeioc village, they were shocked by the primitive longhouses. They were rough-built and "covered with boughes of trees as every man lusteth or liketh best."

Grenville had allowed himself very little time to complete his exploration of the southern sound, following a characteristically ambitious schedule that forced him to depart from Pomeioc on the same day that he had arrived. The reluctant men trudged back to their boats and Manteo once again took his position at the helm, guiding them towards a tributary of the great Pamlico River. They paused briefly at the Indian settlement of Aquascogoc, but the tribesmen showed no inclination to meet the Englishmen, who quickly returned to their boats. It was only later that Grenville noticed his silver drinking cup was missing. Unable to control his fury, he dispatched Amadas back to the settlement to have his revenge. "We burnt and spoyled their corne and towne," records the *Tiger* journal with relish; and the men probably would have killed the villagers as well had they not already fled. This wanton act of violence provoked no immediate revenge, but it was extraordinarily foolish behaviour on the part of men who would shortly be forced to rely on the Indians for food.

The last village that Grenville wished to visit was Secotan, on a secluded stretch of the Pamlico River. The tribesmen here were reputed to be "very cruell and bloodie," and the English were wary of coming under fire. A few of the gentlemen clattered through the undergrowth in full armour, while others donned buff jerkins that would protect them from arrow fire. In the event, their arrival was peaceful. Grenville was welcomed by the chieftain, and after Manteo had explained their reasons for coming, the Englishmen were "well intertayned there of the savages."

It is unclear how much Manteo told the tribesmen about his time in London, but the unannounced arrival of a troop of heavily armed Englishmen provoked the superstitious Indians to lay on an evening of lavish entertainment. These included a terrifying hullabaloo, possibly a corn festival, in which ten men and four women writhed and danced their way around a circle of posts carved with phantom human heads. One of the women was virtually naked, others exposed various limbs, while the men rattled gourds and brandished arrows.

"Every man [was] attyred in the most strange fashion they can devise," wrote a bewildered Harriot. "They dance, singe, and use the strangest gestures that they can possiblye devise. Three of the fayrest virgins of the companie are in the myddst which, imbrassinge one another, doe, as-yt-wear, turn abowt in their dancinge."

Harriot had a keen eye for the human figure and was none too impressed with the maidens of Secotan, even though they were scantily clad. He was prepared to concede that they were "of reasonable good proportion," but was not persuaded that facial tattooes showed them to their best advantage. "They have small eyes, plaine and flatt noses, narrow foreheads, and broade mowths."

The village resembled the settlement of Pomeioc, except for a strange barrel-roofed structure which aroused Harriot's curiosity. He begged to be taken inside, only to find himself face to face with "dead corpses." This was the charnelhouse for the village elders, whose mummified bodies lay in tidy rows in front of a "terrible" idol. The manner of their preservation fascinated Harriot, and he dutifully noted how it was performed. "First the bowells are taken forthe," he wrote, "then, layinge downe the skinne, they cutt all the fleshe clean from the bones, which they drye in the sonne, and well dryed they inclose in matts and place at their feete." That was the easy part. "Then their bones (remaininge still fastened together with the ligaments whole and uncorrupted) are covered agayne with leather and their carcase fashioned as yf their flesh wear not taken away." They were then placed in the ossuary temple and one "poore soule," allotted to live with the corpse, "mumbleth his prayers nighte and day."

Grenville and his men so enjoyed their visit to Secotan that they spent the night in the village. They might have stayed longer, but Grenville was anxious to return to the *Tiger*. In exactly a week he had explored more than two hundred miles of uncharted territory. It was a considerable achievement.

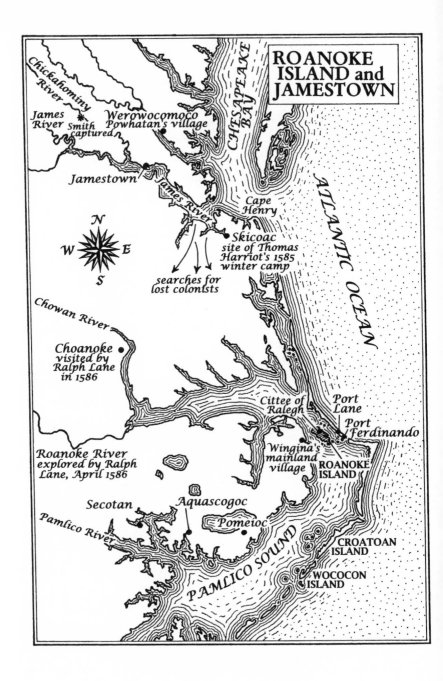

ROANOKE
ISLAND and
JAMESTOWN

Chickahominy
River

James
River   Smith
captured

Werowocomoco
Powhatan's village

CHESAPEAKE
BAY

ATLANTIC OCEAN

Jamestown

James River

Cape
Henry

N
W   E
S

Skicoac
site of Thomas
Harriot's 1585
winter camp

searches for
lost colonists

Chowan River

Choanoke
visited by
Ralph Lane
in 1586

Cittee of
Ralegh

Port
Lane

Port
Ferdinando

Wingina's
mainland
village

ROANOKE
ISLAND

Roanoke River
explored by Ralph
Lane, April 1586

Secotan

Aquascogoc

Pamlico River

Pomeioc

PAMLICO SOUND

CROATOAN
ISLAND

WOCOCON
ISLAND

John White won the confidence of this Indian child by handing her an Elizabethan doll complete with bonnet and buskin. "They are greatlye delighted with puppetts and babes [dolls] which wear brought oute of England."

As the exploration party neared the beach at Wococon, Grenville was overjoyed to see that *Tiger* was no longer lying helpless on the shore. Instead, she had been refloated and was riding at anchor with the rest of the fleet. Once all the men were aboard Grenville ordered his ships to proceed northwards to the largest gap in the Outer Banks, Port Ferdinando, where supplies could at last be unloaded in preparation for the construction of a settlement.

Grenville had by now realised that this would be almost impossible to achieve without the consent of the Indian tribes. He also knew that Amadas and Barlowe had met with considerable goodwill the previous year and been at the receiving end of much hospitality. He decided to renew contact with Granganimeo and, with Manteo's help, inform him of his wish to settle a small group of men. The details of the meeting have been lost. The *Tiger's* journal records only that on July 29, 1585, "Granginimeo, brother to King Wingina, came aboard the Admirall, and Manteo with him." The two sides appear to have reached an amicable agreement that allowed Grenville to settle his colonists on Roanoke Island, probably at Shallowbag Bay on the northeastern coast. This was far enough away from the Indian village to prevent the English from encroaching on their land, and also ensured that the settlement would be hidden from the sea by the dunes of the Outer Banks.

After the disaster at Wococon, Grenville knew better than to attempt to sail the *Tiger* into the shallow sound. Instead, he ordered the fleet to anchor some three miles offshore, from where his men faced the exhausting task of unloading the supplies into boats and rowing them through heavy surf to a holding depot on the Outer Banks. Once here, they could be transferred to Roanoke Island in relative safety.

It was no small undertaking: livestock, barrels, and tools—all had to be rowed ashore in pinnaces that were hard to manoeuvre in the breaking waves. But by August 5 the first of the ships was empty and Captain John Arundell "was sent for England" to inform the queen

The villagers of Secotan welcomed the English with a terrifying dance (bottom right) in which they writhed around a circle of posts. "Every man was attyred in the most strange fashion they can devise."

that the country at last had a toehold on American soil. The queen was so delighted that she knighted him.

Ralph Lane now began to assume his role as the colony's governor, posting himself at the depot on the Outer Banks and overseeing the transferral of supplies to Roanoke. He was in his element. In the rare moments of quiet, he wrote letters home in his characteristically eccentric spelling, describing the paradise that was now his to govern. He boasted that "all ye kingedomes and states of chrystendom . . . doo not yealde ether more good, or more plentyfulle, . . . [than] is needefull or pleasinge for delighte." Since he had arrived at Roanoke less than two weeks previously, his critics might have justifiably accused him of overoptimism, but Lane already had proof of the healthfulness of the land. His men had arrived with the "reumes"—colds, catarrh, bronchitis, and tuberculosis—but had made a spectacular recovery. "The clymate ys soo whoollesome," he wrote, "[that] wee have not had one sycke synce wee enterdde into ye countrey; but sundry yt came sycke, are recovered of longe dyseases."

Once the supplies had been landed, Governor Lane's most urgent task was to build a fort. This had been given much advance thought; Ralegh had commissioned an expert—probably Sir Roger Williams—to design a bastion of sufficient strength to deter both Spanish and Indians alike. Sir Roger more than fulfilled his brief, proposing an enclosing structure strong enough to withstand cannonfire, hurricanes, and tidal waves. It was to be shaped like a pentangle, with "five large bulwarkes," sloping curtain walls, and commanding ramparts. Military strength was his only concern: "I would have every streat strayt to every bulwarke," he wrote, "so as standying in the market-plase, yow may see all the bulwarkes, curtyns and gates." Such a fortress would have required a garrison of some 800 soldiers armed with arquebus guns, longbows, pikes, and halberds.

Lane quickly realised that Williams's planning was all in vain. The only stone to be found on Roanoke was "a fewe small pebbles"—hardly adequate for curtain walls—and any ramparts would have to be built of sand and timbers. He had no option but to construct a fort very much like the makeshift defences on Puerto Rico—a bank of sand, a deep ditch, and a few heavily fortified gun emplacements. It was quickly cobbled together, for Lane was keen to finish the work before Grenville sailed for England with much of the available manpower.

As soon as the fort was complete, Lane ordered his men to begin work on their lodgings. These were extremely rudimentary. Although Lane, Harriot, and the other gentlemen built themselves "decent dwelling houses," the rest of the men lived in roughly thatched wooden shacks. More care went into the construction of the communal buildings. There were a church and a storehouse, an armoury for the weapons, and stables for the few animals that had survived the disaster of Wococon. There was also a jail equipped with "bylboes"—an immovable iron bar with sliding leg irons.

By the third week of August, the work was almost complete and Grenville decided it was time to leave. The *Tiger* set sail for England on August 25, leaving behind 107 settlers—a far smaller number than had originally been planned, but more realistic given the lack of supplies. Three weeks later, the *Roebuck* also weighed anchor and headed off into the Atlantic. The colonists' last link with England was broken.

The departure of the ships filled the colonists with dread. From now on they were alone and totally dependent upon their own skills for survival. There were no women to keep them company, all their alcohol had been lost, and food supplies were critically low. Many already had severe doubts about the wisdom of remaining in America. Now that it was too late to leave, their frustration turned to anger. They became "wylde menn . . . whose unrulynes ys suche as not to gyve leasure to ye goovernour to bee allmost at eny time from them."

Many were alarmed that their governor took such perverse enjoyment in their precarious existence, and there were few who shared his passion for hardship. "For myne owne part," wrote Lane, "[I] do finde myselfe better contented to lyve with fysshe for my dayely foode, and water for my daylye drynke." He added that he would rather eke out an existence in an uncharted wilderness than enjoy the "greatest plenty" that London's courtly circle could offer.

The colonists were horrified and began to protest, a defeatist attitude that incensed Lane and saddened Harriot. "Some . . . were of a nice bringing up," he wrote, "[having lived] only in cities or townes, or such as never (as I may say) had seene the world before." He claimed that they were unwilling to accept the inevitable hardship, and "because there were not to bee found any English cities, nor such faire houses, nor at their owne wish any of their olde accustomed daintie food, nor any soft beds of downe or feathers, the countrey was to them miserable." Few showed any willingness to join the various expeditions planned by Lane and Harriot, nor did they have any desire to trade with the Indians. Many "were never out of the iland where wee were seated," and once they realised there was no gold or silver with which to make their fortunes, they "had little or no care of any other thing but to pamper their bellies."

This was not easy, for few of the colonists had the necessary skills to fend for themselves. Abraham Kendall had trained as a mathematician, Marmaduke Constable was fresh out of Oxford University, and Anthony Rowse appears to have been a former member of Parliament. A good number called themselves gentlemen and, as such, had no intention of digging and sowing their own fields.

As many as half the colonists were soldiers, divided into two small companies under captains Edward Stafford and John Vaughan. Their task was to guard the defences and spearhead expeditions into the interior—vital concerns. But there were too many soldiers in proportion to such a small colonist population. Edward Nugent, Darby Glande, Edward Kelly, and John Gostigo had already proved themselves in Ireland and had been hand-selected by Lane himself.

Governor Lane intended to build a massive fortress with curtain walls and ramparts, but the only stone to be found was "a fewe small pebbles." His sand-and-timber fort probably resembled this contemporary makeshift bastion

Others were less well disciplined, and Harriot reported that several soldiers, "for their misdemeanour and ill-dealing in the countrey, have beene there worthily punished." Such rowdy elements were a constant concern; they were accused of having "badde natures" and blamed for having "maliciously not onelie spoken ill of their governours, but for their sakes slaundered the countrie itselfe."

Lane had no time for such men; he had "sette downe a discipline" before the Roanoke landing, and it was "severely executed, first at sea, and then afterwarde by me in lyke sorte continued at lande." It is likely that at least one unruly soldier was hanged, and his rotting corpse left dangling from a tree as a grim warning to the others.

There were, of course, a number of artisans, farmers, and labourers among the colonists, but these saw no earthly reason why they should do the gentlemen's dirty work. There was a shoemaker called John Brocke, John Fever was a basketmaker, and Richard Sare was a labourer; there were also smithies, carpenters, brewers, and bakers. Many of these skilled workers found themselves unable to carry out the work for which they had been hired. There was little need for "roughe masons" on an island where the biggest stone was the size of a pea, and the "mynerall men," headed by Joachim Ganz, a Jew from Prague, soon discovered that the land was devoid of anything more exciting than shingle. Although there was a brief moment of excitement when a strange rock "was founde to holde yron richly," neither Ganz nor the other mineral men could find the precious metals so requested of them. They might have had more luck with alchemy.

It was some weeks before the colonists received their first visit from Chief Wingina, a capricious individual whose rule extended over all the Indians on Roanoke as well as a small settlement on the mainland, some thirty minutes away by dugout canoe. Wingina was a *weroance*, a "big" or "great" chief, and a man who had absolute power "to governe the people" and dispense his own brand of justice, occasionally with the help of the village elders. His majestic title—which was both barbarous and slightly comical—quickly captured the imagination of the English colonists, and they began referring to their own queen as *Weroanza* Elizabeth. The difficulties they had in pronouncing the word were nothing to the problems they had with its spelling. It is variably written as *werowans, weroance, herowan, cheroun,* and *weroans.*

The colonists' previous dealings with Wingina had been through his brother—for the chieftain himself was nursing a war wound—and they were all anxious to meet this powerful ruler whose stockpiles of food they were already viewing with greedy eyes. When he at last appeared, they found him rather disappointing. He was a skinny man with a sinewy body and bulging eyes, and he lacked the customary tattoos. Indeed, his only concessions to adornment were strings of pearls in his earlobes and a gleaming copper gorget around his neck, a sign of his authority. His wife proved rather more interesting. With her plump lips and saucy expression, she so impressed John White that he immediately reached for his paintbox.

Wingina was wary of the English settlers and unsure how to react. Word had spread that these uninvited strangers had supernatural powers—and dangerous ones at that—that were already being deployed with deadly effect up and down the coastline. "Within a few dayes after our departure from everie such towne," wrote Harriot, "the people began to die very fast, and many in short space; in some townes about twentie; in some fortie, in some sixtie, and in one six score, which—in truth—was very manie in respect of their numbers." He added that "the disease was so strange that they neither knew what it was, nor how to cure it."

Unbeknown to the Indians, the English community was carrying measles and smallpox, which had a devastating effect upon tribesmen with no immunity. "This marvelous accident," continued Harriot, "wrought so strange opinions of us that some people could not tel whether to thinke us gods or men."

Big Chief Wingina had firsthand experience of Lane's magical powers, but he drew back from believing them to be gods. "[He was] perswaded that it was the worke of our God through our meanes, and that wee—by Him—might kil and slaie whom wee woulde without weapons, and not come neere them." Keen to learn the secrets of their sorcery, he jumped at the opportunity to join Lane and his men at prayer in the large wooden chapel.

"Wingina and many of his people would be glad many times to be with us at our praiers," wrote Harriot, "and many times call[ed] upon us both in his owne towne, as also in others whither he sometimes accompanied us, to pray and sing psalmes."

He thoroughly enjoyed the communal singing, and, although he was not about to abandon his traditional beliefs, his superstitious nature got the better of him. On two occasions he "was so grievously sicke that he was like to die and, as he lay languishing . . . sent for some of us to praie . . . either that he might live, or after death dwell with Him in blisse." Wingina's interest in the colonists' religion was by no means exceptional. All of the neighbouring tribes were intrigued by the Englishmen's form of worship and even more curious when Harriot began preaching from the gospels in his best Algonkian. This caused considerable confusion among the Indians, for they were convinced that the book itself contained some sort of supernatural power: they snatched it from Harriot's hands, "glad to touch it, to embrace it, to kisse it, to holde it to their brestes and heades." Such displays became rather embarrassing when the scantily clad chieftains began to "stroke over all their bodie with it [and] to shew their hungrie desire of that knowledge which was spoken of."

When Lane's men had first arrived at Roanoke, they had been welcomed with blue skies and oppressive heat. But now, September was approaching and the temperatures had slumped. The barn swallows that White had enjoyed painting were starting to migrate, replaced by the red-breasted merganser, first harbinger of cold weather. This filled the men with dread; their houses were flimsy (many still had only rush matting for walls) and their clothing was inadequate. Of far greater concern was the lack of provisions. Their late arrival at Roanoke had made it impossible to plant any seeds, while the disaster at Wococon left them desperately short of meat to salt and store for the lean winter months. Thomas Harvey, the chief merchant, tried to acquire "beastes, fishe and foule," but these "coulde not bee so suddenly and easily provided for us, nor in so great number and quantities, nor of that choise as otherwise might have bene to our better satisfaction and contentment."

Harvey's experiences left him deeply disenchanted with life on Roanoke. He began to regret having settled on the island. In London, he had been a respectable member of the Grocer's Company with income to spare. When he had learned from Manteo of America's rich resources—news of which had spread like wildfire after being discussed in Parliament—he had leaped at the opportunity to combine trade with adventure, hoping to exchange trinkets for the

This is probably Wingina, *weroance* of Roanoke. He was a skinny man with a sinewy body and wore a gleaming copper gorget round his neck. His attitude towards the settlers was by turns wary, friendly, inquisitive, and ultimately hostile

abundant furs and skins he assumed he would find on arrival. But now that he had firsthand experience of the meagre food supplies, he felt cheated. He would later complain that he had not only lost "the greatest parte of his own wealth," but had also "borrowed divers sommes of money of others" which he had been obliged to spend on essential foodstuffs.

It was only when the Indians had harvested their crops that the men could buy maize, beans, spinach, and sunflower seeds — some of which were dried and placed in the storehouse. They also managed to brew "good ale" from the maize, considerably boosting morale, and salted a little meat for storage. But they seriously underestimated the quantities they would need to keep them alive.

They found it all but impossible to catch fish in the shallow waters of the sound and failed to master the Indian skill of fishing with traps, which were made by "settinge opp reedes or twigges in the water." Nor were they able to learn the Indian practise of fishing with arrows, "shooting them into the fish after the maner as Irishmen cast dartes; either as they are rowing in their boats or els as they are wading in the shallowes for the purpose." They even had difficulty shooting the deer and bear that abounded in the forests, perhaps because their gunpowder had been spoiled in the *Tiger* disaster.

For the moment, none of this mattered; the Indians appeared willing enough to help out by supplying them with food. But if the English had known that Indian goodwill was already being stretched to the limit, they might have redoubled their efforts to collect wild berries, chestnuts, and acorns before it was too late.

Once the settlement was finished, Lane began planning a series of explorations through Pamlico Sound. His first goal was the northern settlement of Skicoac, an important village, which Manteo grandly described as a "citie." Lane himself did not accompany this expedition: instead, he sent Harriot and White, who were charged with producing an accurate map of the northern end of the sound, all of it still uncharted territory. The men's equipment was rudimentary, even by Elizabethan standards. Harriot's principal tools were the dial, crossstaff, and compass; White's must have been similar to the standard toolkit carried by Elizabethan surveyors: "a good store of parchment, paper ryall, quills and inck [and] black powder to make ynck." The two men worked slowly and methodically: Harriot took the readings and coordinates and White recorded his findings on a large sheet of paper, using a selection of colours and symbols to denote features in the landscape. It was painstaking work, not made any easier by the fact that their workshop was an unstable pinnace exposed to the elements. It is testament to their skill that they were able to present Lane with a finely drawn map on their return.

The men edged their way slowly northeastwards, at one point pushing their boat out of the sound and into the Atlantic swell, before turning west towards the opening to Chesapeake Bay. Both were struck by the friendliness of the Indians and the richness of the land, and were particularly interested in the possibilities presented by the deepwater Chesapeake Bay. They remained in the area for more than a month, a period of punishing hardship, for it was now "the time of winter [and] our lodging was in the open aire upon the grounde." Governor Lane's love of the outdoor life appears to have rubbed off on Harriot, who was thoroughly enjoying the rigours of the journey and went so far as to praise the Indians for their spartan winter diet. "I would to god wee would followe their example," he wrote. "For wee should bee free from many kynes of diseasyes which wee fall into by sumptwous and unseasonable blanketts, continuallye devisinge new sawces, and provocation of gluttonnye to satisfie our unsatiable appetite."

Harriot and White's party headed back to Roanoke in early spring to find the settlers in poor spirits. Food stocks were perilously low. Although the colonists did manage to acquire a little seed grain, the Indians seemed reluctant to part with their scarce supplies. Wingina was still outwardly friendly, but he was fast losing patience with the colonists' constant demands for food. It is quite possible—although information is sketchy—that his tribe had been at the receiving end of a number of violent clashes with the English and that these had caused a dangerous rift between the two communities. It certainly helps to explain his sudden conversion from friend to foe, and his dramatic decision to rid Roanoke of the English once and for all. "The king was advised and of himselfe disposed," writes Lane, "to have assuredly brought us to ruine."

Wingina was unsure how to achieve this, and his feeling of help-lessness led him to make wild boasts about a massive army "to the number of 3,000 bowes" that was about to sweep down on Roanoke and wipe out the colonists. Lane was not unduly worried, but he was sufficiently intrigued to plan an expedition to the Choanoke River, where this army was supposedly gathered. When Wingina offered guides to lead him there, the governor realised something strange was afoot, and took with him a substantial contingent of men, all of them bristling with weapons.

The journey proved easy enough, for the river "shewe[d] no cur-rant in the world," and the men made rapid progress to the settle-ment of Choanoke, "the greatest province and seigniorie lying upon that river." Lane displayed all the qualities of leadership that had led Ralegh to employ him as governor. Bold, decisive, and supremely confident, he marched a phalanx of forty soldiers into the village and seized the chieftain—a task made considerably easier by the fact that the old man, called Menatonon, was paralysed from the waist down. Outwitted and surrounded, the tribal elder realised the game was up and admitted that he was indeed assembling an army, but only because Wingina had "sent them continuall worde that our purpose was fully bent to destroy them." Lane corrected him, Menatonon mumbled an apology, and the two men sealed their newfound friendship with a chat around the campfire. "For a sav-age," wrote Lane, "[he was] a very grave and wise man, and of very singular good discourse." He added that "for [the] two dayes that we were together, he gave mee more understanding and light of the countrey than I had received by all the searches and salvages that before I or any of my companie had had conference with." Menatonon gave Lane the tantalising information that if he continued upstream for three days, then continued overland for four more, he would arrive at the territory of a powerful chieftain who lived on the shores of a bay of such depth that even the greatest vessel could anchor in safety. Lane suspected that these were the same shores as those discovered by Harriot and White, and began to form plans for a great expedition.

Lane also learned that the nearby Roanoke River would repay further investigation. His captive chieftain informed him that if he pushed deep inland he would find a tribe with so much copper "that they beautifie their houses with great plates." This was music to Lane's ears. Copper was a sought-after commodity in England, and a cheap source would delight Ralegh's profit-hungry financiers. He decided that this must be his first goal, and he set off to explore immediately, keenly aware that he needed some good news before the expected supply fleet arrived in the summer.

Lane took two boats and forty of his hardiest soldiers on his expedition up the Roanoke River. But they soon found themselves struggling to propel their boats, for the river "hath so violent a current" that it was scarcely navigable. Manteo told them that this was the easy part. Further upstream, "it passeth with many creeks and turnings, and for the space of thirtie miles rowing and more it is as broad as the Thames betwixt Greenwich and the Ile of Dogges."

The oarsmen were quickly exhausted and hungry. They had hoped to buy food from the Indians, but they discovered that all the tribes living close to the riverbank had fled into the forest. "Having passed three dayes voyage up the river, we could not meete a man, nor finde a graine of corne in any of their townes." Despite this, Lane pushed them to the limits of their endurance; they managed to cover a remarkable thirty miles a day.

After several days of this punishing regime, Lane realised that he faced a difficult choice. He had few supplies left and was, by his own reckoning, some 160 miles from Roanoke Island. The weather held the prospect of "contrarie windes or stormes," and he suspected that they might be ambushed by "savages." It seemed clear to him that they should continue—endurance, after all, was one of the pleasures of exploration—but he took the unusual step of allowing his men the choice. "I willed them to deliberate all night upon the matter, and in the morning at our going aborde, to set our course according to the desires of the greatest part." The men talked late into the night, debating whether to risk their lives by continuing upstream or return to the safety of Roanoke. As dawn broke, Lane asked for their decision. "Their resolution fully and wholly was . . . that whiles there was left one halfe pinte of corne for a man, that we should not leave the searche of that river."

They set off with renewed hopes of success, forcing their passage against an increasingly swift current. But two more days of exhaustion finally began to break the spirit of these hardy but hungry men. They moored their boats and wondered if they would lose their lives in this dank, inhospitable forest.

As night fell and the temperature plummeted, they noticed small fires flickering in the twilight and hoped that this signified the existence of a settlement where they might find food. "In the evening," wrote Lane, "we heard certaine savages call as we thought, 'Manteo,' who was also at that time with mee in the boate." The men were heartened by this, "hoping of some friendly conference with them, and willing him to answere them, they presently began a song, as we thought, in token of our welcome to them." But Manteo was not so convinced that this was a welcome cry; as he strained to catch their words, he suddenly leaped up and grabbed his weapon. "[He] tolde mee that they ment to fight with us," wrote Lane, "which word was not so sooner spoken by him . . . [than] there lighted a vollie of arrowes." The men on shore were fortunate to be wearing their buff jerkins, so the arrows "did no hurt—God be thanked—to any man." Those still in the boat primed their weapons, jumped ashore, and chased their Indian quarry into the woods. But the tribesmen vanished without trace. With "the sunne drawing then towards the setting," Lane wisely ordered all his men back to the riverbank. They hastily built a makeshift fort, elected a guard to stand watch throughout the night, and agreed to start the long journey back to Roanoke "before the rising of the sunne."

The men were now so hungry that they began to look greedily on the two bullmastiffs that they had brought on the expedition. These huge animals terrified the Indians and were valuable as watchdogs, but such was the desperation for food that they were now put to more practical use. They were slaughtered, mixed together with leaves of the sassafras tree, and made into a "pottage." The half-starved men ate as much of this revolting mixture as their stomachs would hold, then—after a brief rest—climbed into the boats and headed back downstream, keeping a careful watch for any surprise attack from the forest.

The return journey was much faster, for the little wherry was whisked downstream by the current. They covered in one day what had previously taken four. Even so, by the time they reached the open waters of Pamlico Sound, the congealed bullmastiff was finished and "wee had nothing in the world to eate but pottage of sassafras leaves." Even the ebullient Lane records that this was virtually inedible. He took the opportunity to crack the only joke in his entire journal. "This was upon Easter eve," he wrote, "which was fasted very trulie."

He now realised that he had been extremely fortunate to have brought all his men back down the river alive, having narrowly escaped starvation. Their hardship was not quite over, for they found themselves unable to row across the sound. "The winde blewe so strongly, and the billow so great, that there was no possibilities of passage without sinking of our boates." But the storm ceased on the following morning, and after a hard day's rowing the men finally arrived back at their settlement on Roanoke. "God," wrote Lane, "was pleased not utterly to suffer us to be lost."

Their arrival was a source of amazement to both the English and the Indians. In their absence, Wingina had been busy making mischief, informing both parties that Lane's expedition had been wiped out—"part slayne and part starved." This, he told his tribe, was proof that the English were not the immortal spirits that the superstitious elders believed them to be. The tribesmen took Wingina at his word and, feeling they had been duped by the English, "grew not onely into contempt of us . . . [but] began to blaspheme and flatly to say that our Lord God was not God, since hee suffered us to sustaine much hunger and also to be killed."

Wingina's strategy had worked well. Had Lane not unexpectedly returned, he would have withdrawn his tribe from Roanoke and moved to the settlement on the mainland. This would have had dire consequences for the colonists, for they had "no weares for fish . . . [nor] one grayne of corne for seede to put into the grounde." Indeed, Lane later wrote that such an action would have "brought us to ruine." The English colony would have starved to death.

The return of the expeditionary force changed everything. It undermined all that Wingina had told his tribe and dramatically weakened his authority. It also forced him to listen once again to his most influential advisor, Ensenor, who had consistently supported the English cause and believed their presence on Roanoke to be beneficial to the Indians. Ensenor had pleaded with his fellow tribesmen to treat the English with respect, arguing that they "were the servants of God and . . . not subject to be destroyed by them." He believed Lane's men to be phantoms and spirits who, "being dead men, were able to doe them more hurt then now we coulde do being alive."

Wingina's tribe now sided with Ensenor, convinced that the English were indeed reincarnated spirits. They rejected their chieftain's fiery rhetoric, returning to their former belief "that we be dead men returned into the worlde againe."

This heartened the English colonists, and they soon received even better news. An Indian runner arrived at Roanoke with a message from Menatonon, the disabled chieftain, informing them that he had been so impressed with Lane's tales of the might of Queen

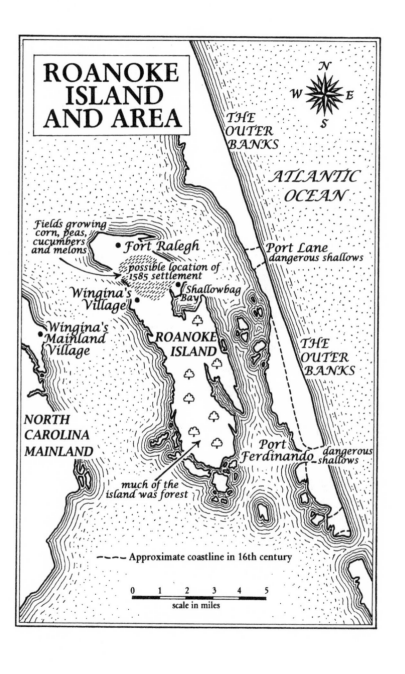

ROANOKE
ISLAND
AND AREA

N
W E
S

THE
OUTER
BANKS

ATLANTIC
OCEAN

Fields growing
corn, peas,
cucumbers
and melons

• Fort Ralegh

Port Lane
dangerous shallows

possible location of
1585 settlement

• Shallowbag
Bay

Wingina's
Village

Wingina's
Mainland
Village

ROANOKE
ISLAND

THE
OUTER
BANKS

NORTH
CAROLINA
MAINLAND

Port
Ferdinando

dangerous
shallows

much of the
island was forest

- - - - Approximate coastline in 16th century

0   1   2   3   4   5

scale in miles

Elizabeth that he had commanded one of his lesser chieftains "to yelde himselfe servant and homager to the great *weroanza* of England, and after her to Sir Walter Ralegh." This chieftain, Okisko, demonstrated his loyalty by sending "foure and twentie of his princi-pllest men to Roanoke" with the news that "from that time forwarde, hee and his successours were to acknowledge her Majestie [as] their onely sovereigne."

This news was greeted with great joy by the colonists. After just eight months in America, an entire Indian tribe was prepared to accept Queen Elizabeth as their supreme chieftain. The queen now had a new and exotic title to add to her list—one that would cause her immense pride. Henceforth, she was *Weroanza* Elizabeth of Virginia.

When Wingina learned what had happened, he was finally convinced that his anti-English policy was doomed. Since he could no longer count on the support of either his own tribe or the neighbouring Indians, he reluctantly ordered his men to assist the English. They set up fish traps, and by the end of April "had sowed a good quantitie of grounde; so much as [would have] bene sufficient to have fed our whole company (God blessing the grouth) and that by the belly for a whole yere." He also gave the English some fields—something he had previously resisted—so they could sow grain on their own land.

For the first time in many months, there was a feeling of optimism among the English on Roanoke. With a supply ship due to arrive at the beginning of July—when the first grain would be ready for harvesting—the colonists had just two months more to rely on the Indians for food.

7

Enter Sir Francis

Sir Richard Grenville's voyage back to England was blessed with good fortune. He set sail in the third week of August 1585 and steered his course towards Bermuda, where he had the good fortune to cross the path of the *Santa Maria*, a straggler from the Spanish treasure fleet.

The ship's captain nervously saluted the *Tiger*, firing a round of blank artillery "in token of amity." In a flash, Grenville was firing back—not with blanks but with weighty cannonballs—aiming his heaviest weaponry at the hull of the *Santa Maria*. "He opened fire and bore down on them . . . and so cut up their rigging that they were disabled." Rejoicing in the carnage, Grenville pumped more and more shot into the ship's weakened timbers. "One man on board was killed, four or five were injured, and two shots struck her near the waterline so that they were sinking." To avoid catastrophe, the Spaniards hauled in their sails and shifted the ship through a ninety-degree turn so that her crippled hull was no longer facing the waves; but "they could do nothing else because their ship was badly damaged."

Grenville was anxious to board the vessel and seize her cargo, but he realised he had a problem. He had foolishly left his pinnace and all his small boats with Ralph Lane on Roanoke, and had absolutely no means of getting his men onto the Spanish ship. As he pondered his predicament, one of his crew had the bright idea of constructing "a boate made with boards of chests." This was duly knocked together, but the boat was flimsy and began to fall apart as soon as she was lowered into the water. As Grenville and his boarding party rowed across to the *Santa Maria*, watched by jeering Spaniards, there was a sudden crack and she "fell asunder and sunke at the shippes side." Grenville and his men had to grapple up the ship's ropes and haul themselves aboard.

The wounded Spanish crew had no stomach for a fight and willingly capitulated to Grenville. He promised "that he would do them no bodily hurt"—little consolation to the dead and dying—on condition that they handed over the ship's register. When he realised the size and value of her cargo, he could scarcely believe his luck. According to the official Spanish records, the *Santa Maria* was heavily laden with gold, silver, and pearls, as well as 200 boxes of sugar, 7,000 hides, and 1,000 hundredweight of ginger, "to a total value of 120,000 ducats."

There was far too much to be transferred to the *Tiger*, so Grenville decided to repair the shattered hull of the *Santa Maria* and take command of the vessel, aided by a small contingent of his soldiers. After transferring his belongings, he made his way slowly back to England, eventually dropping anchor at Plymouth in October 1585.

News of his triumph had already reached London; Grenville suddenly found himself the most popular man in the land. "[He] was courteously received by diverse of his worshipfull friends," reads one account, and doubtless plied with wine. Many of these hosts also happened to be investors in the Roanoke enterprise and, as such, hoped to receive their share of the prize. Prattlers and tavern gossips said the ship was worth a million, maybe more, but however much the London merchants pestered Grenville for an accurate breakdown of her cargo, they learned nothing. The wily Sir Richard kept a stony silence and devoted his time to selling off the seized goods in great secrecy.

It was some weeks before he wrote to Sir Francis Walsingham, also an investor, with the sad news that the *Santa Maria* had been grossly overvalued. "The whole estimate of the shippe . . . amountethe only to 40,000 or 50,000 ducats." Such a low amount was clearly nonsense, yet even with such modest proceeds Grenville was able to repay "the retorne of your adventure, with some gayne." This was a most important boast, for it proved to London's financiers that England's colony could be a profitable enterprise, if only as a base for privateers and pirates. Grenville had given them tangible evidence of the advantages of a fortified stronghold on Roanoke—a supply depot and warehouse—from where their doughty captains could launch raids on the Spanish treasure fleet. It was an exhilarating prospect, and men began to talk excitedly about how the colonisation of America would enable them "to possesse king Phillippes pursse, which is the sure waie to ruine, att one instant, both him and all the usurers depending on him."

Grenville presented Ralegh with a mixed account of the fledgling colony on Roanoke. He proudly informed him that a settlement had been constructed and—never shy of blowing his own clarion—added that through his own exertions it had been planted "with suche cattell and beastes as are fitte and necessary for manuringe the countrey." But he also brought news of the loss of the *Tiger's* stores, and explained that he had left the colonists with empty bellies and mouldy seeds.

Ralegh was alarmed by what he heard. The colony's first supply ship was due to have sailed some months previously, but it had been unexpectedly delayed by an event in Spain that had not only brought the two countries to the brink of war, but now threatened the very existence of the first English colony in America.

King Philip had grown increasingly frustrated with Queen Elizabeth's hawkish foreign policy in the Spanish Netherlands and was infuriated by her refusal to call a halt to the piratical activities of sea captains like Sir Richard Grenville. When crop failures in Spain threatened a famine, he decided to make mischief. He invited English merchants to dispatch a large flotilla of grain ships, with the intention of seizing their cargoes and imprisoning their sailors as the prelude to a total embargo on English trade.

It was a bold idea and it almost worked. But a single slip caused the operation to backfire, and this in turn caused a serious domino effect on the fledgling colony on Roanoke. Things went awry in the spring of 1585 when King Philip's officers came to board the *Primrose*, a large English vessel anchored in the bay of Bilbao. The *Primrose*'s captain was ignorant of the seizure of the other English ships and had given a warm welcome to the boarding party, showing particular courtesy to the lieutenant general of Biscay. The lieutenant general repaid his kindness by ordering him to "yeeld yourselfe, for you are the king's prisoner." The captain lamely called to his men, "We are betrayed."

But the English mariners had no inclination to surrender. They knew that capture would lead to incarceration and torture, and resolved "to die and be burned in the middest of the sea, rather than to suffer themselves to come into the tormentors' hands." They braced themselves for an onslaught and, "in very bold and manly sort . . . tooke them to their javelings, lances, bore-speares and shot . . . [and] did shoote up at the Spaniards."

Carnage ensued, in which the upper decks of the *Primrose* were turned into a human abbatoir. "Now did their blood runne about in the ship in great quantitie, some of them being shot in betweene the legges, the bullets issuing foorth of their breasts, some cut in the hand, some thrust into the bodie, and many of them very sore wounded." The Spanish quickly realised they had made a grave error of judgement. The English crew were sea-toughened ruffians who fought with such tenacity that they had soon recovered the greater part of the vessel. The Spaniards threw in the towel and, without further ado, "tumbled as fast over boord on both sides, with their weapons in their handes, some falling into the sea and some getting into their bootes."

The lieutenant general followed them into the water and clung to the ship until, "for pities sake," he was hauled aboard. Realising that the game was up, he reached inside his clothes, "which were wet, [and] did plucke foorth the king's commission by which he was authorized to doe all that he did."

Only now did the crew of the *Primrose* realise that they had an extremely valuable hostage. The lieutenant general was carrying proof that King Philip had masterminded the whole affair. The English captain immediately weighed anchor and headed for England to present both the document and the Spaniard to Queen Elizabeth.

The queen was livid when she learned what had happened and vowed to have her revenge. England's merchants were no less indignant and clamoured for war with Spain. Soon the whole country was demanding action. Elizabeth, answering the cries of her nation, threw caution to the wind and ordered a retaliatory embargo on Spanish goods, as well as issuing letters of reprisal to the merchants. This was tantamount to a declaration of war, for the queen's measure made it "lawful for the said merchants . . . to set upon by force of arms, and to take and apprehend upon the seas, any of the ships or goods of the subjects of the King of Spain." Henceforth they were allowed to act "as if it were in the time of open war between her Majesty and the said King of Spain." The queen showed that she meant business by ordering her trusty servant, Sir Francis Drake, to prepare a fleet to rescue the seized vessels.

The furore that followed had an unfortunate consequence for Ralph Lane and his hungry colonists on Roanoke. Ralegh's supply ship, the *Golden Royal*, was already laden with tools and victuals and was about to sail for America when Queen Elizabeth announced that she had a more urgent task for its captain, Bernard Drake, the brother of Sir Francis. Concerned that the English fishing fleet in Newfoundland was in danger, she ordered him to alert the fishermen to the turn of events and to protect them from attack.

Young Bernard carried out Her Majesty's orders to the letter, and even found time in the coming weeks to attack nineteen Spanish vessels, much to the fury of their owners. Elizabeth rejoiced in his success and added salt to the Spaniards' wounds by knighting him on his return.

English piracy quickly became so rife in New World waters that Spain's Council of the Indies was moved to write a desperate plea to the king. "Since the damage is becoming greater every day, and since, if the arrogance of these corsairs remains unchecked, we will always be troubled, we again, with all humility, beseech your majesty to find a remedy." The council added that it was imperative that the English colony be located and destroyed, since it was believed to be harbouring the piratical English vessels.

The Spanish were hindered by a lack of reliable information. Although dozens of reports were delivered to the king's magnificent palace, El Escorial, few contained anything more concrete than rumour. "The plan and principal objective of these corsairs is not yet understood," reads one report; another claims that Ralegh had dispatched more than 500 colonists to America. Anger bred desperation, and the Council of the Indies prepared a warship, "strong and well armed . . . with settlers, arms, powder, necessary military stores and any other cargo considered desirable." This was to have a defensive and offensive role—capable of protecting Spain's military outposts in Florida but also equipped to strike at the English colony.

King Philip fully supported such measures, aware that he would almost certainly have to use force to drive England out of America. But unbeknown to either the Spanish or the English, Ralph Lane's settlers were proving more than capable of destroying themselves.

Ralph Lane had every reason for optimism after surviving his ill-fated expedition up the Roanoke River. Crops had been planted and fish traps set, and he noted in his journal that the crops could be harvested in just two months, at which point the colony would become self-sufficient. "All our feare was of the two moneths betwixt," he wrote, "in which meane space, if the savages should not helpe us . . . we might well starve."

But on April 20, 1586, Lane was awakened with some dreadful news. Ensenor, "the only frend to our nation," had dropped dead, depriving the English of their most loyal supporter. He alone had "opposed himselfe in their consultations against al matters proposed against us." And he alone commanded sufficient respect to force a climbdown from Wingina. More bad news arrived a few days later when Lane learned that Wanchese, along with several others, had finally deserted the English cause, leaving Manteo as Lane's only Indian ally.

With Ensenor dead and the collapse of the pro-English camp, Wingina's hostility to Lane was renewed; he privately vowed to wipe out the colonists once and for all. He was tired of their "dayly sending . . . for supply of victuall" and forbade his tribesmen from selling any food to the English. He also moved his base to the mainland and forced his tribe to destroy all the fish traps, which, "once being broken, [were] never to be repaired."

This was a serious development. "The king stood assured," wrote Lane, "that I must be enforced, for lacke of sustenance, there to disband my company into sundry places to live upon shell-fishe." This was exactly the course that the English now adopted, "for the famine grewe so extreeme among us . . . that I was enforced to send Captaine Stafford with 20 with him to Croatoan [Island]." Lane further reduced numbers by dispatching another band of men to the Outer Banks "to live there and also to wayte for shipping." He sent a rotating team to the mainland to forage for berries and shellfish.

It was not long before Wingina felt that the English were sufficiently weakened for him to attempt an assault on their fort, and he spent considerable effort persuading other tribes to join him, promising them the spoils of war as their reward. Lane knew in advance of the planned ambush, for the information had been leaked to him by a renegade Indian. It was a carefully planned operation that involved several hundred warriors. Two of Wingina's advisors, along with twenty bowmen, were to row across to Roanoke Island, and then, according to Lane, "in the dead time of the night, they would have beset my house and put fire in the reedes." If all had gone to plan, a panic-striken Lane "woulde have come running out of a sudden, amazed, in my shirt [and] without armes, upon the instant whereof they woulde have knocked out my braynes." As soon as Lane was dead, the Indians would have killed Harriot and the other "gentlemen" and then set upon the shocked survivors. In the space of a few short hours, England's colony in America would have been wiped off the map.

When Lane learned of the proposed ambush, he decided to wrest the initiative with a characteristically audacious plan. He began by sending a message to Wingina informing him that he was about to lead a small party to Croatoan Island, as he "had heard of the arival of our fleete." This was a fabrication, and Lane admits in his journal that "in trueth, [I] had neither heard nor hoped for so good adventure," but he knew it would so alarm Wingina that it would force him to postpone his attack.

Lane now got down to business. There was no time to be lost, for Indian scouts would soon learn that the story was a hoax. He called his men to a secret council of war and informed them that he was planning an attack on Wingina's village that very evening, May 31. It was to be a night attack or "camisado"—so called because the attackers left their shirt-tails hanging behind them so that they would not be fired upon by their own men.

It was planned in two stages. On the eve of the attack, Lane's men were to "sease upon all the canoes about the island" so they would have enough boats to get quickly across the sound. It was imperative that every canoe be captured, or word of the impending attack could easily be carried to Wingina. Once this operation was complete, the men would wait until nightfall before rowing across to the mainland and mounting a frontal assault against Wingina's settlement.

The attack misfired right from the outset. A group of men was sent "to gather up all the canoas in the setting of the sunne," but two

Indians managed to escape and began rowing furiously towards the mainland. The Englishmen chased after the canoe, captured it, and promptly "cut off two savages heads." Unfortunately for Lane, several Indians on Roanoke were witness to the slaughter, "whereupon the cry arose; for in trueth they, privie to their owne villanous purposes against us, held as good espial upon us, both day and night, as we did upon them." The tables were now turned and the Indians launched their own attack; within minutes, Lane found himself locked into a desperate struggle for the island. "[The Indians] tooke themselves to their bowes and we to our armes," he wrote; "some three or foure of them at the first were slayne with our shot, the rest fled into ye woods." Lane's position was precarious, for although he knew that none of the Indians could cross the sound to warn Wingina of events on Roanoke, he felt he had lost the initiative. He now had no option but to press ahead with his attack on the mainland, although the fear of ambush meant it would have to take place at dawn.

Lane's men passed a tense night in their settlement, half-expecting trouble from the warriors in the woods. They had good reason to be frightened, for the Indians' favoured method of attack was, as Manteo had previously warned, "by sudden surprising one an other, most commonly about the dawning of the day, or moone light." All night the men clutched their weapons, but the attack never materialised. It was with considerable relief that they watched the first streaks of dawn light the eastern sky.

Lane split his men into two groups, leaving forty soldiers to guard the fort on Roanoke while he led twenty-seven men across the sound to punish Wingina and his tribe. Their boats were sighted by the Indians long before they reached the mainland, but Lane's heavily armed men were not unduly troubled. Some had donned breastplates, others wore jerkins, and all carried loaded pistols.

As the boats neared the foreshore, Lane called to an Indian at the water's edge and asked him to tell Wingina that he was heading to Croatoan Island but would first like a word with the chieftain. The

Wingina's warriors were itching to wipe out the English colony. Lane said their plan was to storm his house, "put fire in the reedes," and "knock out my braynes."

tribesman duly ran to the settlement and returned shortly after with the news that Wingina "did abide my coming to him." Lane's bluff had worked; he would not have to fight his way into the settlement after all.

His men were jumpy as they entered the village and looked for any hint of suspicious activity. Wingina was seated on the ground surrounded by seven or eight of his principal advisors, but most of the "common sort" were still in their houses. Lane realised that this was the opportune moment to attack: "I gave the watchword agreed upon, (which was 'Christ our Victory')," and the men fired their muskets straight at the little group of tribal elders. Never before had Lane led such a devastating offensive. Wingina was the first to be hit, "shot thorow by the colonell with a pistoll," while others lay stunned and bleeding, unsure as to whether they were dead, wounded, or as yet unhurt. Lane ordered his men to halt firing for a moment, "for the saving of Manteo's friends," then blasted a second round of grapeshot into the group.

Wingina, who had been "lying on the ground for dead," suddenly scrambled to his feet "and ran away, as though he had not bene touched, insomuch as he overran all the companie." He had not been seriously hurt, and was desperate to flee before Lane's troops could reload their muskets for a third time. A band of men set off in hot pursuit, anxious not to lose him in the thick undergrowth.

The chieftain had a very real chance of escape. He was familiar with the forest trails and skilled at moving quickly through the bracken. He was also extremely lucky. One of Lane's Irish contingent lifted his cavalry pistol and, with Wingina in his sights, discharged his lead. The chieftain was "shot thwart the buttocks," which momentarily stunned him, but he was not badly injured and he continued his desperate dash through the forest. He had now shaken off all but two of his assailants, and these found it hard to run through the forest in their heavy garments.

Lane, who had remained in the village, had no idea whether Wingina was alive or dead and was "in some doubt lest we had lost both the king and my man." But after a long interval, the two exhausted foot soldiers emerged from the forest. When Lane stepped forward to ask what had happened, he saw that one of the men, Edward Nugent, was clutching Wingina's bloody head, severed with his trusty blade.

The events that followed immediately after the attack remain a mystery, for there is a week-long break in Lane's journal. It is probable that the village elders surrendered to the English as soon as they saw this grisly trophy, but whether Lane exacted more revenge is unclear. It would certainly have been in keeping with his reputation for clinical efficiency, and Thomas Harriot hinted at further bloodshed when he wrote that "some of our companie, towards the ende of the yeare, shewed themselves too fierce in slaying some of the people." What is certain is that Lane's offensive gave the English breathing space. There was no chance of an Indian attack in the immediate future. All they now had to do was survive the short period before their harvest could be gathered.

On June 8, just over a week after the attack, one of Lane's soldiers, Captain Stafford, arrived breathless from his post on the Outer Banks with the news that Lane had long wanted to hear. A great fleet lay at anchor—no fewer than twenty-three ships—and they flew from their masts the flag of St. George. Sir Francis Drake had come to the aid of Ralegh's half-starved colony on Roanoke.

Drake had long taken an interest in Ralegh's project. He had served on the parliamentary committee that had scrutinized his plans, and welcomed the news that Sir Richard Grenville had successfully planted the colonists on Roanoke. But his arrival at the island in the summer of 1586 was as unplanned as it was unexpected: Drake was more than four thousand miles from his original destination.

He had set sail with a commission to free the English grain ships in Spain, and he was also expected, and encouraged, to ransack and loot whichever Spanish coastal towns took his fancy. But Drake had

Lane led a devastating attack on Wingina's village. The chieftain was pursued into the forest where he met with a grisly end

set his mind on a far more ambitious agenda, which included an attack on the Spanish treasure fleet and a series of raids in the Spanish Caribbean. He had been encouraged by reports—filtering back from both Grenville and Lane—that suggested the Caribbean islands were not as strongly fortified as had first been thought. Lane had written in a letter that any attack would be "most honorable and feasible and profytable," and added that Spain's forces were "soo meane" that it would be easy to capture their strongholds with "eny small force sent by hyr majeste." Grenville had only increased Drake's impatience to set sail with his reports of "sugar, ginger, pearle, tobacco and such like commodities." What neither man had asked for, nor expected, was for Drake to pitch up at Roanoke.

He had set sail on his Spain-bound voyage in September 1585, having secured the backing of many of the most prestigious names in Elizabethan England. The queen herself had invested £20,000, while courtiers such as Leicester, Hatton, and Ralegh had offered money, ships, and supplies. London's populace sent the thirty-strong fleet on its way "with great jollity," as well they might, for it was the largest squadron ever to leave English shores.

King Philip was seriously alarmed by rumours of its departure and wrote desperate letters to his former ambassador to England—Mendoza—urging him "to use the utmost diligence in obtaining very frequent and very trustworthy news from England." In the absence of concrete information, everyone in Spain had their own theory about Drake's mission. Mendoza believed his objective was to make "a landing in Portugal"; the Marques de Santa Cruz, Spain's high admiral, thought he was heading for Brazil; and a few harboured naïve hopes that Drake was sailing directly to Ralegh's colony, avoiding Spanish territory altogether.

Whatever the goal of his mission, his fleet sent a wave of panic through the Spanish Admiralty, which called for immediate action: "despatch caravels with all possible diligence to the viceroyes and goverours of the Indies," wrote Santa Cruz, "advertising them of the newes of the English army, that they may be provided and make themselves ready for them."

Drake headed directly for Spain, where he learned that most of the seized grain ships had already been released, thus deflecting his planned onslaught. This enabled him to proceed towards the Caribbean, a voyage of such monotony that the on-board chroniclers were clearly delighted when the steward of the *Talbot*, Thomas Ogle, was caught with his hose around his ankles and two young lads in his bunk. Here, at last, was something to write about. After being convicted of sodomy by his peers, Ogle cheerfully "confessed the fact" and was "hanged . . . for buggery, committed in his stewards rome with 2 boyes."

Once Drake had entered tropical waters, he pointed his fleet in the direction of Santo Domingo, the fabled Spanish city on the southern coast of Hispaniola Island. He had set his heart on executing the most brazen raid that England had ever launched against its old adversary. Santo Domingo was the original seat of Spanish government in the New World, its "chief jewel," whose opulence and splendour had long been the subject of ballads and songs. Drake wished to sack this "goodly builded cittie" not just for the spoils of war, but because it stood as the very symbol of King Philip's power.

He had chosen a formidable target. From the sea, Santo Domingo looked impregnable, its stone bulwarks dominating the entrance to the harbour. The Spanish governor boasted of commanding "the strongest [city] in Christendom," a fortress defended by "handsome and effective troops," and was confident that the place would never come under attack.

Shortly after ten o'clock on the morning of December 31, 1585, a breathless messenger arrived at the fort with the disconcerting news that a fleet "believed to be English" had been sighted. Word spread quickly through the city, but few chose to believe such a story, doubting that English ships would dare to sail so close to the island without first asking permission. A captain was nonetheless put to sea to investigate; when he returned to the city a few hours later he confirmed the rumours. Not only were the ships flying the flag of St. George, they were also commanded by "*el Capitan* Francisco."

Drake was reviled throughout Spain's New World empire, largely because he had spent the greater part of his sea career filching from its treasure fleet and silver mines. His audaciousness stunned King Philip's seamen, who claimed he was a wizard who had a secret mirror that enabled him to peep over the horizon. Since returning from his triumphant voyage around the world in 1580, a "large winde" had carried him forward, both in the queen's favour and in the fear he engendered in Spain.

The citizens of Santo Domingo panicked when they learned that *el Capitan* was in command of the fleet. Harbour defences were bolstered, ships were sunk to block the entrance to the port, and guns were primed in readiness for his arrival. Then, with the city's defences on a war footing, the townsfolk retired into the hills, confident that even Sir Francis would have difficulty in silencing the city's great cannon.

But Drake had planned his attack with considerable cunning. He knew that although Santo Domingo looked impressive from the sea, the city was exposed on its land side, where only cactus hedges blocked the path of would-be invaders. This had never troubled the inhabitants, for it was a commonplace that the city could not be attacked from the land. Drake decided to exploit this weakness, a high-risk gamble that required him to land his soldiers at the treacherous Hayna Beach, where the "sea surge" was notoriously unpredictable. The Spanish held that it was impossible to bring a pinnace to shore at Hayna, and for this reason there was no sentry on duty to see the English disembark. The first they knew of anything untoward happening was when astonished city officers saw one thousand English soldiers marching towards Santo Domingo's poorly defended west wall. "To have landed there," wrote one, "is a thing more incredible than I can express."

The Spanish *licentiate*, Cristobal de Ovalle, rode out with a troop of horsemen and prepared to attack. But the English were well prepared and seized the initiative: "our small shot played upon them . . . [and] they were thus driven to give us leave to proceede towardes the two gates of the towne." This first skirmish ended well for the English, and it encouraged them to press home their assault.

Drake's land commander, Christopher Carleill, divided his forces so that he could attack two of the city gates simultaneously. The Spanish put up a heroic defence, and came within a whisker of

Sir Francis Drake terrified the Spanish. He vowed to sack Santo Domingo, Spain's "chief jewel," before heading to Roanoke

killing Carleill, but the speed of the onslaught proved decisive. "We marched or rather ranne soe roundly into them," wrote one of the attackers, "as pell mell we entered the gates with them." Carleill had vowed to his subordinates that "he woulde not rest until our meeting in the market place." Yet even he was surprised at the ease of his victory. Spain's proudest colonial bulwark had fallen with scarcely a fight, and by late afternoon on New Year's Day, 1586, the flag of St. George was flying over the city's crenellated battlements. "Thus," wrote the author of one journal, "the Spaniards gave us the towne for a Newyeers gifte."

Drake's attack marked a turning point in relations with Spain. For decades, English adventurers had been chancing their luck in New World waters, ransacking vessels and attempting trade. Ralegh had increased the tensions by settling men in North America, in blatant disregard of Spain's claim to the continent. Now, in attacking Santo Domingo, Drake had declared war on everything that King Philip II represented—trade restrictions, control of the seas, Catholicism, and absolute mastery of the Americas. He had also opened a new chapter in the history of North America, one that would decide who would ultimately control the land adopted and named by the Virgin Queen.

Drake chose not to be magnanimous in his hour of triumph. He vowed to reduce Santo Domingo to rubble unless he was offered a suitable ransom. "We spent the early mornings in firing the outmost houses," reads one English account, "but they being built very magnificently . . . gave us no small travell to ruine them." It was back-breaking work, "[and] for divers dayes together we ordained eche morning by daybreake . . . [and] did nought else but labour to fier and burne the sayd houses." The churches and fortifications were the most popular target for destruction. "Wee set parte of ther castle on fire," wrote another who took part in the pillage, "and burned all ther images of woode, brake and distroied all there fairest worke within ther churches." Nothing was spared, and it was not until a large part of Santo Domingo had been gutted that the shocked citizens agreed to offer *el Capitan* 25,000 ducats if he spared the buildings still standing.

Drake's work was now complete: he exchanged three of his ships for more seaworthy vessels, and cheekily renamed the largest the *New Year's Gift*. The remaining Spanish ships were burned, including the royal galley, and all the slaves were set free. Many of them were so pleased to have escaped the Spanish yoke that they chose to sail with Drake.

While he was plundering the Caribbean Sir Francis heard rumours of a Spanish plot to destroy Ralegh's colony on Roanoke. Although he was unsure if these contained any grain of truth, he was inclined to believe them, and later claimed to a visitor at Queen Elizabeth's court that he had unearthed hard evidence that the Spanish were organising "an expedition to Virginia in order to root out utterly the British colony." This was a serious development that required urgent action. After a lightning raid on the Spanish main, Drake "set course for Virginia, with the object, commendable of course, of rescuing Ralph Lane . . . and his people from death."

He knew that any Spanish attack was likely to be dispatched from one of their military outposts in Florida, probably St. Augustine, where the local governor himself was stationed. It was there that Drake now headed, hoping to preempt any assault on Roanoke by wiping out its garrison.

The fleet arrived at the end of May. Carleill was once again sent ashore with his crack troops, with orders to "lodge himselfe intrenched as neare the fort as that he might play with his muskets and smallest shot upon anie that should appeare."

The Spanish garrison had already heard news of the fate that had befallen Santo Domingo and were reluctant to sacrifice their lives for a decrepit log fort on the edge of a wilderness. "Taking the alarum, [they] grew fearefull that the whole force was approaching to the assault, and therefore with all speede abandoned the place after the shotting of some of their peeces." So reads the English account, adding that the defending troops were "fainte-harted cowardes." The Spanish report reads rather differently, recalling how the garrison bravely fought off repeated waves of attackers. "Behind certain sand dunes, they [the English] drew up in formation, flags flying and drums beating . . . [They] attacked the fort, which met them with such fire from its artillery that they again withdrew with the loss of one pinnace which was sunk." The report concludes that it was only when the English had landed an overwhelmingly superior force that the defenders finally capitulated.

Once the fort was destroyed, Drake's men moved on to the town, where they encountered unexpected resistance. One English sergeant was "shot through the head and, falling downe therewith, was by the same and two or three more, stabbed in three or foure places of his bodie with swords and daggers before anie could come neere to his rescue." Although this understandably disheartened the English, they continued to press home their attack and soon captured the town.

Drake hesitated to torch St. Augustine, for he realised there was much that could be of use to Lane and his men. He sent instructions that all the transportables were to be brought aboard his ships, including windows, doors, locks, and metalwork. Only once all of these had been removed could the town be burned, a task that his men carried out with unusual enthusiasm. They had arrived at St. Augustine to find "abowte 250 howses in this towne." By the time they left "not one of them [was] standinge."

Drake had hoped to repeat his success on the Spanish fort of Santa Helena, further to the north, but "the shols appearing dangerous, and we having no pilot to undertake the entrie, it was thought meetest to go hence alongst." So, at the beginning of June, he put to sea once again and "sailed alonge the coast of this lande untill wee came to the place where those men did lyve that Sir Walter Raleghe had sente thither to inhabitt the yeere before."

It was a "speciall great fire" on the Outer Banks that alerted Drake to the location of the English colony. Correctly assuming it was a signal to the fleet—it had been lit by Captain Stafford for exactly this purpose—he ordered his ships to drop anchor and sent his skiff ashore. There he "found some of our English countrymen that had bene sent thither the yeare before by Sir Walter Ralegh."

Stafford immediately set off overland to break the good news to Lane, aware that Drake was in no hurry to continue northwards towards Roanoke. He covered more than twenty miles a day across terrible terrain, and arrived at the settlement with so many scratches and blisters that even Governor Lane was impressed. "I must truly report of him from the first to the last," he wrote, "he was the gentleman that never spared labour or perill either by land or water, faire weather or fowle, to performe any service committed unto him."

Stafford was carrying a letter from Drake which pleased Lane enormously, for it contained "a most bountifull and honourable offer . . . not onely of victuals, munitions and clothing, but also of barkes, pinnaces and bootes, they also by him to be victualled, manned and furnished to my contention."

On June 10, 1586, the small colony of Englishmen on Roanoke awoke to a marvelous sight—one not to be repeated in American waters for many years. Drake's huge array of ships lay at anchor off the Outer Banks, their flags flying proudly in the offshore breeze. Most were far too large to enter the shallow waters of Pamlico Sound and Drake ordered them all to anchor out at sea.

The following morning, Lane rowed out to meet Sir Francis. After much pomp and ceremony, the governor was ushered into the great cabin for discussions. He spoke with frankness and honesty, informing Drake that the colony was in desperate straits, manned by disillusioned layabouts who were keen to return to England. "I craved at his hands that it would please him to take with him into England a number of weake and unfit men . . . and in place of them to supply me of his company with oaremen, artificers and others." Lane also asked for fresh victuals, pinnaces, and boats that would enable him to complete his exploration of Chesapeake Bay, and a vessel large enough to weather the Atlantic storms.

Drake graciously agreed to all these requests "according to his usuall commendable maner of governement." Not only did he offer Lane the *Francis*, a vessel of seventy tons, but "further appointed for me two fine pinnaces and four small boats" as well as two "experienced masters." With a deal struck, the two men shook hands and Drake told Lane to send his best officers aboard his flagship so they could make a note of everything they needed "for 100 men for four months." These would then be transferred onto the *Francis*.

On June 13, just as Lane's men were in the process of loading supplies, disaster struck. The two commanders were conferring onshore when a ferocious storm raced up the coastline, smashing its way through the anchored fleet. "The weather was so sore and the storme so great that our ankers woulde not holde, and no shipp of them all but eyther broke or lost ther ankers."

The wind churned the sea into troughs and mountains, crushing pinnaces and tossing the smaller boats through the air. Canvas was shredded, anchor cables were snapped, and unstowed supplies were washed overboard by waves so huge that they were breaking on the ships' upper decks. "We had thunder, lightning and raigne with hailstones as bigge as hennes egges. There were greate spowtes at the seas as thoughe heaven and earth woulde have mett."

It was three days before the storm died. The scattered fleet slowly reassembled in the roadstead off the Outer Banks, but one ship failed to reappear: the *Francis*, which had on board many of Lane's men as well as stores and victuals, had disappeared without trace. It was several weeks before Drake had to conclude that the disillusioned men had used the storm as an excuse to sail back to England.

Drake offered Lane a new vessel, the *Bark Bonner*, but she was too cumbersome to enter Pamlico Sound and not suited to his needs. The governor also faced a serious shortage of manpower. Realising that his colony had reached crisis point, he reluctantly called a meeting of "such captaines and gentlemen of my companie as then were at hand." As the men discussed their options, they realised that there was very little they could do. They had lost not only their ship and the greater part of their provisions, but also two of the captains whom Drake had appointed to serve under Lane. Their numbers were perilously low and there was little likelihood of any supply ships arriving in the near future, given the state of virtual war that now existed between England and Spain. With heavy heart, Lane declared that the only solution to their plight was to return to England. If his men agreed, he would immediately "make request to the generall, in all our names, that he would bee pleased to give us present passage with him."

Drake listened to Lane's request and "most readily assented," aware that it was the only sensible option. Without further ado, he sent his surviving pinnaces to Roanoke to pick up the supplies and men. As he watched them crash through the surf towards his off-shore fleet, he was surprised to see a small, dark-faced figure seated at the helm of one of the boats. Manteo, friend of the English, had decided to return to London.

8

Smoke into Gold

Ralph Lane's departure from Roanoke was chaotic. Sir Francis Drake's sailors were so fearful the hurricane would return that they threatened to leave the colonists behind if they did not immediately assemble on the foreshore. "The weather was so boysterous," admitted Lane, "[that] the greater number of the fleete [were] much agrieved with their long and daungerous abode in that miserable road."

Lane was the first to climb aboard the waiting pinnace, followed by Harriot, White, and the other gentlemen. They were rowed out to Drake's vessel, the *Elizabeth Bonaventure*, leaving a few sailors in charge of their trunks and chests. These contained virtually everything that had been collected over the previous year—charts, maps, specimens, paintings, and seeds. It was a scientific treasure trove—a complete record of Queen Elizabeth I's Virginia.

To Lane's surprise, the pinnace assigned to bring these trunks to Drake's flagship was empty when it arrived at the ship's side. His immediate concern was that his belongings had been left unattended on the beach, and he ordered the men to row the two miles back to shore to retrieve them. But the sailors refused. They had already made the journey several times and were worried by the growing strength of the wind. When Lane repeated his order, he was told by one of the men that there was no point. The trunks, chests, and crates, he explained, had all gone to a watery grave.

There was a moment's stunned silence before a horrified Lane demanded to know more. The sailors nonchalantly explained that the heavily laden pinnace had repeatedly grounded in the shallow waters of Pamlico Sound, and they had lightened it by simply hurling everything overboard. "Most of all wee had," wrote a distraught Lane, "with all our cardes, bookes and writings, were by the saylers cast over boord." The scale of the catastrophe soon became apparent. Many of Lane's notebooks had been hurled into the sea, Harriot's priceless scientific notes were lost, and even a "fayre chaine" of pearls was jettisoned. This caused Harriot no less distress than the loss of his notes, for they were of such "uniformitie in roundenesse [and] orientnesse" that he had intended to present them to the queen on his return. Even some of John White's watercolours had been cast overboard. Of the enormous amount of material gathered from Roanoke, only a few boxes of seeds and a book of Harriot's notes had made it to the *Elizabeth Bonaventure*. It was a setback that devastated Lane, Harriot, and White.

The maps and notes were not all that had been left behind. Such was the rush to set sail that three of the colonists had the misfortune to be left on shore. "[They] had gone further into the country," explained Lane, "and the wind grew so that we could not stay for them." Their fate was to remain a mystery for more than three decades, and was to become entwined in one of the great riddles of the early seventeenth century, one which would involve Ralegh, Harriot, and White as well as two Indian chieftains and dozens of tribesmen.

Drake's ships were extremely crowded. In addition to Lane's colonists, he was still carrying 500 African and Indian slaves that had been picked up in the Caribbean. There were far too many mouths to feed on the long journey back to England. After guaranteeing safe passage to a small group of Turkish galley slaves, Sir Francis set the rest of the slaves ashore on the Outer Banks and left them to fend for

themselves. It was a cruel decision, for he knew they had little hope
of survival. Abandoned and hungry, they must have either starved to
death or been butchered by the Indians. They were never heard
from again.

The fleet made its hurried departure from the Outer Banks in the
third week of June 1586, and arrived "in Portesmouth, the 27 of Julie
the same yeere." Drake was given a triumphant welcome when he
stepped ashore. Stories of his voyage of destruction had already
reached England and the harbour was thronged with townsfolk anxious to glimpse not only Sir Francis, but the "great spoyles and
riches" that were said to be stashed in the holds of his ships. The fact
that he had failed in his key objective—to attack the Spanish treasure fleet—was brushed aside in the rush to celebrate his "large scale
villainy." The audacity of his attack on Santo Domingo thrilled even
England's most peace-minded courtiers, and "so inflamed the whole
countrie with a desyre to adventure unto the seas yn hope of the lyke
good successe, that a greate number prepeared shipps, marynors and
soylders and travelled every place at the seas where any proffite
might be had."

After a brief rest, Drake made his leisurely progress to London,
where he was royally entertained at Richmond Palace. "I happened
to meet Francis Drake, the knight, on the next day," wrote a Ger-
man visitor to the court. "He filled the whole palace with a very special joy. His friends and relatives are celebrating his safe return
from such a long journey with its difficulties and dangers overcome."

Drake's return totally overshadowed that of Ralph Lane and his
men. The court was far more interested in the sack of Santo
Domingo than in the failed experiment on Roanoke, and even those
who had been keeping themselves informed of developments did
not rush to make contact with Lane. When Richard Hakluyt learned
of his disorderly departure, his moral indignation got the better of
him: "[He] left all thinges so confusedly," he wrote, "as if they had
bene chased from thence by a mightie armie, and no doubt so they

were, for the hande of God came upon them for the crueltie and outrages committed by some of them against the native inhabitantes of the countrie."

The records of Ralegh's first meeting with Lane have been lost, but the content of their discussion is not in doubt. Enough of Lane's letters have survived to show that his opinion of America—and more particularly of Roanoke—had changed dramatically in the twelve months he spent living there. His earliest reports had been bursting with optimism; he had assured the court that "the Lord, to hys glory, dothe dayely blesse here with a dayely discoverye of sumwhat rare growynge." In a note to Hakluyt he was more expansive, informing him that the land "has the goodliest soile under the cape of heaven" and adding the tantalising news that "the people [are] naturally most curteous, and very desirous to have clothes, but especially of course cloth rather than silke." This, he knew, would gain the attention of England's merchants, for woollens and broadcloth were among the country's most profitable exports. If anything was guaranteed to ensure the survival of Ralegh's American colony, it was a new export market.

Now, one year on, Lane had changed his tune. The natives, he had discovered, where not quite as "curteous" as he had first supposed. Far from wanting woolly jerkins and cloaks, they were desperate to get their hands on muskets and calivers—items that even England's hard-pressed merchants were reluctant to sell. Then there was the geographical position of the colony to consider. Pamlico Sound was certainly hidden from the prying eyes of the Spaniards, but there was a high price to pay for such security. The water was so shallow that even relatively small craft had to remain at anchor several miles offshore, and all three inlets to the sound were treacherous. Wococon had already displayed ample proof of its dangers; Trinity had just seven feet of water at high tide; Ferdinando was only a few feet deeper. The only boats that could move freely in and out of the sound were wherries and pinnaces, fragile craft that had not been built to withstand the Atlantic breakers. Since a secure harbour was critical to the success of any colony, Lane had grave reservations about this entire stretch of coastline.

His greatest disappointment was the lack of success of his "myn-erall men." In the early days he had written excitedly about "many sortes of apothecorie drugs" and had held out the hope of finding, if not gold, then certainly silver and copper. Metallurgist Joachim Ganz had been so confident of success that he built a smelting labo-ratory and devoted hours of his time to bubbling up heady concoc-tions of crushed stone and dirt. It was a forlorn task, for his men had been unable to find anything more valuable than "ragge stones" or pebbles. Although there was a brief moment of celebration when they discovered a vein of kaolin, useful for colonists with diarrhoea, they soon realised that short of a nationwide outbreak of food poi-soning, it was unlikely to make Ralegh the fortune he craved. Lane still held out the hope that precious metals would be found in the interior of the country, but his forced evacuation had brought to a halt all of his planned expeditions. His final assessment of the reali-ties of American colonisation was blunt and uncompromising: "The discovery of a good mine, by the goodnesse of God, or a passage to the South Sea, . . . and nothing els, can bring this country in request to be inhabited by our nation."

For all the doom and gloom, there was a faint glimmer of hope in his prognosis. America's soil was fertile and the country could boast "the most sweete and healthfullest climate." If Ralegh could dis-cover even a small amount of gold, concluded Lane, then the "many other rootes and gummes there found [will] make good marchandise . . . which otherwise, of themselves, will not be worth the fetching."

Sir Walter must have been disappointed in Lane's assessment of the Roanoke experiment and dismayed that Lane had abandoned his colony. His only consolation was the fact that the crippling costs of equipping the settlers had been more than covered by pillage from Spanish vessels—a tidy sum that could yet persuade London's merchants to try their luck once again in America.

But he soon found his efforts hampered by an unexpected development. Lane's men had suffered appalling hardships during their year on Roanoke and were furious at having been duped into thinking that life in the New World would be comfortable. Now that they were back in London, they gave vent to their rage, vilifying the organisation of the colony and spreading scurrilous tales about the gentlemen in charge. Their criticisms were not entirely unwarranted: it was all very well for their governor to brag of surviving on a diet of congealed dog gristle and leaves, but they—unlike him— were not war-hardened soldiers. Nor were they enamoured with living alongside neighbours who showed an alarming propensity for murder and bloodshed—a very different picture from the one they had been given by Manteo during his time in London. One of the wealthier colonists, Thomas Harvey, was virtually bankrupted by his year on Roanoke; unable to settle his debts, he found himself in the dock. He used the court as a platform from which to pour out his grievances, further widening the damaging publicity. He publicly complained of the colonists' "very miserable case" and said that as a direct consequence of his year in America, "he became poore and [was] unable to pay his creditors." The court was not impressed and he was thrown in prison, but his plight found a ready audience among tavern dwellers and gossips who delighted in the colourful stories of colonists scavenging for acorns while fighting off murderous Indians.

"There have bin divers and variable reportes," wrote a despairing Harriot, "with some slaunderous and shameful speeches bruited abroad by many that returned from thence." He was concerned that these "envious, malicious and slaunderous" tales would dissuade "many that otherwise would have also favoured and adventured in the action."

With Ralegh's active encouragement, Harriot now began work on his A *Briefe and True Report* about America, a brilliant and well-crafted work of propaganda that set out to scotch many of the "lies" being told by the settlers. "I have therefore thought it good," he writes in the preface, "to impart so much unto you of the fruites of our labours, as that you may knowe how injuriously the enterprise is slaundered." He added that he was uniquely qualified to tell the truth, since he alone spoke the Indian tongue and had "seene and knowne more then the ordinarie."

Published in 1588, *A Briefe and True Report* was neither brief nor was it always true. Harriot had been hired to write a book whose principal aim was to persuade London's merchants that America was a land of glittering opportunity that could be a great source of "profit and gaine." He urged them not to lose sight of the New World's potential, and gave his assurance that trade with the Indians would "enrich yourselves the providers, those that shal deal with you; the enterprisers in general, and greatly profit our owne countreymen."

Harriot's breadth of knowledge was remarkable, especially since so much of his material had been lost in the departure from Roanoke, but he worked in tandem with Manteo, his unacknowledged collaborator, who explained the customs of the Indians and provided information about the produce of the land. The two men had renewed their chambers at Durham House on their return to England and, shortly afterwards, begun work on what was to prove an exhilarating project.

Their hardest task was to present the Indian population in a positive light. Men like Davy Ingrams and Sir George Peckham had led the colonists to expect that they would arrive in America to find cheery natives falling over themselves in their desire to be helpful. The reality had proved rather different. Many of the native Americans had looked upon the English adventurers with deep suspicion, and although they had saved Lane's men from starvation on more than one occasion, they had also come close to wiping them out. Harriot chose to gloss over the murders and butchery; he made only one oblique reference to the slaughter of Wingina, and even then he blamed the bloodthirsty settlers. His purpose was to persuade future colonists that "in respect of troubling our inhabiting and planting, [the Indians] are not to be feared."

He took great exception to the popular view that they were ignorant savages: while admitting that they were somewhat lacking in
"skill and judgement in the knowledge and use of our things," he
made the startling assertion (for the Elizabethan age) that they were
"very ingenious"—clever and talented—"for although they have no
such tooles, nor any such craftes, sciences and artes as wee, yet in
those things they doe, they shewe excellencie of wit." He added that
if future colonists behaved themselves and taught by example, the
natives "may in short time be brought to civilities and the imbracing
of true religion."

He was enough of a realist to foresee considerable difficulties in
converting a native population whose interest in the Bible had so far
been limited to stroking their bellies with its vellum jacket. Many of
the Indians believed the English to be imbued with supernatural
powers, and however much Harriot tried to correct them, he found
himself fighting a losing battle. When the tribes were decimated by
sickness, the Indians believed that the English spirits were killing
their people "by shooting invisible bullets into them." They even
managed to prove it; the Indian "phisitions" punched holes into the
veins of their tribesmen and told Harriot "that the strings of blood
that they sucked out of the sicke bodies were the strings wherewithall the invisible bullets were tied and cast."

They "could not tel whether to thinke us gods or men," wrote
Harriot; partly because there was "no man of ours knowne to die,"
but also because "we had no women amongst us, neither that we did
care for any of theirs." How the men gratified themselves remains
unanswered, but Harriot's disdain for the appearance of the Indian
women suggests that he, for one, was never going to share his eider-
down with a shaven-headed maiden.

One of the most persistent complaints made by Lane's colonists
was the lack of any victuals more nourishing than acorns and oysters.
Harriot dismissed such stories and launched into a withering attack
on the returnees, accusing them of an unhealthy obsession with
"daintie food." He proceeded to describe dozens of mouth-watering

viands and fruits that were readily available to anyone who had the sense to go hunting: "turkie cockes and turkie hennes, stockdoves, partridges, cranes, hennes and, in winter, great store of swannes and geese." He was tempted to include "wolves or wolvish dogges" in his list of tasty meat, but declined from doing so "least that some would understand my judgement therein to be more simple then needeth." But he could not stop himself from informing his readers that he himself had tucked into a plate of "wolvish dogges," adding that "I could alleage the difference in taste of these kindes from ours"—a reference to the unfortunate bullmastiffs that were eaten on the expedition up the Roanoke River.

Harriot's list was less convincing when he came to record Virginia's edible fruits and nuts. What was scrumptious to him was unlikely to find favour with everyone, and although many English settlers were happy to munch their way through "chestnuts, walnuts, grapes and straberies," they baulked at the idea of tucking into a plate of acorns. To Harriot, this was yet another example of fussiness. "They make good victual," he wrote defensively, "either to eate so simply, or els being also pounded to make loaves or lumpes of bread."

Harriot strongly believed in the virtues of a simple diet and was convinced that bland food was better for the digestion than "sawces" and "blanketts." The Indians, he said, were living proof of his theory: "they are verye sober in their eatinge and drinkinge and, consequentlye, verye longe lived because they doe not oppress nature." Unfortunately, this was exactly the message that Elizabethan England did not wish to hear. People had no desire to swap roast capons for roast acorns, for the country was in the process of discovering the delights of gluttony and sumptuous foods. Household accounts reveal that even quite modest families thought nothing of tucking into a hearty lunch of pottage, stewed meat, bacon, pork, goose pie, roast beef, and custard. And those were merely appetisers. For the main course, it was not unusual to serve a platter of roast lamb, rabbit, and capon, along with chicken, venison, and tarts. A

Harriot did not find the Indian women to his liking. "They have small eyes, plaine and flatt noses, narrow foreheads, and broade mowths."

growing interest in elaborate recipes had also led to households' competing to produce ever more outlandish dishes. Almond tart, for example, was no longer the plain dish of the past. Now it was de rigueur to make it with blanched almonds, cream, sugar, rosewater, butter, and egg yolks.

None of this was particularly good for the health, as Harriot was well aware. But he also knew that he had discovered something in America that worked wonders on those with aching bellies and sluggish circulation. It was this miracle cure that he now hoped to unleash on a plump but far from jolly population. His fellow Londoners were the most sickly, "bursten with bancketing and sore and sick with surfeting," although many country folk were also beginning to discover the delights of "bellicheer [and] drunkenesse." Some physicians had abandoned all hope of promoting a healthy diet and, aware that their patients paid more for advice they wished to hear, began recommending hearty meals centred firmly on meat. The suggested diet for those wishing to strengthen their blood was to eat plenty of capons, pheasants, turtledoves, blackbirds, and mutton. Vegetables were not recommended; fresh herbs were forbidden.

But not all were convinced that you could eat your way to good health. As early as 1541, the dietary expert Sir Thomas Elyot used his book *The castel of helth* to castigate England's growing love of excess, "banqueting after supper and drinking much, specially wine." He urged people to reduce their meat intake, particularly in summer, and attributed a rash of hitherto unknown illnesses to England's gluttony. In particular, he noticed an alarming increase in cases of the rheums, an energy-sapping disease of the mucous glands whose symptoms were obvious to all: "wit dull; much superfluities, sleep much and dull."

The problem that physicians faced was finding a cure that would be acceptable to the gorging gluttons of the court. Elizabethan medicine was still extremely primitive. Most remedies hinged on the theory of "humours" or bodily fluids. The body was believed to contain four humours, and the balance of these determined the character

Harriot chastises the settlers for their obsession with "gluttonnye." He said the simple fare of the Indians—fish and maize—was the reason why they were "verye longe lived."

and temper of the individual. Since gluttony and the rheums made the head more watery, the obvious cure (short of eating less) was to ingest something hot and dry, thereby bringing the humours back into balance. But what no one had yet discovered was a suitable hot and dry substance.

It was here that Harriot felt he had something to contribute—a substance so efficacious that he believed it could be the saving of Ralegh's American colony. "There is an herbe which is sowed apart, by itselfe," he wrote, "and is called by the inhabitants, *uppowac*. In the West Indies it hath divers names, according to the severall places and countreys where it groweth and is used: the Spaniardes generally call it tobacco."

What made tobacco particularly effective was the manner in which it was consumed. Unlike most herbal remedies, which were infused in water or wine, tobacco was inhaled directly into the lungs, a novel procedure that was said to bring immediate relief.

"The leaves thereof being dried and brought into pouder," explains Harriot, "they [the Indians] use to take the fume or smoke thereof by sucking it thorough pipes made of claie, into their stomacke and heade." The effects were quite extraordinary, both in the speed with which the smoke took effect and in the herb's healing properties. "It purgeth superfluous fleame and other grosse humors, [and] openeth all the pores and passages of the body." Harriot added that regular smokers were the most likely to be blessed with a good constitution: "their bodies are notably preserved in health, and know not many greevous diseases wherewithall wee in England are oftentimes afflicted."

His extraordinary claims for the efficacy of tobacco were not altogether new. More than two decades previously, an adventurer accompanying one of Sir John Hawkins's slave-trading voyages had noticed the Indians smoking tobacco and learned that it "causeth water and phlegm to void from their stomachs." Several of London's rheumatic physicians had managed to lay their hands on some tobacco, and after smoking themselves into a stupor, they concluded that it was indeed a remarkable drug. But it was far too expensive to catch on, and it was also difficult to acquire, since any consignment had to pass first through the hands of numerous Spanish middlemen.

Harriot quickly realised that tobacco could prove the saviour of Ralegh's colony, if only he could make smoking a popular pastime. His motives were not purely cynical, since he himself was already a convert. "We, ourselves, during the time we were there used to suck it after their maner, as also since our returne, and have found in manie rare and wonderfull experiments of the vertues thereof; of which the relation woulde require a volume by itselfe." Harriot himself did not have the time to write such a book, but he was able to point his readers to the work of the Spaniard Nicholas Monades, whose *Joyfull Newes out of the Newe Founde Worlde* had recently become available in English translation.

Monades had devoted time and effort to conducting tobacco

experiments on sick patients, with results that were little short of spectacular. He claimed that the drug provided an instant cure for numerous ailments, including chilblains, dropsy, and constipation. He particularly recommended it for pregnant women and young children, claiming that a moderate use of the weed "doth take awaie their naughtie breathyng and it doth make that thei goe to the stoole." For worms, "it killeth them"; for aching joints, "it maketh a marveilous woorke"; and for swellings, "it dooeth disolve and undoe them." The Spaniard had even experimented on patients suffering from festering and cankered wounds; on every occasion, the results had proved startling.

"I sawe a manne that had certaine old sores in his nose whereby he did caste out from hym muche matter," he wrote, "and daily did rotte and canker inwardes." Monades's solution was to apply tobacco juice to the affected areas, which, to his amazement, took immediate effect. The patient "did caste out from hym more than twentie little wormes, and afterwarde a fewe more, untill that he remained cleane of them." Even Monades was astonished, claiming that "if he had tarried any longer, I thinke that there had remained nothyng of his nose, but all had been eaten awaie."

Many of his cures involved chewing the leaves or drinking tobacco cordials; he recommended smoking the herb only for dropsy and a few other ailments. This was a complex procedure in which the smoker first had to sit with his head covered with a heavy blanket. Then the tobacco was "caste on a chaffying dishe of coales to bee burned," and the patient was told to suck "through a tonnell or cane." Monades also recommended tobacco for insomniacs, advising that it be taken on a daily basis. Heavy smokers, he declared, slept soundly and "remaine as dedde people . . . thei bee so eased in suche sorte that when thei bee awakened of their slepe, thei remaine without wearinesse . . . and be muche the lustier."

Ralph Lane and his settlers had eagerly adopted the Indian habit of smoking. When they returned to England, they "brought pipes with them, to drink the smoake of tobacco." It was a novelty that found instant popularity among courtiers. According to an early English book on tobacco, "since that time, the use of drinking tobacco hath so much prevailed all England over, especially among the courtiers, that they have caused many such like pipes to be made to drink tobacco with."

One of the most enthusiastic smokers was Sir Walter Ralegh, who loved the rarity and exotic nature of the substance. The fact that it was used by the Indians in their wild, ritualistic dances only enhanced its darkly romantic appeal, and he delighted in Harriot's account of their smoking sessions, which were accompanied by "strange gestures, stamping, sometime dauncing, clapping of hands, holding up of hands, and staring up into the heavens, uttering therewithal and chattering strange words and noises." It was not long before Ralegh had persuaded more and more of his fellow courtiers to take up smoking, a habit they adopted with gusto. Most smoked pipes made of "a walnutshell and a straw," but Ralegh's was altogether more extravagant—a chiselled silver bowl with a long and elegant stem.

Not everyone was smitten with the new fad. There were those who claimed that Ralegh was trying to poison the queen with his pipe—he certainly persuaded her to try it—while his critics said that his love of tobacco, turning substance into smoke, epitomised his insubstantiality. With characteristic flair, Ralegh turned such jibes to his own advantage, boasting to the queen that he would weigh his pipe smoke—an impossible feat—if the reward was suitably large. When the queen challenged him to do just that, Ralegh weighed his tobacco, smoked it, then weighed the ash. The difference, he jested, was the weight of the smoke. The queen chortled with delight and said that she had heard of men who turned gold into smoke, but had never before met anyone who could turn smoke into gold.

Harriot's report on America mentioned few other commodities that offered the same potential as tobacco. Sassafras was said to cure syphilis, and was supposed to be particularly effective on those whose private parts were covered in "knobbes and moister of matter." But

Thomas Harriot believed he had stumbled across a plant that would save Ralegh's colony. "There is an herbe called *uppowac*," he wrote. "The Spaniardes generally call it tobacco."

prices were already low, and there were a good many syphilitic men who could testify to the fact that it did not work. There were skins and furs, and walnut oil was plentiful, while the ubiquitous cedarwood was much sought after for "bedsteads, tables, deskes, lutes, virginalles, and many things else." But these were small crumbs of comfort for Ralegh. As he studied the draft of Harriot's book, it remained unclear whether he would abandon the entire project. Richard Hakluyt urged him not to give up, pleading that "if you persevere only a little longer in your constancy, your bride will slowly bring forth new and most abundant offspring, such as will delight you and yours, and cover with disgrace and shame those who have so

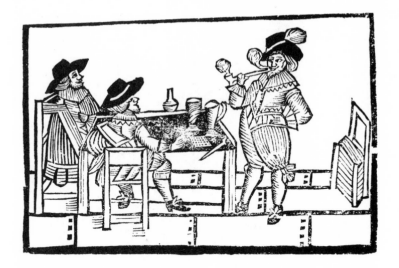

Ralegh introduced smoking to the court and even persuaded the queen to have a puff. Tobacco was particularly recommended for pregnant women and children

often dared rashly and impudently to charge her with barrenness." He added that "no-one had yet probed the depth of her hidden resources and wealth" and, pandering directly to Ralegh's ego, begged him to "leave to posterity an imperishable monument of your name and fame, such as age will never obliterate."

It was a challenge that Sir Walter couldn't resist.

Some three or four days after Ralph Lane's departure from Roanoke, Ralegh's first supply ship had belatedly dropped anchor just off the Outer Banks. She was "fraighted with all maner of things in most plentiful maner for the supplie and relief of his colonie" — everything that had been so desperately needed by the colonists. The only drawback was her late arrival.

Sir Walter had always intended his supply ship to arrive in America shortly after the first colonists, but it was delayed by a series of complications and it was not until the spring of 1586, more than nine months behind schedule, that it was ready to leave England. This vessel might have reached Lane in time if it had left port immediately, but once again there were unexpected delays and "before they set saile from England it was after Easter." This was not Ralegh's fault. The English Channel was notoriously unpredictable in winter and spring and bad weather often prevented ships from setting sail.

The vessel did not leave port until the first week of April, and by the time it arrived at Roanoke, "the paradise of the worlde," Lane's men had already been evacuated. The sailors were truly shocked by what they found. The wooden shacks and shelters had been ripped apart by the hurricane; broken trunks lay scattered over a wide area. It was immediately apparent that the colonists had left—although the supply party had no idea why—and "after some time spent in seeking our colonie up in the countrie, and not finding them, [the ship] returned with all the aforesayd provision into England."

This was not the only ship to narrowly miss the colonists. Ralegh had long intended to settle a second batch of colonists on Roanoke. At the same time as organising the supply vessel, he was overseeing the preparation of a major new fleet, once again under the command of Sir Richard Grenville.

Grenville was never one to do things by halves, and the flotilla he assembled was a sizeable one: "six ships, one of 150 tons, and the rest from 100 down to 60 tons . . . with 400 soldiers and sailors and provisions for a year." It was to sail in a wolf pack, so as to increase its effectiveness in the event of sighting any Spanish vessels.

When Sir Richard arrived at Roanoke in the first week of July, he was stunned by what he found. He had expected to be welcomed by a flourishing colony as well as Ralegh's supply ship, and although he cannot have been overly excited at the prospect of seeing Ralph Lane, he did at least hope the governor would have the place in order. Instead of happy colonists and a flourishing settlement, he found Pamlico Sound empty, the island colony deserted, and many of the buildings destroyed. All around him lay evidence of destruction, not least "the bodies of one Englishman and one Indian hanged." Neither he nor his crew could identify the flyblown corpse of the Englishman, but he was almost certainly a mutinous crew member from the supply ship.

Grenville split his soldiers into small groups. With himself taking command, he led them "up into divers places of the contrey, as well to see if he could here any newes of the colony left there by him the yere before." For two weeks the groups scoured the landscape, but when they returned they each had a similar story to tell. There was no trace of Lane and his men.

"After some time spent therein, not hearing any newes of them, and finding the place which they inhabited desolate," Grenville prepared to depart. It was only as the men were returning to the fleet that he had a stroke of good fortune. He captured three Indians. Two of them escaped, but the third spoke enough broken English to explain to Sir Richard that there had been some sort of trouble between the settlers and the Indians and that "Francis Drake had brought away the people who had been on that island."

This news put Grenville in a quandry. It was clear to him that blood had been spilt, and he also deduced that Lane must have been near starvation to have agreed to the evacuation of Roanoke. But he was "unwilling to loose the possession of the countrie, which Englishmen had so long helde," and began toying with the idea of leaving behind a small garrison of soldiers.

"After good deliberation, he determined to leave some men behinde to retaine possession of the country." He landed fifteen soldiers under the leadership of the unfortunately named Master Coffin, a Barnstable man, and "furnished [them] plentifully with all maner of provision for two yeeres." He also provided them with four pieces of heavy artillery.

He had chosen the very worst option. Such a small group of men were at great risk of attack and would find it difficult to fend off a concerted assault, even with small arms and artillery. But the bullish Master Coffin was confident of success and ordered his men to begin transferring their possessions to the ruined settlement. These troops watched Grenville's departure with heavy hearts. They had no idea when the next English vessel might enter these waters, and were uncertain as to which of the Indian tribes they could trust. Anxious and scared, they built rough shelters from the wreckage on Roanoke and repaired the fort, preparing themselves for attack. Many of them wondered if they would ever see their homeland again.

The Indian captive aboard Grenville's flagship was also deeply unhappy about his predicament. He soon discovered that Grenville had no intention of allowing him to go free, and that he was being taken across the Atlantic to England. His life was destined to be short and almost certainly miserable. He was landed in Bideford, where church records reveal that he was baptised Ralegh on March 27, 1588. Just over a year later, the same Ralegh was buried.

When Sir Walter learned that Grenville had landed a new batch of men on Roanoke, he was unsure how to react. The terms of his American charter meant that he was officially responsible for these men, but he was so deeply involved in his Irish colonial projects, attempting to settle men and women on his vast estates, that he simply did not have time to organise another voyage to America. Nor did he wish to pour any more money into what was likely to be a costly, ill-conceived, and profitless venture. But in the spring of 1587 his financial situation was transformed by the capture of Anthony Babington, the fabulously wealthy Catholic whose treasonable plot to murder the queen ended in his being mutilated to death. When Elizabeth came to dispose of his estates, which sprawled across Lincolnshire, Derbyshire, and Nottinghamshire, there was only one name on her lips. Sir Walter Ralegh, guardian of Virginia, was to receive the lot.

Ralegh now had the necessary fortune to turn, once again, to America. He let it be known that "no terrors, no personal losses or misfortunes" would tear him away "from the sweet embraces of . . . Virginia, that fairest of nymphs."

There would, after all, be another expedition to the New World.

9

The Unfortunate Master Coffin

Master Coffin set his men to work as soon as they had landed on Roanoke. Most of the storm-damaged dwellings were abandoned and the earth-and-timber fort was hurriedly broken up so that it could be rebuilt on a much smaller scale. "Four pieces of artillery of cast-iron," left by Grenville, were polished and primed in anticipation of an attack.

The fifteen soldiers made little effort to explore their surroundings. Once they had repaired a few essential buildings, they allowed themselves the luxury of gorging on their plentiful victuals. Grenville had provided them with "all manner of provision for two years," and there was no immediate necessity to hunt and fish for their food. Besides, they had his assurance that a supply vessel would arrive within a few months.

The men must nevertheless have taken the departure of the fleet with a mixture of fear and foreboding, aware that their last link with England was now broken. Their sense of isolation is apparent in the long silence that followed. They kept no journal and wrote no letters, for there was no ship to carry their news back across the Atlantic. These reluctant colonists were charged with playing a waiting game, and their hopes were pinned on one day sighting through the mists the white and red flag of St. George.

The rituals and dances of the Indians terrified the English. "They be verye familiar with devils," wrote Harriot, "from whome they enquier what their enemies doe."

It is possible that some of Coffin's men had volunteered to stay on Roanoke, relieved to have escaped the return journey to England. Life on board was perilous and unpredictable, particularly when the ship was captained by such a chimerical spirit as Sir Richard Grenville. But what none of them realised—for they had left England before Harriot's return—was that their long months on the island would be even more dangerous and uncomfortable.

It was a far cry from the grandiose dreams espoused by London's colonial enthusiasts. Hakluyt's vision of colonisation aspired to lofty principles. In a letter to Ralegh, originally written in Latin, he saw the goal as inherently noble. "No greater glory can be handed down than to conquer the barbarian, to recall the savage and the pagan to civility, to draw the ignorant within the orbit of reason, and to fill with reverence for divinity the godless and the ungodly." But Hakluyt had never experienced the backbreaking work of building a colony, nor did he know the perils of the long voyage to America. The furthest he had travelled was to Paris, where he dined off porcelain and lived a splendid existence in the cosseted surroundings of England's embassy.

The reality of colonisation had more to do with willpower and survival, a constant battle of wits between the English and the Indians. Coffin and his men were all too aware of the dangers of clashing with the local tribes and decided that their safest option was to dig themselves in on their island stronghold. This seemed like a sensible course of action, for they lay out of reach of Indian arrows. But cocooned behind mud walls, Coffin failed to detect that deadly forces were conspiring against his little battalion, and that the surrounding woodlands were home to a growing band of vengeful and warlike tribesmen.

His hope that a supply vessel would soon be under way was not altogether misplaced, for Ralegh was seriously considering shipping a new colony across the Atlantic. But he had no intention of landing more men on Roanoke. His eyes were now set on Chesapeake Bay, some eighty miles to the north, which had none of the drawbacks of

Wingina's former fiefdom. Lane himself had proposed this new site, assuring Ralegh that "the territorie and soyle of the Chespians . . . was for pleasantnes of seate, for temperature of climate, for fertilitie of soyle, and for the commoditie of the sea . . . not to be excelled by any other whatsoever."

Sir Walter had been given considerably more information by Harriot and White, who had led the winter expedition to the "Chespians," rowing their pinnace through the mouth of the bay and exploring its irregular southern shoreline. Their small-scale map is remarkably accurate, and they also produced a much larger copy—which has been lost—on which they marked villages, harbours, hills, even fruit trees and wild vines. They reported that the land was much less forbidding than the swamps of Pamlico Sound. "We found the soyle to bee fatter," wrote Harriot, "the trees greater and to growe thinner, the grounde more firme and deeper mould, more and larger champions, finer grasse and as good as ever we saw any in England."

For once, his account was not mere hyperbole. Later adventurers also declared themselves impressed by the "faire meddowes and goodly tall trees." One enthusiast was so enraptured by the bucolic delights that he was "almost ravished at the sight thereof." There was not a peat bog in sight: indeed, the ground was "full of fine and beautiful strawberries"—not like the miniature ones served up in England, but "foure times bigger and better than ours."

Ralegh also learned that Chesapeake Bay was ruled by jovial chieftains who had shown a hearty friendship towards the English. They had lavished meat and fruit on the exploratory party and gone out of their way to provide wholesome and nourishing food throughout the lean winter months. Harriot had enjoyed their "deers' flesche" and "broiled fishe," especially when accompanied by maize, but his favourite dish was a thick peasant stew cooked in earthenware with "special cunninge." "Their woemen fill the vessel with water," he explained, "and then putt in fruite, flesh and fish, and lett all boyle together." The result was not unlike the tasty

Spanish dish *olla podrida,* and it was always eaten with "good cheere."

Harriot's enthusiasm soon convinced Sir Walter of the merits of Chesapeake Bay, but before he took any final decisions he once again sought advice from his trusty friend Richard Hakluyt. He had chosen his moment well, for Hakluyt was putting the finishing touches to his investigation into Spanish forays in North America. After months of research, the chronicler was able to give some straightforward advice: "Yf yow proceed, which I longe much to knowe, in yor enterprise of Virginia, yor best planting wilbe about the bay of Chesepians." He added the tantalising information that the colonists would be in striking distance of "rich sylver mynes up in the country."

Ralegh's mind was now made up, and he launched himself into his new enterprise with customary gusto. His most pressing concern was to find someone of a suitable calibre to lead his new colony. Ralph Lane showed no immediate desire to return to America. Thomas Harriot, for all his enthusiasm, preferred to try his hand at being a colonist in Ireland, and he set off for Munster, where he began the arduous task of mapping Ralegh's huge estates.

John White alone was anxious to return to the New World. He had thoroughly enjoyed his year of adventure on Roanoke. When Sir Walter began casting around for someone to appoint as prospective governor, he let it be known that he was itching to take up the position.

Ralegh was more than happy to reward White for all his previous hard work. He had been astonished by the quality of White's maps and portraits. Although it was unorthodox to appoint an artist as governor, he did not hesitate in giving his backing. In January 1587, he "nomynated, elected, chose, constituted, made and appoynted John White of London, gentleman, to be chief governor theare."

It was an impressive appointment for a man whose origins were probably humble and certainly obscure. His date and place of birth are unknown, his family history has passed unrecorded, and his early years are a complete mystery. It is not until 1580 that a John White is listed as a member of the Painter-Stainers' company, a guild which embraced everyone involved in the painting crafts.

It is almost certain that the young White served his apprenticeship as a limner or miniaturist, a gentleman's profession that saw itself as being a cut above the tawdry world of the common artist. "None should meddle with limning but gentlemen alone," wrote the famous miniaturist Nicholas Hilliard, adding that "the fierst and cheefest precepts which I give is cleanlynes." Hilliard instructed aspiring miniaturists to wear silken blouses and breeches and suggested that they work in a reverent silence, although he conceded that "discret talke or reading, quiet mirth or musike offendeth not."

John White must have cut a very different figure from his fellow miniaturists. While they honed their skills in oil painting, he began experimenting with an altogether more eccentric medium—watercolour—which was shunned by professional portrait artists and only commonly used as a wash for line drawings and maps. Nor was White content to spend his life painting the sycophants and flatterers of the Elizabethan court. His love of adventure had been kindled by the yarns of merchants and explorers, and from an early age he had yearned to take his skills to far-off climes. His chance came at last in 1577 when he heard rumours that the explorer Martin Frobisher was setting off to the Arctic in search of a northwest passage. He seems to have won himself employment as expedition artist, for the earliest of his surviving works depict skin-wrapped Eskimos paddling kayaks through the ice floes. These paintings persuaded Ralegh to commission him to portray the Indians of Roanoke Island.

Painting in the swamps of Pamlico Sound was frustratingly hard and taught him that the strange rules of limning had their limitations. It was hardly practical for him to powder his hair and wear silk pantaloons, yet he never forgot the first and most important rule of portraiture: "[to] drawe to life . . . the figures and shapes of men and woemen in their apparell." Speed was crucial to success, and White developed a system that enabled him to capture a likeness in a flash, making quick field sketches which he later used to produce his watercolours. These sketches were lost in the hurried departure from Roanoke, as were many of his finished watercolours, but others survived and they were bound into a set on his return to England.

News of White's talent soon spread across Europe, and within two years of his return, the great Flemish printer, Theodor de Bry, was begging permission to make engravings of his portraits. These eventually became the illustrations for de Bry's magnificent four-language edition of Harriot's writings, published in 1590 under the title *America*.

Although White had amply demonstrated his ability as an artist, he had yet to prove he had the leadership skills necessary to govern unruly and dissolute layabouts. Nor had he displayed much resourcefulness or initiative during the 1585 experiment. It was Harriot who had masterminded the great winter expedition to Chesapeake Bay, and Lane who had kept his colonists alive throughout a period of unremitting hardship. Both of these men were shrewd enough to brag about their successes in writing, ensuring that the Elizabethan court was well apprised of their heroics. White, by contrast, is the invisible man of Ralegh's 1585 colony. He is scarcely mentioned in dispatches and never commended for his bravado; were it not for his watercolours, it would be easy to forget that he was one of the lynchpins of Ralegh's team. His new appointment as governor was a high-risk gamble, and it remained to be seen if his artistic temperament was capable of commanding respect from his men.

He was not, of course, to govern the colony on his own. Ralegh also created a body that was given the grandiloquent title of the Governor and Assistants of the City of Ralegh in Virginia. This provided White with twelve assistants, like-minded adventurers who had been fired with enthusiasm by Harriot's account of America.

It was unfortunate that the majority of these men lacked the flair and skill of the gentlemen who had set sail in 1585. England's most sought-after mariners were too preoccupied with plundering Spain's treasure ships to take any part in John White's expedition, and the few who put their names forward as assistants were wholly unknown and quite without breeding. The only exception was Simon Fernandez, Grenville's skillful navigator on the *Tiger*, whose arrogance had made him one of the most hated men in Lane's team. His nickname among sailors was "the swine," yet he retained the full confidence of Ralegh and was welcomed into the new organisation.

Another of White's assistants was Ananias Dare, his son-in-law, who had trained as a bricklayer and tiler. His practical skills would be useful when it came to building houses, but were not what was needed to govern a colony. Dare was a wild card who had sown his oats at an early age and unwittingly sired an illegitimate child. In the wrong circles, this would have seriously tarnished his reputation; but there were plenty among London's adventurers who had a sneaking admiration for such knavish behaviour and agreed with the adage that "untill everyone hath two or three bastards a peece, they esteeme him no man."

Dare's indiscretion left White untroubled and he willingly consented to him marrying his daughter, Eleanor. The couple lived in London's Fleet Street, close to St. Bride's, and young Eleanor had recently fallen pregnant, a situation that would have deterred most women from a seven-week voyage to an unknown wilderness. Childbirth, after all, was always dangerous and usually painful, and there was little to comfort the woman in labour. Many still relied on traditional methods of pain relief, such as swallowing a spider coated in treacle, while the devout and superstitious pinned their hopes on religious relics, objects of devotion, and even church bell ropes. Had Eleanor stayed in London, she might well have borrowed the ropes from St. Bride's to wrap around her aching belly; but she insisted on accompanying her husband to America, and the couple began preparations for the long voyage.

John White's other governing assistants remain a mystery, known only by their names: Roger Baylye, Christopher Cooper, John Sampson, Thomas Steevens, William Fullwood, Roger Pratt, Dyonise Harvey, John Nicholls, George Howe, and James Plat.

Eleanor Dare insisted on sailing to America while pregnant. Childbirth was
as dangerous in London as on board ship, and many still used traditional
remedies for labour pains, such as swallowing treacle-coated spiders

None of them had any social status in England, being without line-age or land; they probably came from London's artisan class, involved in skilled trade.

This troubled Ralegh, who wanted his self-styled Cittie of Ralegh to be ruled by men of standing. To this end, he dreamed up an inspired stunt which would automatically make them gentlemen and give them a lineage. He approached the chief officer of arms, William Dethick, an unscrupulous individual who sold blazons and crests to anyone who gave him a sufficient bribe. Ralegh offered golden rewards if he devised coats of arms for John White and his twelve assistants, a task that Dethick accomplished with aplomb, linking even the lowest-born assistants to ancient and arms-bearing gentility. He paid particular attention to the governor's coat of arms, producing a whimsical shield that showed descent from no fewer than eight distinguished White families. It was a complete fiction, but none of this troubled Ralegh, for the exercise was little more than a publicity exercise that would assure potential investors that his colony was run by men of quality. He probably presented the arms at a public ceremony in Durham House, declaring—in the words of the grant—that the twelve gentlemen were remarkable per-sonages who should "in all tymes and throwgh all ages be honoured, rewarded and, [in] their remembrance by sondry monuments, pre-served."

Ralegh had not forgotten the ever loyal Manteo during the flurry of activity in those early weeks of January. Manteo had supported his project from the very outset and—increasingly anglicised—had come to see an English presence on his land as both desirable and beneficial. He had been the catalyst for Lane's colony, providing much of the information that had allowed the 1585 expedition to set sail, and had played a critical role in ensuring the survival of Ralph Lane and his men. Sir Walter now decided to reward him for this loyalty by making him a feudal ruler in the New World, entrusting him with the island of Roanoke and giving him the title of "lord therof . . . in reward of his faithfull service." Although Ralegh had no intention of settling his new colony on Roanoke, he did not wish to abandon his hold over that stretch of coastline and almost certainly promised to supply Manteo with troops—perhaps the fifteen men currently serving under Master Coffin.

Manteo's appointment was truly extraordinary—and shocking to many—for Ralegh was effectively making him his local governor, subject to *Weroanza* Elizabeth but with important powers over the Indians on his land. To give such responsibility to a "savage" sat uneasily alongside the prejudice and intolerance of Elizabethan England and proved to both the court and populace that Ralegh was quite content to fly in the face of the prevailing mood. Not everyone greeted the news with mute acceptance; it was probably the objections of some of the more fusty courtiers that led to Ralegh's making Manteo's baptism a condition of his governorship—a ceremony that was to take place on his arrival at Roanoke.

Attracting prospective colonists to Chesapeake Bay proved far more difficult than attracting governors. The Roanoke settlers had brought much damaging publicity to Ralegh's 1585 enterprise, and their tales of munching acorns and berries had lodged in people's minds. But this was not all that hindered John White in his drive to recruit settlers. Throughout England, hundreds of agents were searching for colonists for the new plantations in Ireland, making a particular effort to attract artisans and farmers—the very people White needed for his settlement. Given the choice between Ireland and America, few would hesitate to choose the former, which, for those living in the West Country, was less than two days' journey.

White knew that he could not compete with these agents and avoided recruiting in the countryside, preferring instead to bang his colonial drum in the streets and alleys of London. This was a wise move, for the overcrowded capital was such an unsanitary and plague-ridden "dunghyll" that a great many people were keen to escape. The city's diseased population already stood at around 90,000 and was expanding with every month that passed. The majority lived "within the bars"—the city's twenty-six wards—but a growing underclass had spilled out into the suburbs, where they were packed like herrings into stinking cellars in Southwark and Hounditch, the "places of the begging poor." Many were only too willing to chance their luck in America, especially as it gave them the opportunity to escape the rogues, bawds, and cutpurses who stalked the streets at night. The records of violent crime in Aldgate, one of the poorer areas of town, make for horrific reading. Stabbings, knifings, and child murders were so commonplace that the courts had grown weary of the endless hearings. One "murderous strumpett cast hir child into a privie," drowning it in effluent, while others "smothered" their victims to death in the course of a robbery. Dozens were killed in knife fights. There were few among the poor who died of infirmity or old age.

White could offer the honest citizens of such areas the chance to escape forever. The reason that people listened to him was that he was offering something extremely attractive: a "temperate and holesome" climate in a disease- and crime-free land. He could justifiably trumpet the facts that Lane's colonists had returned in rude health and that "but foure of our whole company . . . died all the yeere." This was a remarkable achievement in the eyes of the poorer citizens of London. Quite apart from the plague, which regularly swept through the unsanitary backstreets of the capital, many illnesses afflicted the weak and malnourished. The biggest killers were consumption and ague, followed by the scouring flux, smallpox, worms, dropsy, scurvy, colic, pleurisy, jaundice—the list was endless. "Bursten" or ruptured haemorrhoids claimed a surprisingly large number of victims—they quickly got infected—while "bursten" scrotums reaped a similarly grisly toll. Those who underwent surgery for such ailments rarely survived the rusty blades and infected hacksaws. Sir William Wenter entrusted his "bowells" to the surgeons after years of painful gallstones. Just hours after his operation, he "endid this lyfe . . . beinge cutt of the collick and the stone." It is scarcely surprising that depression was on the increase and an ever growing number of people were recorded as having died from "some inward griefe"—the polite expression for suicide.

White promised his settlers more than life in a disease-free land. He also offered them an escape from the "corruption, whoredom [and] drunkeness" that were ubiquitous in London, a city that had "more sins than Ninevah contains." Bankside was particularly notorious for its "stews" or brothels, and whoring was a popular pastime among high-spirited youths, even though the majority of strumpets were diseased with the "French pox" or syphilis. Whoring went hand in hand with drunkenness, and crawling from tavern to tavern enjoyed widespread popularity. It was a dangerous pastime, even for those with cavernous bellies, for there were hostelries on every alley and thoroughfare. One short stretch of Southwark High Street, particularly popular with revellers, boasted no fewer than twenty taverns. Drinking bouts were often followed by rowdy games of football, "a bloody and murthering practice" that the authorities were forced to ban when gangs of youths went on the rampage, smashing shop fronts and kicking passersby.

White worked hard to assure potential colonists that his settlement on Chesapeake Bay would be better organised than the disasterous experiment on Roanoke. It had become clear to both him and Ralegh that any long-term colony would have to be a farming community, largely self-sufficient, that would in time produce such bumper harvests of tobacco and grain that surplus crops could be shipped back to England. The fact that he was recruiting the majority of his settlers from London was not necessarily a problem; many city dwellers grew their own vegetables in plots and gardens and would bring with them at least some knowledge of self-sufficiency.

A few men signed up immediately, but to the waverers Ralegh offered an added incentive. He was extremely "liberall . . . in giving and granting land there," promising every colonist no less than 500 acres, irrespective of any financial investment, and guaranteeing that it would be fertile farmland. This was a veritable windfall, for 500 acres was far larger than most English farms, and served to

arouse great interest in the project. Ralegh further heartened potential colonists by assuring them that the settlement was being built as
a safe haven for English privateering vessels. There was no question
of them having to cut their ties with England, since ships would be
coming and going all year round. These would bring with them
essential supplies and, in good years, carry the surplus foodstuffs
back to England. Enterprising settlers were likely to get rich.

White hoped to sail in the spring, giving him just three months to
recruit his colonists. His target was to attract about 150—both men
and women—but this proved difficult in the time available. By April
only 100 had signed up. Many were single men or fathers who
elected to leave their wives and children in London until they had
established themselves in the new land. But White did score a few
notable successes, persuading some fourteen families to set sail, along
with seventeen women, several of whom were single. These may well
have been wives of the men left behind by Grenville, or even the
spouses of the three men inadvertently left behind by Drake in 1586.
There were also several young boys with no apparent relatives to
accompany them.

The drawback of recruiting in London was immediately apparent:
there were simply not enough country folk to contribute a wider experience and knowledge to the colony. Settler Mark Bennett was a hus-
bandman and William Berde a yeoman—both of whom would bring
usefull skills—but they were joined by few others from the farming
fraternity. William Nicholes appears to have been a tailor and Thomas
Hewet a lawyer. William Brown may have been the London goldsmith
of the same name; if he hoped to find himself fashioning jewellery out
of nodules of gold, he was likely to be disappointed.

The colonists came from all across the social spectrum. John
Spendlove described himself as a "gentleman"; John Hynde and
William Clement had both served time in Colchester prison.
Roanoke veterans were conspicuous by their absence. Only James
Lassie and John Wright were willing to return to America to try their
luck on a second attempt.

John White needed farmers for his colony. He recruited in London's streets and markets, such as Eastcheap, where he found city dwellers with some knowledge of country life

The women who signed up for the adventure remain something of a mystery, partly because the eccentricity of Elizabethan spelling makes them hard to identify with any certainty. Elizabeth Glane appears to have been the wife of Darby Glande, while Agnes Wood had links through marriage with either Audry Tappan, Thomas Topan, or perhaps both. Margaret Lawrence, Joan Warren, Jane Mannering, and Rose Payne all seem to have been unmarried; Elizabeth Viccars was almost certainly the mother of young Ambrose Viccars. It comes as a shock to learn that at least two of the women—Eleanor Dare and Margery Harvie—were pregnant; another brought along a baby that was still being breastfed.

All of these women were about to embark on an adventure that would have seemed inconceivable just a few months earlier. The wifely role in Elizabethan England was one of obedience and subservience, and women like Elizabeth Glane and Agnes Wood had been brought up to be neither seen nor heard. "A wyfe ought to be dyscrete, chaste . . . shamefaste, good, meke, pacyent and sober," advised one Elizabethan guide for housewives; others added that she should stay indoors, eschew frivolous costumes, and avoid alcohol. One author went so far as to claim that kissing one's wife should not be a sign of affection, but to check whether she had been drinking wine. If so, a sound thrashing was in order, "not to offende or despise hir, but . . . lovingly to reform hir."

Many of White's female recruits would have smiled wearily at the bawdy wife jokes that did the rounds of London's playhouses. "Wife!" runs a jest in one comedy, "There's no such thing in nature. I confess, gentlemen, I have [only] a cook, a laundress [and] a housedrudge that serves my necessary turns." Others joshed that women existed solely for men's comfort, claiming that "wives are yong men's mistreses, companions for middle age, and old men's nurses."

To such women, the thought of entering the man's world of spills and adventure must have been both daunting and exciting. But White was not recruiting women out of compassion or charity. He had once been married—his wife appears to have died—and knew that many Elizabethan women worked long hours in the home and were in possession of many more practical skills than their gaming, drinking husbands. The housewife's daily routine included baking and brewing, churning butter, tending the chickens, and spinning wool. She was also in charge of the potager—a most important skill for the colony— and had a well-trained eye for "good seedes and herbes, . . . specyally suche as be good for the potte." She planted them and harvested them, and when the flax reached ripeness it was the wife who would make sure it was washed, beaten, and woven "into shetes, bordeclothes, towels, shertes, smockes and such other necessaries." The day ended in reckoning the accounts; only then did she have the dubious pleasure of jumping into bed in order to "make merry."

Preparations for the voyage progressed rapidly as winter drew to a close. White had secured three ships—the *Lion* of 120 tons, an unnamed flyboat to carry supplies, and a small pinnace captained by Edward Stafford, who had served under Lane in 1585.

The ships left London at the end of April 1587, fully laden with supplies but not yet carrying their full complement of colonists.

Many were dreading the voyage and had chosen to join the expedition at Portsmouth or Plymouth, where the ships stopped to take on fresh water. The fleet then headed west down the English Channel, hoping to reach Chesapeake Bay by the end of June.

White's diary entry for May 8, the day of their departure, leaves much to the imagination. "We waied anker at Plymouth," he wrote, "and departed thence for Virginia." Nor does he give any account of the first week of the voyage, when the colonists—many of whom had never before seen the sea—were growing accustomed to life on board ship.

The next note in White's diary is much more interesting. On May 16 he records that Fernandez, his navigator, had allowed the fleet to disperse, with the unfortunate consequence that the *Lion* had lost sight of the flyboat carrying all the provisions. "[He] lewdly forsooke our flie-boate," writes White, "leaving her distressed in the baye of Portugall." This was a serious allegation; in using the word *lewdly*, White suggests that Fernandez had *deliberately* abandoned the smaller vessel. He adds fuel to the fire by claiming that his navigator "stole away from them in the night" in the hope that the captain would be unable to locate Chesapeake Bay, "or else, being left in so dangerous a place . . . they should surely be taken or slaine."

White gives no explanation why Fernandez would act with such malice, nor does he provide further details. But if the allegation is in any way true, then Fernandez was guilty of a criminal recklessness that threatened everyone on board with starvation. In normal circumstances, this would deserve the harshest punishment, to be carried out by the expedition's commander. Yet White did nothing—no whipping, no flogging, no dunking from the yardarm. His inaction is the first indication that he lacked the most important requirement of an Elizabethan commander—ruthlessness. He had shown that he was unable to impose his own terms and conditions over the expedition, and, after just eight days at sea, had effectively forfeited his authority to Fernandez.

It was forty-four days before the *Lion* reached the Caribbean. The weary colonists stumbled ashore at the Virgin Islands and built temporary shelters on the beach. To these impoverished and scurvy-ridden Londoners, the sight of trees laden with tropical fruit was so welcome that they began plucking whatever was within reach. It was a big mistake, for they were eating a poisonous species of pome. "Some of our women and men, by eating a small fruite, like green apples, were fearefully troubled with a sudden burning in their mouthes and swelling of their tongues so bigge that some of them could not speake." The baby on board had a more violent reaction to the fruit. "A child, by sucking one of those women's brestes, had of that instant his mouth set on such a burning that it was strange to see how the infant was tormented for the time." White had ne-

"A wyfe ought to be chaste, pacyent and sober," reads one Elizabethan guide for housewives. She also needed to be hardworking, for her daily routine included baking, brewing, harvesting, spinning, and bookkeeping. Women were to be the life-blood of the colony

glected to warn the colonists against eating unknown fruits, and it was fortunate that they escaped lasting damage.

Other colonists made the mistake of drinking from "a standing ponde, the water whereof was so evill that many of our companie fell sicke with drinking thereof . . . their faces did so burne and swell that their eies were shut up and could not see in five or sixe daies or longer."

White was growing increasingly worried at the lack of food, water, and salt, especially since there was still no sign of his flyboat. He knew that if he did not acquire these in considerable quantity, his colonists would starve to death soon after arriving at Chesapeake Bay. Fernandez had sailed through the Caribbean on numerous occasions and knew the islands well. His failure to steer the *Lion* towards livestock and saltponds confirmed White's suspicions that he was deliberately trying to sabotage the colonial project. The tone of his diary becomes increasingly irritable as he records a litany of real or imaginary grievances, claiming that Fernandez had "assured" him that sheep could be found on St. John Island when in fact there was nothing more nourishing than old droppings.

It was now the first of July—late in the year to be planting a colony, and still the settlers were nowhere near their destination. Two of the company had jumped ship—though White does not explain why—and relations between the governor and Fernandez had broken down completely. On the rare occasions that he did address his pilot, he always found his requests rebuffed. When he demanded that the vessel stop again to "gather yong plants," he was overruled. And when he begged Fernandez to pause at Hispaniola to buy cows, he was brusquely informed that there were no cattle on the island. Having failed to find any supplies, the *Lion* headed for Virginia in the hope that the flyboat would have already arrived.

White's first port of call was Roanoke Island, where he hoped to find Master Coffin and his men in rude health. He was looking forward to meeting Coffin, "with whome he meant to have conference concerning the state of the countrey and savages," and particularly keen to hear how the Indians had reacted to the hurried departure in 1586. He also hoped to persuade the fifteen English soldiers to remain on the island to protect Lord Manteo. Then, once he had overseen the baptism of Manteo, White intended to "passe along the coast to the Baye of Chesepiok where we intended to make our seate and forte, according to the charge given us . . . under the hande of Sir Walter Ralegh."

The *Lion* dropped anchor some two miles off the Outer Banks, and the governor began preparations to take the large pinnace across Pamlico Sound to Roanoke, "accompanied by fortie of his best men." Many of these were anxious to step ashore after the long voyage, and keen to see the settlement that White had helped to build two years previously. They had just pushed off from the *Lion* when one of Fernandez's trouble-making deputies leaned over the edge of the flagship and, on the orders of his superior, shouted to the colonists that they would not be welcomed back on board and should chance their luck on Roanoke. The same man then "called to the sailors in the pinnesse, charging them not to bring any of the planters backe againe, but leave them in the island."

The colonists could scarcely believe their ears. They were used to all kinds of setbacks and changes of plan, but this was an extraordinary development that ran contrary to everything that had been meticulously planned in England. Fernandez was disobeying not only the orders of John White, but the very word and command of Sir Walter Ralegh.

More observant men might have realised that a showdown between White and Fernandez had been brewing for some weeks, and that Fernandez had shown himself to be distinctly uninterested in the fate of the colonists ever since he "lewdly" forsook the flyboat in the Bay of Portugal. White's journal, though partisan, makes it clear that his navigator had always been more interested in Spanish bullion than in Ralegh's settlement, and it was quite possible that Fernandez had accepted the commission from Sir Walter for the sole reason that it gave him a free passage to the Caribbean. Now, having missed one opportunity of privateering, he was determined to seize the initiative, curtly informing the governor that "summer was farre spent, wherefore hee would land all the planters in no other place." He added that he would remain at anchor only long enough for all the colonists to be taken ashore.

White should have hanged the truculent Fernandez on the spot— as Drake would have done—but the curious weakness that had afflicted him throughout the voyage now struck once again. Faced with what was technically a mutiny, he did not clamber back on board the *Lion* to impose his will over the lawless Fernandez. He vacillated and dithered. When he learned that the vessel's prize-hungry crew were also itching to return to the Caribbean, "it booted not the governor to contend with them." That very night, "at sunne set," he abandoned all thoughts of settling in Chesapeake Bay and weakly acquiesced in Fernandez's change of plan. After a brief discussion, he agreed that the rest of the colonists, totalling 112 men and women, would be rowed across to Roanoke over the following few days.

It was dusk on July 22, 1587, by the time White and his advance party drew their pinnace ashore at the eastern end of Roanoke. Although they were several miles from the English settlement, they were certain that Master Coffin would have seen where they landed and would soon arrive to greet them. But they waited in vain, and when they began calling into the dark woodland, their cries were met with ghostly echoes. "We found none of them," wrote a puzzled White, "nor any signe that they had bene there." It was most mysterious. Coffin's men were all battle-hardened soldiers who had been trained to survive in the harsh terrain of Ireland. Unless there had been a massacre—which White doubted, for the Indians had clearly not reoccupied the island—the only possible explanation was that they had set off on an expedition inland.

The colonists searched up and down the coast for further clues. As night arrived one of them called over to White in an urgent, desperate voice. There on the ground, half-covered with dust, were "the bones of one of those fifteene which the savages had slaine long before." The discovery came as a terrible shock to the landing party. Although a concerted search turned up no more bones, the men now began to fear that the entire party had indeed been massacred.

They passed a fitful night in the open air and resumed their search at first light, walking to "the north ende of the island where Master Ralfe Lane had his forte, with sundrie necessarie and decent dwelling houses." White was still hoping to find "some signes or certaine knowledge of our fifteene men," but he soon realised that this was wishful thinking. "When we come thither, wee found the forte raised downe"—it appeared to have been demolished—"but all the houses standing unhurt . . . [which] were overgrowen with melons of divers sortes, and deere within them feeding on those mellons."

The abandoned and overgrown village made a sorry sight and was deeply disconcerting for White's settlers. Master Coffin and his men had disappeared and were presumed dead. "We returned to our companie without hope of ever seeing any of the fifteene men living."

Manteo suggested to White that they visit his own tribe on Croatoan Island, some ten miles from Roanoke, in the hope that they would know what had happened. White agreed and selected twenty of his men, who "passed by water to the island of Croatoan with Manteo, who had his mother and many of his kindred dwelling in that island, of whom we hoped to understande some newes of our fifteene men."

Their arrival almost ended in disaster. Manteo's tribe did not recognise their kinsman and assumed that the Englishmen were a hostile force. "At our first landing," writes White, "they seemed as though they would fight with us: but perceiving us begin to marche with our shot towards them, they turned their backes and fled." It was only when Manteo "called to them in their owne language"—to their great joy—that they "threwe away their bowes and arrowes and some of them came unto us, embracing and entertaining us friendly, desiring us not to gather or spill any of their corne for that they had but little."

White asked if they had any news of the mysterious disappearance of Master Coffin and his men, expecting to be told little more than he already knew. But to his surprise, one of Manteo's kinsmen was able to tell him every detail of what had happened. He had watched as the Englishmen were "set upon by 30 of the men of Secota, Aquascogoc and Dasamongueponke."

The Indian attack had been well planned and executed, relying on deceit to draw the English from their fort. The attackers had "conveied themselves secretly behind the trees, neere the houses where our men carelesly lived." Several of the Indians had stepped forward with smiles, "calling to them by friendly signes" and suggesting that "two of their chiefest men should come unarmed to speake with those two savages."

Master Coffin had suspected nothing, "wherefore, two of the chiefest of our Englishmen"—probably himself and Chapman—"went gladly to them." They walked straight into a trap. The leading Indian grabbed one of the men and, "with his sword of wood, which he had secretly hidden under his mantell, stroke him on the head and slewe him." The other Englishman managed to escape unharmed and rejoin the rest of his men, but before they had a chance to regroup, the "savages" charged out of the woods. The English retreated to the relative safety of their supply house, but even this was not secure for long. "The savages foorthwith set the same on fire, by meanes whereof our men were forced to take up such weapons as come first to hand, and without order to runne foorth among the savages with whome they skirmished above an howre."

The fighting was fierce. Although the English were at a considerable disadvantage, having lost the initiative and most of their weapons, they fought with courage. One of their number proved skillful with his longbow and gave a triumphant cry when "one of the savages was shot into the side . . . with a wild-fire arrowe, whereof he died presently." These arrows were deadly: with a flaming ball of fire on the tip, they caused a lingering and agonising death.

For a long time Coffin's battalion held its own, with only one man lost in action. But as the battle intensified, "another of our men was shotte into the mouth with an arrowe whereof he died." It slowly became apparent to the outnumbered English that the Indians had chosen a field of battle that perfectly suited their tactics. "The place where they fought was of great advantage to the savages," White later noted in his journal, "by meanes of the thicke trees, behinde which the savages, through their nimblenes, defended themselves and so offended our men with their arrowes that our men being some of them hurt, retired fighting to the waterside where their boate lay." They now realised that their only hope of survival lay in flight; without further ado, they jumped into the boat and pushed away from the shore.

Once they were out of the range of the Indian arrows, they counted their losses. Two men were dead, including their leader, and several of them had received severe arrow wounds that needed urgent treatment. They were also concerned for the four men who had been gathering oysters at the time of the attack. If these returned to Roanoke before they could be alerted to the situation, they were certain to be slaughtered by the Indians. But as the soldiers rowed across Pamlico Sound, "they espied their foure fellowes comming from a creeke thereby, where they had bene to fetch oysters: these foure they receaved into their boate . . . and landed on a little island" — probably on the Outer Banks.

The events that followed remain something of a mystery. These injured and defenceless men were caught in a terrible predicament, pursued by bellicose Indians who saw a very real chance of annihilating the English once and for all. Yet the tribesmen also knew that Coffin's men were resourceful and ferocious, and must have concluded that another assault was unthinkable until they had repaired their bows and restocked their arrows.

Food was the most pressing concern of the English survivors, for every last pea and bean had been lost in their flight from Roanoke. Their only hope of survival now lay in living off the land — scratching a diet from the shellfish and berries that could be found on the

Outer Banks. White believed their plight to have been so hopeless that he was convinced they had either sailed for England in their pinnace—a huge gamble—or chanced their luck and headed for the Caribbean. "They remained a while [on the Outer Banks]," he recorded, "but afterward departed, whither, as yet, we knowe not."

He held out little hope that such a desperate group could have survived on the shores of Pamlico Sound, yet perhaps he underestimated the gritty determination of these men. Unlike his own colonists, Master Coffin's band were battle-hardened soldiers who were trained to live off their wits and used to surviving in the desolate terrain of Ireland, where the native population was no less hostile than in America. If anyone was able to endure hardship, it was this little band of thirteen men.

White was intrigued to discover more about their fate, but was unable to learn anything else from Manteo's kinsmen. He concluded that only time would reveal whether these men's stamina and willpower had enabled them to survive.

Master Coffin relied on heavy weaponry to defend his fort. When the Indians staged an ambush, the English had to flee, losing all their cannon. They were now unarmed and in a terrible predicament

10

Arise, Lord Manteo

While Master Coffin's men battled to save their skins on the Outer Banks, Sir Walter Ralegh found himself facing mounting hostility to his intimate relationship with the queen. England's highborn courtiers were fast tiring of his flirtatious antics and annoyed that their own attempts to parley with Elizabeth were constantly frustrated by her thirst for "Water." Protocol demanded that they could only address the queen when she herself wished it, but this was something that occurred with less and less frequency. She infinitely preferred the company of Sir Walter to her doting but decrepit elder statesmen.

None of the lords dared to criticise the queen in public, for to do so would earn them at the very least a frosty rebuke. But Tarleton, the court jester, had arisen from a quite different stable from the lordly courtiers, and had no truck with their artificial world of honeyed charm and deceits. His raison d'être was to entertain with cheeky good humour, and now—at a state dinner—he prepared to give the queen's favourite a comeuppance that he would not forget.

He chose his moment well, waiting for a pause in the music before rising from his bolster and jabbing a finger in Ralegh's direction. "See," he roared, "the knave commands the queen." There was a momentary silence as people awaited her reaction. But Elizabeth kept her composure—although she was clearly angry—and, according to the chroniclers, "corrected him with a frown." The cocksure Tarleton took this as a cue for another jibe and added that Ralegh "was of too much and too intolerable a power." He then sat down, aware that he had probably said enough.

Tarelton's jest was popular with the revellers, but it was only a half-truth. Ralegh did indeed wield enormous influence, in part due to his wealth, but his power over the queen was emotional, not political. He did not sit on the Privy Council, nor did he hold any of the great offices of state. Although he could argue with the queen, he never forgot that theirs was a precarious relationship that was dependent upon charm and wit on his part. A false step or an indiscretion could quickly bring about his fall.

This did not look likely in 1587, for the queen had just heaped yet another honour upon her favourite. She had made him Captain of her Guard, a position of great prestige that kept him close to her side. He was now in charge of the corps of bodyguards that escorted her to chapel and accompanied her on great state occasions. While his governorship of Virginia had made him a guardian of her Western empire, his new position entrusted him with her very flesh and blood.

The job came with a uniform allowance of "six yards of tawny medley at thirteen shillings and fourpence a yard, with a fur of black budge, rated at £10." It also obliged him to dress with even greater flamboyance than usual. His orange tunic had stretched and puffed sleeves, while his knee-length skirt was splayed outwards at a daring angle. On his head he wore a splendid plumed hat warped with silk, and his chin was thrust heavenwards by a starch-stiffened lace ruff.

He and the men under his command had a hectic schedule, for as well as accompanying the queen in public, they also served her food, delivered messages, and eavesdropped on the maids of honour who shuttled gossip between the queen and her courtiers. The maids were "like witches," said Ralegh; "they could do hurt, but they could do no good."

Shortly after he had been promoted to the position of Captain of the Guard, the queen decided to make one of her "progresses" or royal tours, a shrewd piece of statecraft that enabled her to display herself to her people at the expense of her unfortunate lords. Queen Elizabeth never had any problem loosening other men's purse strings, and these tours were planned on an epic scale. More than 220 carts were required to carry her baggage, which included everything from her oak-carved bed to portable pavilions, hales, and picnic tents.

As few roads were built to withstand the pounding of such a huge baggage train, the royal entourage made painfully slow progress, never advancing more than twelve miles in a day. Many a lord sighed in despair as the horde approached, aware that he was about to play host to some of the most skillful spongers and welshers in the kingdom. Each time the court visited Lord Burghley's home, Theobalds, he was forced to spend "two or three thousand pounds" on entertainment, while a brief visit to Canterbury cost the archbishop more than £2,000, the same as a prolonged privateering voyage in the Caribbean. One unwilling nobleman was so horrified by the prospect of hosting a royal pit stop that he kept an itemised account of everything he spent on victuals: £105 on chickens and herons, £28 on sheep's tongues, cows' udders, and calves' feet, and a further £57 on wine.

Food was not the only expense. New ovens had to be built, damasks and Turkish carpets borrowed or begged, and players hired for Her Majesty's pleasure. Courtly rivalry drove hosts to stage ever more lavish entertainment. One lord tried to impress the queen by digging an artificial lake and staging a sea scene from antiquity. Another, not wishing to be outdone, tried (unsuccessfully) to launch live dogs and cats into the heavens on specially built fireworks.

The queen's 1587 progress was to be a relatively modest affair—a short stay with the Earl of Warwick, followed by a longer sojourn at Theobalds. The entourage made a magnificent spectacle as it passed through the mud-splattered villages of Hertfordshire. The queen herself rode sidesaddle or in a coach, and all around her were members of her bodyguard, led from the front by Sir Walter. As this blaze of colour clattered along the highways, country folk would emerge from their wattle dwellings, blinking in amazement at the pageantry of the Elizabethan court.

A few cynics tried to glimpse the queen's midriff, for although she was dearly loved by her subjects, there were a good number who were less than convinced by her purity, and said that far from being a Virgin Queen, she only sallied forth into the countryside to hide a pregnancy. But most people cheerfully waved their kerchiefs at a figure who inspired genuine affection. "She was received everywhere with great acclamations and signs of joy," reads one account, "[and] would order her carriage sometimes to be taken where the crowd seemed thickest, and stood up and thanked the people."

While the queen herself was feted and adored, her Captain of the Guard was not greeted with quite the same enthusiasm. His highly lucrative monopoly on woollen broadcloth was widely resented as a tax on the poor, while his foppish silks and velvets only served to remind the common folk that much of his wealth had been earned at their expense. Few bothered to disguise their contempt for Ralegh, prompting one courtier to write that "no man is more hated than him; none more cursed daily by the poor, for whom infinite numbers are brought to extreme poverty by the gift of cloth to him."

Sir Walter reacted to any criticism with disdain, and had such an "awfulness and ascendancy in his aspect over other mortals" that even his fellow courtiers were genuinely shocked. "[He] is the best hated man of the world," wrote one, while another noted that "he was so far from affecting popularity as he seemed to take a pride in being hated of the people, either for that he thought it a point of policy, or else because he scorned the approbation of the multitude." But the courtiers who delighted in such assessments were his sworn enemies who would have willingly danced a jig at the merest hint of

fama:

The queen's royal tours were led by Sir Walter Ralegh whose pride and foppish dress made him "the best hated man of the world."

his downfall. Sir Walter also had his champions, his West Country brethren, who were inspired by his audacious rise to the top. He commanded a fanatical loyalty that never faltered, even towards the end of his life, and this support was not confined to his kinsmen and friends. The "rough and mutinous" tin miners of Cornwall—who fell under Ralegh's authority as Lord Warden of the Stanneries— were quickly won over to their new master. "Yours ears and mouth have ever been open to hear and deliver our grievances," wrote Robert Carew, "not always as a magistrate . . . but also very often as a suitor and solicitor of others at the highest place." It was an acknowledgement that Ralegh had frequently used his influence with the queen to further their cause.

Few in the court cared to hear Ralegh's name praised in such a manner, and his enemies were waiting for the moment when his star would go into decline. Their time seemed suddenly to have arrived in the summer of 1587, for a new and dangerous suitor had recently been introduced to the queen—one who was not content to compete with Ralegh for her affections. Robert Devereux, Earl of Essex, was a formidable opponent who was determined to crush his rival. Twenty years old, handsome and quixotic, he was so well versed in the arts of wooing that he could even charm a wizened old lady of fifty-four.

The queen was immediately smitten with Essex and made him her Master of Horse, a position that kept him at her side from dawn till dusk. Even when the horses were asleep in their stables, Essex remained with the queen. "When she is abroad," wrote Anthony Bagot in 1587, "nobody [is] near her but my lord of Essex; and at night, my lord is at cards, or one game or another, with her, till the birds sing in the morning."

Essex was proud, argumentative, and a "great resenter," and he quickly learned to resent Sir Walter's cosy dalliance with the queen. He was determined to besmirch Ralegh's reputation, using his newfound influence to undermine his rival's position and status. Matters came to a head during the royal progress of 1587 when Essex's sister, who had been banished from the court for a marital indiscretion, suddenly turned up at North Hall in Hertfordshire. The queen was furious at such disregard for her authority and sent the impertinent lady to her room, a disgrace that Essex believed to have been arranged by Ralegh. He reproached the queen in no uncertain terms, adding that Her Majesty had only acted with such anger "to please that knave Ralegh." The queen found herself trapped in a tangle of affections, aware that she could not champion both of her suitors at the same time. On this occasion she jumped to Ralegh's defense, much to the disgust of Essex, who said that "it seemed she could not well endure anything to be spoken against him." He was now in a fury and, speaking with "grief and choler," told the queen that he had difficulty serving anyone who "was in awe of such a man."

While this row was taking place inside the queen's chamber, Ralegh—as Captain of the Guard—was stationed on the other side of the door and listening to every word. He was delighted when the queen rushed to his defence and even happier when Essex stormed out of the chamber and rode off into the night. But his triumph was not to last for long, for the queen suddenly panicked and begged her courtiers to discover where Essex had gone. When she learned he was heading for the Low Countries, she broke down, for her beloved Sir Philip Sidney had been killed in the Netherlands less than two years previously. She immediately sent a messenger galloping after her Master of Horse, promising to reward him with a loving reconciliation. Essex accepted graciously and rejoined the tour, but he warned the queen that if she tried "to drive me to be friends with Ralegh," she would not only fail, but would "drive me to many other extremities."

The heady events of that summer led to much speculation as to the timing and manner of Ralegh's expected fall from grace. Most in the court felt that he had met his match in the aristocratic Essex, and that it was only a matter of months before he was sent packing. "Sir Walter Ralegh is in wonderful declention," wrote one, "and [it] is thought he will never rise again." Ralegh himself was also aware of the precariousness of his position and was momentarily struck by a melancholy that would become more and more pronounced in his later years. He sat down to write a despairing verse that tried to imagine a life bereft of courtly splendour:

> My foode shall be of care and sorow made,
> My drink nought else but teares falne from mine eies,
> And for my light in such obscured shade,
> The flames shall serve, which from my hart arise.

He had reached the zenith of his career: now, he could only fall. As yet, no one could predict when and how that fall would occur, but it was certain to have profound consequences for John White and his 110 settlers on Roanoke.

Governor White's colony faced a summer of extreme peril. His settlers had been horrified to learn that Master Coffin's battalion had been attacked by an alliance of three tribes that had traditionally fought among themselves. What made it worse was that one of these tribes came from Secotan, a village that White himself had visited two years previously. On that occasion, the English had been accorded the heartiest of welcomes. Now they were an object of hatred.

The governor's first task was to rally his men. Morale was extremely low, for there were few soldiers to defend the colony's women and children, and the dilapidated state of the village on Roanoke was a constant reminder of the precariousness of their position. With uncharacteristic decisiveness, White issued an order that "every man should be imploied for the repairing of those houses, which we found standing, and also to make other new cottages for such as shoulde neede."

The construction work was not as difficult as it sounded. Elizabethan houses were built around a cagelike framework of timber that was held in place by stout uprights called "studding posts." In England, builders used shaped wood, but it was perfectly possible to use the same method of construction using roughly hewn tree trunks. White's men threw themselves into their work with energy and within a couple of days the skeletal village was once again taking shape.

On July 25, White was astonished to see a largish craft heading towards the island. As it drew nearer, he realised it was the flyboat which had been last sighted in the Bay of Portugal. It contained "the rest of our planters, arrived [and] all safe . . . to the great joye and comfort of the whole companie." Ever since it had been "lewdly" forsaken, White had been nervous about his lack of supplies. Now, at last, his settlers had enough food to stave off starvation.

Three days after this joyous reunion, George Howe, one of White's assistants, set off to hunt for crabs in the shallows of Pamlico Sound. There were now many more mouths to feed, and Howe believed it would raise the colonists' spirits if he could collect enough crabs for a hearty feast. It was a warm day and he stripped off his hose and breeches and waded "almost naked" through the water. Without a thought for his safety, he plucked crabs and oysters from the mud, unaware that he was being watched and tracked by sixteen pairs of eyes.

These Indian huntsmen had set out to stalk deer in the "high reedes," but they quickly abandoned their search when they spied this human quarry. They bided their time, "secretly hidden" in the overgrown reed beds, and were pleased to see that Howe was "wading in the water alone, almost naked, without any weapon save only a small forked stick [for] catching crabs."

The Englishman was in very real danger, for he had "strayed two miles from his companie" and was now a sitting target, unarmed, alone, and defenceless. Suddenly, a crackle in the reed beds caused him to spin around. He was shocked by what he saw: the Indian warriors always made a terrifying sight, and these paint-daubed hunters had already raised their bows and taken aim. A split second later, their piercing arrows had hit their target, biting deep into Howe's flesh. "They gave him sixteene wounds with their arrowes: and after they had slaine him with their wooden swordes, beat his head in peeces and fled over the water to the maine." His battered and mutilated corpse was discovered later in the day by a group of settlers. This was a devastating blow to their morale as well as a graphic reminder that they were all in deadly peril.

Characteristically, White's immediate reaction was to do nothing. He had no idea who had perpetrated the attack and knew that to do battle with the wrong tribe would only add to his woes. He sought advice from the men of Croatoan, Manteo's tribe, who had so far accepted the English presence on Roanoke with an outward show of friendship.

White repeated his reassurance that "neither their corne, nor any other thing of theirs, should be diminished by any of us." He informed them that supply ships were already under way and added that "our comming was onely to renew the olde love that was betweene us and them at the first, and to live with them as brethren and friendes." This "old love" was not exactly reciprocated by the Indians, who had suffered at the hands of Ralph Lane's soldiers after being mistakenly identified as supporters of Wingina. They complained that "divers of them were hurt the yeere before"; to stress their anger, "they shewed us one [of the wounded] which at that very instant laye lame, and had lien of that hurt ever since." Their proposed solution was sensible and was quickly adopted: that they be given "some token or badge" so that White's men "might know them to be our friendes when we met them anywhere out of the towne or island." Henceforth, there would be no chance of these Indians' being attacked by mistake.

White's men spent the night on Croatoan Island. As soon as it was light, the governor summoned a "conference" to ask the village elders if they would help him to organise a gathering of all the tribes on Pamlico Sound. White intended to address this gathering in person, to inform the assembled Indians of his peaceful intentions. He wished to tell them "that if they would accept our friendship, we would willingly receave them againe, and that all unfriendly dealings past on both partes should be utterly forgiven and forgotten."

White's proposal was accepted by the elders, who "answered that they would gladly doe the best they could." They were given a week to arrange the conference. After White had said his farewells, he spent the intervening days transferring the last of the supplies from ship to shore. Once this was completed, there was nothing to do but wait.

The big day—August 8—arrived at last. White had "expected the coming" of the tribesmen at some point during the morning, but noon came and went without any sign of life on the shallow sound. His anxieties increased when he learned that the various chieftains had neglected "to send their answers by the men of Croatoan," and was further alarmed when told that George Howe had been killed by the remnants of Wingina's tribe, who were still living in the settlement just across the water.

White now concluded that the time for conciliation was over. The majority of Indians were evidently not interested in his peace overtures. "He thought to differre the revenging thereof no longer," and planned a surprise attack that would wipe out the most hostile tribesmen once and for all. "Whereffore the same night, about midnight, he passed over the water, accompanied with Captaine Stafford and 24 men." They were also accompanied by Manteo, "whome wee tooke with us to be our guide to the place where these savages dwelt."

The men crossed the water long before dawn—"so earely that it was yet darke"—and landed close to Wingina's old settlement, "the dwelling place of our enemie." It was a tense moment. The men "very secretly conveyed our selves through the woods to that side, where we had their houses betweene us and the water." In absolute silence, the troop crept towards the palisade that surrounded the village and soon "espied their fire, and some sitting about it." These were the hostile survivors of Lane's 1586 attack, and they had learned to hate the English.

White knew they were unlikely to surrender without a fight, and also realised that it would be to his advantage to seize the initiative. "We presently sette on them," he writes; but scarcely had his men blasted their muskets than the Indians leaped back from the fire and "fledde into a place of thicke reedes growing fast by." Although this provided good cover, White's band was determined to flush them out and kill them. "Our men, perceaving them, shotte one of them through the bodie with a bullet, and therewith wee entred the reedes, among which wee hoped to acquite their evill doing towards us."

Many thought it strange that none of the Indians had yet fired back, for they were normally swift with their arrows. The reason for this soon became apparent. As White and his men crashed through the reed beds, they heard an urgent cry from Manteo, begging the English to halt their attack.

White held his fire to learn more, only to discover some horrific news. These were not Wingina's tribe at all; he had mistakenly attacked a group of friendly Croatoans—the very men with whom he had feasted just a few days before. Their identity badges had not prevented the tragedy. A dejected White was now left with a lot of explaining. "We were deceaved," he wrote, "for the savages were our friendes, and were come from Croatoan to gather the corne and fruite of that place because they understoode our enemies were fledde immediately after they had slaine George Howe."

The attack had been swift but deadly. One Indian was seriously wounded, others were bleeding from shot wounds, and many were still shaking with fear, pleading for mercy from the men they recognised from their feast a few days earlier. The timing of the offensive had compounded the problem. "It was so darke," wrote White, "[that] we knew not but that they were all men; and if that one of them, which was a *weroance*'s wife, had not had her childe at her backe, she had beene slaine in steede of a man."

White found himself presiding over a disaster that threatened to turn his only Indian friends against him. His attack had failed in every respect, in striking contrast to Ralph Lane's ambush the previous year. Lane's trophy had been Wingina's severed head. All White had achieved was a new hostility from a hitherto friendly tribe. As both sides came to terms with what had happened, the governor fell into despair and was forced to admit that the Indians "have paide deerely for it."

Once the injured had dressed their wounds, the English and

Indians sat down to discuss what had gone wrong. Manteo explained that his kinsmen had rowed across to the abandoned settlement because the native villagers—George Howe's murderers—had been so terrified of reprisals that they had sought refuge in the forest. "[They] had left all their corne, tabacco and pompions standing in such sorte that all had beene devoured of the birdes and deere if it had not beene gathered in time." Manteo was clearly torn between defending the English and standing up for his old tribe, but he eventually realised that he was now so involved in the colony that his future lay with England. "Although the mistaking of these savages somewhat grieved Manteo," writes White, "yet he imputed their harme to their owne follie, saying to them that if their *weroances* had kept their promise in comming to the governour at the day appointed, they had not knowen that mischance." The governor added that he was indebted to Manteo, who had "behaved himselfe towards us as a most faithfull English man."

The English desperately tried to make amends by working alongside the Indians, gathering the harvested crops that were stockpiled in the abandoned village. "Wee gathered all the corne, pease, pumpions and tabacco that we found ripe," writes White, "and took Menatoan [a kinsman of Manteo], his wife, with the yong childe, and the other savages with us over the water to Roanoke."

For the next three days, the English kept a low profile, planting crops and repairing their houses. But on Saturday, August 13, the settlers brushed down their doublets in preparation for an important and joyous ceremony. "Our savage, Manteo, by the commandment of Sir Walter Ralegh, was christened in Roanoke." Henceforth, and "in reward of his faithful service," he was to be known as Lord of Roanoke and Dasemunkepeuc, the village across the water. Since no one could spell this latter name, let alone pronounce it, he became known simply as Lord Manteo.

Manteo was now a governor in his own right, with semifeudal powers over the local Indians, as well as being the official representative of *Weroanza* Elizabeth of Virginia. For the time being, his

When John White realised the Indians had no interest in peace, he marched his men against a group occupying Wingina's old settlement, unaware he was making a grave error

power was largely theoretical, for there were few Indians in the area and the English colonists remained under White's command. But it was nevertheless a moment of celebration for the settlers. For the first time, England had forged an Indian in its own image, a tattooed and shaven-headed tribesman who was now so civilised that he would salute the flag of St. George. He spoke English, wore breeches and a doublet, and had even rejected his panoply of gods and devils. This was the very goal that Harriot had dreamed about when he wrote that "if means of good government bee used . . . [the Indians] may in short time be brought to civilitie and the imbracing of true religion."

Five days after Manteo's baptism, the English settlers had further cause for celebration. "Elenora, daughter to the governour and wife to Ananias Dare, one of the assistants, was delivered of a daughter in Roanoke." This was very good news indeed. A high proportion of Elizabethan babies were stillborn, and two out of every three that survived birth were doomed to die in infancy. Many suffered from malnutrition in the womb, and a large number were born "crooked and misshapen." Eleanor's baby was in rude health, which filled the settlers with joy. She "was christened there the Sunday following, and because this childe was the first Christian borne in Virginia, she was named Virginia."

White was delighted to be a grandfather and clearly felt that the events of the previous week represented a turning point in the colony's fortunes. In his journal he suddenly becomes more optimistic and looks to the future with a degree of breezy confidence. "By this time our shippes had unlanded the goods and victuals of the planters," he writes, "[and] the planters also prepared their letters and tokens to send backe into England."

White was at a loss to explain why Fernandez was still anchored two miles offshore and had not set sail for the Caribbean. The ill-tempered navigator had refused to take the settlers to Chesapeake Bay on the grounds that it would give him less time to track down Spanish galleons, yet he had remained at anchor for almost four weeks and showed no sign of setting sail. White could only conclude that Fernandez was taking a perverse delight in torturing the colonists with the constant sight of his vessel, while at the same time refusing to allow them to come on board. Even when a sudden squall forced him out to sea, Fernandez was not gone for long. After six days of riding out the storm, he reappeared off the coastline of the Outer Banks.

Those six days had unsettled the colonists, for they had grown used to the sight of his vessel. A wave of collective panic now passed through their ranks and caused them to reevaluate their position. Although the arrival of their flyboat had been a source of joy, she was found to be weakened by storms and carrying a disappointingly meagre quantity of victuals. This had not unduly troubled White, for he knew that supply ships were on the way, but it suddenly dawned on the settlers that these vessels were due to head directly to Chesapeake Bay. If they did not also call at Roanoke—and there was no reason why they should—then the colony would surely starve to death.

The *Lion*'s reappearance convinced the settlers that they should send an urgent message back to England, alerting Ralegh to the unexpected changes of plan. It was decided that at least two of the assistants should sail back to England; but selecting which two should make the voyage was not easy, since no one wished to spend another few months at sea. It was only after "much perswading of the governour" that Christopher Cooper agreed to sail alone, and the settlers went to their beds relieved that at least one of their number would be heading to England. But their good cheer was not to last for long: Cooper passed a fretful night, during which, "through the perswasion of divers of his familiar friendes, he changed his minde, so that now the matter stoode as at the first." They were back to square one.

A tense situation was made worse by the fact that Fernandez suddenly announced that he was about to set sail and that if the colonists did not choose a messenger promptly, he would miss the boat. White's weak leadership once again became evident. His inability to make a decision forced the colonists to take the initiative. They approached their governor and "with one voice requested him to returne himselfe into England, for the better and sooner obtaining of supplies and other necessaries for them."

It was an extraordinary request that caught White completely off his guard. The colonists pandered to his vanity, arguing that only he had the necessary stature to be taken seriously by Sir Walter; but the real explanation for their decision lay in their deep dissatisfaction with their governor. White had proved a poor leader whose indecision had landed them in their terrible predicament. The settlers were so disillusioned by his incompetence that—astonishingly—they felt their chances of survival to be greater without him at the helm.

White refused to countenance the idea of abandoning his colony, citing many "sufficient causes" as to why he could not sail. Principal among these was that "some enemies to him"—whom he does not name—would spread rumours that he had never had any intention of settling in America. "[They] would not spare to slander falsely both him and the action," he said, "by saying that he went to Virginia but politikely . . . to leade so many into a countrey in which he never meant to stay himselfe, and there to leave them behind him."

This argument did not cut much ice with the settlers, who claimed that his only concern was that his possessions would be stolen in his absence. White admitted as much in his diary, revealing that he was concerned that "his stuffe and goods might be both spoiled and most of it pilfered away." He added that he would "be either forced to provide himselfe of all such things againe, or els at his comming againe to Virginia, finde himselfe utterly unfurnished."

Time was ticking and still he refused to sail for England. The colonists were by now determined to rid themselves of White. On the following morning, they "beganne to renewe their requests to the governour againe." Aware that his possessions were the sticking point, they promised "to make him their bonde, under all their handes and seales, for the safe preserving of all his goods for him at his returne to Virginia." They added that "if any part thereto were spoiled, or lost, they would see it restored to him or his assignes, whensoever the same should be missed and demanded." Their final offer proved the clincher: "a testimonie, under their handes and seales," which guaranteed the safety of his personal possessions, and stated that White was sailing "much against his will" and "through our importunacie."

Only now did the governor agree to set sail, leaving his daughter and granddaughter to an uncertain fate. He had no idea whether he would ever see them again, nor could he be sure that Ralegh would allow him to resume his post of governor when he learned of all the mishaps and disasters. It was, after all, a difficult train of events to explain to Sir Walter, and this latest development was the hardest of all. White's mutinous men were telling their leader—in no uncertain terms—that he was no longer welcome on Roanoke.

It is possible that he was so deluded by the trappings of power that he failed to realise he was being evicted by the colonists; but more likely, given the tone of his journal, he realised his leadership had been a disaster. With a heavy heart, he bid his farewells, vowing to return as soon as possible with the desperately needed provisions. It was a sorry moment. At a critical juncture in the fortunes of the colony—and with hostile forces gathering apace—White had voluntarily abnegated his responsibilities. Roanoke was about to enter its darkest days, and it was to do so without the steadying hand of a governor.

He makes no mention in his journal of what must have been an emotional parting with his daughter, nor does he spare any thought for his baby granddaughter, Virginia, just nine days old. Even more surprising, he neglects to say whom he was putting in charge of the colony during his absence, and he further muddies the waters by stating that while he was in England, the colonists "intended to remove fifty miles further up into the maine."

This throwaway line—so characteristic of White—lacked any coherent sense. He can only have meant that the settlers had expressed their intention of moving to Chesapeake Bay, yet this would have removed the whole point of his going to England. It would also have been a tricky operation with only three or four boats at their disposal. But the governor clearly expected them to move, for he gave them precise instructions on what to do when they left the island, telling them to carve letters into a tree revealing where they had gone. "[I made] a secret token agreed betweene them and me," he wrote, "to write or carve on the trees or posts of the dores the name of the place where they should be seated."

He added that if they were leaving Roanoke of their own will, they were to write only their destination, but "if they should happen to be distressed in any of those places, that then they should carve over the letters or name a crosse, †, in this forme."

White was never a master of clarity; on the eve of his departure from Roanoke, his journal became even more confused than usual. He was tired, depressed, and emotionally drained; yet he would surely have paid more attention to detail had he known that these few scraps of information were to be remembered and examined for years to come—the only clues in a mystery that was to haunt England's New World adventurers for almost two decades.

When Fernandez learned that he would have to spend several more months in the company of White, he brusquely informed the governor that he intended to depart before midday, giving him "halfe a daies respite to prepare himselfe for the same." The only good news for White was that he managed to secure himself passage on the flyboat rather than the *Lion*. This small craft was captained by his friend, Edward Spicer, who was sure to whisk him back to England in as short a time as possible.

Misfortune struck the flyboat as it prepared to set sail. The vessel's anchor was raised by a capstan, a vertical drum which gathered up the cable as the twelve mariners pushed on its horizontal bars. The strain was tremendous, for the anchor was snagged on the rocky seabed, and there was a sickening crack when it was finally freed. One of the capstan's great bars had snapped, flinging several of the seamen to the deck. The sudden loss of equilibrium and tension caused the drum to spin wildly out of control, its bars smashing into the sailors.

To White, who had just stepped aboard, the accident was a dreadful sight. "Twelve of the men . . . were throwen from the cope-stone," he wrote. The bars "came so fast about upon them, that the other two barres thereof stroke and hurt most of them so sore that some of them never recovered it." Several had broken bones while others were shaken and bruised. It was some time before enough of the men were sufficiently recovered to make a second attempt.

Once again they were "throwen downe and hurt," and at this point the crew gave up: they were "so bruised and hurt" that they decided to "cut their cable and lose their anker." White adds, with characteristic understatement, that it was an "infortunate beginning."

White set sail with an injured and dispirited crew, but these experienced seadogs managed to shadow the *Lion* for a month. As soon as they sighted the Azores, Fernandez announced that he was going in search of booty, much to the dismay of White and his men. They were dangerously short of supplies, physically debilitated, and still nursing the appalling wounds inflicted by the broken capstan. Of the fifteen crew, only five "were able to stande to their labour"—a very small number to man the watches and sail the boat. They begged Fernandez to reconsider, but he refused. After transferring the settlers' letters into the flyboat, the men swung their vessel northeastwards for England.

"We hoped by the helpe of God to arrive shortly," wrote White. But after twenty days of "scarse and variable windes," there arose "a storme at the north-east." This broke the spirits of the exhausted men, whose fresh water supply was "by leaking [barrels] almost consumed." They were soaked to the bones by sea spray, and every lurch of the boat sent them crashing into timbers, reopening their wounds. More galling was the fact that the wind was blowing from the northeast, pushing them further and further from English shores. "For six dayes [the wind] ceased not to blowe so exceeding that we were driven further in those six days then wee could recover in thirteene daies." They soon found themselves in desperate straits. With their food finished, the scurvy-ridden men quickly began to starve. Ten of the crew were already suffering; now, "others of our saylers began to fall very sicke, and two of them dyed." These unfortunate souls were wrapped in canvas sheeting and dropped overboard. The storm showed no signs of abating. It "continued so close that our master sometimes in foure daies together could see neither sunne nor starre." Nor could he see land, much to the men's discomfort, since they had only "stinking water, dregges of beere and lees of wine which remained . . . but three gallons, and therefore now we expected nothing but by famyne to perish at sea."

At last the winds changed, bringing fairer weather, and for almost a month the men drifted slowly northwards, too debilitated to man the vessel. They had given up all hope of surviving the voyage and hoped only for a quick and painless death. But on October 16, 1587, White noticed a low grey smudge on the horizon that grew more distinct as the morning progressed. He had sighted land. "We knew not what land it was," but it caused enough interest for a few of the men to bestir themselves and hoist a sail. For the rest of the day, the land grew nearer. "About sunne set, we put into a harbour where we found a hulke of Dublin and a pynesse of [South]ampton." This pinnace made contact with White's men and informed them that "we were in Smewicke in the west parts of Ireland."

White and Edward Spicer struggled ashore "to take order of the new victualling of our flye boate for England," but this Irish wilderness outpost had little to offer in the way of food. It took four days to acquire a few provisions, by which time "the boatswane, the steward and the boatswane's mate [had] dyed."

Worse was to follow. Five days later, "the master's mate and two of our chiefe saylers were brought sicke." White no longer had a crew for his flyboat, so he "skipped himselfe in a ship called the *Monkie*." After a few more days at sea, at long last he stepped ashore at Southampton, exhausted and sick but relieved that his mission was finally coming to an end.

All he now needed to do was find Sir Walter Ralegh.

11

Sounding a Trumpet

John White landed at Southampton to be greeted with some extremely bad news. Just two weeks earlier, in October 1587, Queen Elizabeth had issued a general "stay of shipping" that forbade any vessel from setting sail without special licence. This order extended to warships, privateers, and even supply vessels carrying mattocks and seeds to America.

The reasons for such a ban were clear, even to those who had never seen the sea. King Philip II had determined to invade England, and was assembling a mighty armada which—if rumour proved true—was of such strength that it was already being called *invencible*. "There was spread throughout all England," wrote White, "such report of the wonderfull preparation and invincible fleetes made by the King of Spain, joyned with the power of the Pope, for the invading of England." The queen had decreed that all available ships would be needed for the defence of her kingdom.

Soon after arriving in England, White met with Ralegh and broke the news that he had landed his men on Roanoke Island rather than Chesapeake Bay. Ralegh must have been furious. He curtly informed White that the first supply vessel had already left for Chesapeake Bay and that it was most unlikely to call at Roanoke. But he also realised that the settlers on Roanoke were in considerable danger, and offered to dispatch a second ship "with all such necessaries as he understood they stood in neede of." Moreover, he declared his intention of sending a huge fleet under the command of Sir Richard Grenville, carrying many more supplies and a few more settlers. It was to be "a good supply of shiping" and would be laden "with sufficient of all thinges needefull."

When White asked how, exactly, Ralegh proposed to obtain permission to sail, Sir Walter haughtily informed him that he had always considered his own projects to fall outside the purview of the government. Although he fully supported the queen's ban on sailings because of the Spanish Armada threat, and even wrote to his half-brother stressing the importance of ensuring that no vessels left the West Country, he added in a postscript that his own ships, "to whom I have geven leve, you may latt them steale away."

White was relieved that supplies would soon be on their way to his daughter and granddaughter, but he was to find, not for the first time, that luck would fail him in his hour of need. The supply vessel did not sail—perhaps for fear of Spanish attack—and Sir Richard Grenville's fleet of seven or eight ships was delayed by contrary winds. By spring 1588 it was "in a reddinesse" to sail for America when a breathless messenger arrived at Bideford with some unwelcome news. Ralegh had been overruled by the queen. Grenville was "strayghtly charged and commanded in Her Majesties' name, and upon his alleadgeance, to forbeare to go [on] his intended voyage." He was to join Sir Francis Drake in Plymouth, where preparations were under way for the defence of England.

There was only one crumb of comfort in the news: Grenville was given some leeway over what he did with his smaller vessels and was told that any that Sir Francis did not need, "he might dispose of and employ in his intended voyage." Drake had no use for Grenville's two pinnaces, which were so small that a single cannonshot could have sunk them. These were now loaned to White—under the command of Captain Arthur Facy—so that he could dash to the relief of his colonists.

They were not the ideal craft in which to sail across the Atlantic. The *Brave* was just thirty tons, while the *Roe* was even smaller, and there was scarcely enough room for the "fifteen planters and all their provisions." But there was no alternative, and White clambered aboard with a growing feeling that he had been born under an "unlucky star."

He was absolutely right, for less than a week after leaving England, in April, the *Brave* suffered a devastating attack from a French pirate ship. Captain Facy's men were no strangers to marine warfare, but they soon found themselves outgunned by their attackers. Within minutes, grappling irons enabled a large troop of fighters to board the English vessel. This was the turning point in the battle; the French pirates "playd extreemely upon us with their shot," and White, much to his embarrassment, was struck "in the side of the buttoke." Even in an age that glorified battle scars, a black-and-blue bottom was not a wound to boast about.

When the men could fight no more, they capitulated to their attackers and managed to talk themselves out of being put to the sword. The French were rather less magnanimous when it came to claiming their booty. They seized all the supplies that had been intended for the colonist on Roanoke; so much, indeed, that they sank their two pinnaces through overloading. "They robbed us of all our victuals, powder, weapons and provision," recorded a distressed White, "saving a smal quantity of biskuit to serve us scarce for England." He added that their sorry plight was God's way of "justly punishing our . . . evil disposed mariners," and concludes, with more than a hint of bitterness, "we were of force constraned to breake of[f] our voyage intended for the reliefe of our colony left the yere before in Virginia." The *Brave* returned to England, followed soon after by the *Roe*, which had also failed to make it to America.

White was now extremely anxious about the safety of the Roanoke colonists, and feared that nine months without any supplies would have left them "not a little distressed." But he was at a loss to know what to do next. His hands were tied, for the country was now on a war footing with Spain, and Ralegh was far too busy to concern himself with his American colony. England itself was under threat.

It was widely believed that Spanish crack troops would attempt a landing in the West Country, capture a port, and create a beach-head. Since this was Ralegh's territory—he was still vice admiral of the West Country—he was one of the "noble and experienced captains" appointed to advise on how Devon and Cornwall could best "withstand an invasion pretended [intended] by the King of Spain." His advisors were all close friends, and when he was summoned to attend the council of war, he found himself surrounded by the very men who had led his 1585 expedition to Virginia. Sir Richard Grenville was present, as was Ralph Lane, and each of these men was able to draw on his experience in America to second-guess the Spanish strategy. "To invade by sea upon a perilous coast," wrote Ralegh later, "being neither in possession of any port, nor succoured by any party, may better fit a prince presuming on his fortune than enriched by understanding."

Ralegh threw himself into his work with customary enthusiasm. From his headquarters in Plymouth, he issued orders, inspected fortifications, and helped to muster troops. But his activities were not confined to land defences. He also helped to assemble the English fleet, lending several of his privateering vessels to do battle with the Armada. None was more impressive than the mighty *Ark Royal*, the most advanced warship of her day, which Sir Walter had had built two years earlier. Now she was to lead the defence of the realm, commanded by Admiral Lord Howard of Effingham himself. "I thinke her the odd [best] ship in the world for all conditions," the admiral wrote, "and truly, I think there can be no great ship make me change and go out of her."

The Spanish Armada, an astonishing array of 130 frigates and galleons, was sighted off the southwest coast of England at 3 p.m. on Friday, July 19. It was the greatest fleet that had ever approached the shores of Great Britain. Within minutes, the first of Ralegh's beacons was roaring into flame, sending a message of impending danger swiftly along the south coast. News quickly reached the queen at Richmond; then the message flashed inland, carrying the news to Nottingham, Derby, and York. All night, the inhabitants of Plymouth battled against a swift southwesterly to get their ships out of the harbour. By dawn, most of the fleet had been warped to sea and were ready to challenge the great Armada.

It soon became apparent that the Spanish had no intention of landing in the West Country. The fleet continued eastwards, up the Channel, followed by English vessels dancing around their tail. "We pluck their feathers little by little," wrote the Lord High Admiral with relish. With no further danger to the West Country, Ralegh was able to join the fleet, stepping aboard his old flagship in time to witness victory. The English fleet closed on the Spanish ships in the Strait of Dover; in the mayhem that followed, the battered Armada was "chased out of the sight of England." Dozens of ships were sunk, many more were later wrecked on the wild shores of Scotland, and only half of the fleet ever made it back to Spain. Ralegh's account of the battle was withering in its attack on the Spanish commanders and their strategy. "With all which so great and terrible an ostentation, they did not in all their sailing round England, so much as sink or take one ship, bark, pinnace, or cock-boat of ours; or ever burnt so much as one sheepcote of this land."

The queen was overjoyed. To celebrate her victory, she commissioned a special engraving that depicted her in majesterial pose, standing between two columns. These represented the Pillars of Hercules—those chunks of rock that marked the limits of Rome's western empire—and they signalled that England's historic victory stretched far beyond the fringes of Europe. Her Royal Highness, *Weroanza* Elizabeth, now saw herself as the unchallenged ruler in the New World. She was, according to the inscription, "Queen . . . of England, France, Ireland and Virginia."

.   .   .

Queen Elizabeth revelled in her victory over the Spanish Armada. She had saved England from invasion, and now saw herself as the unchallenged ruler of the New World

Sir Walter had been too busy to meet with John White during the Armada campaign, and even after the danger had passed, he was in Ireland to counter any attack from the remnants of King Philip's fleet. He did not return to London until March 1589, by which time nineteen months had passed since there had been any contact with the Roanoke settlers. Only now did he have time to consider his next move. He was reluctant to send yet another fleet to Virginia, for the project was proving a drain even on his not inconsiderable resources. It cost about £2,000 to equip a medium-sized ship for a protracted voyage in American waters, and in the four years between 1584 and 1588 Sir Walter had sent no fewer than eighteen vessels across the ocean, for a total cost of perhaps £36,000. The supplies for these vessels added a further £10,000 to the bill, while the expense of keeping a colony in tools and victuals was reckoned at £10,000 a year. Although there were potential rich pickings to be had in the holds of Spanish treasure ships, not all of Ralegh's captains returned home with silver and gold.

But while the colonisation of America was a considerable burden on the resources of one man — even a wealthy one — it was not beyond the means of a group of merchants. There were few who wished to join Ralegh in his enterprise, but he managed to strike an agreement with a group of London traders by giving them the right to trade with the "Citee of Ralegh," exempt from tax, for seven years. Their side of the bargain was to inject the necessary capital to ensure the survival of the colony.

The agreement was signed with a flourish in March 1589, and White was heartened by the thought that he might, at long last, be reunited with his family. But the merchants showed no interest in organising a fleet, and spring slipped into summer without a single vessel being sent to America. It had slowly dawned on the merchants that the Citee of Ralegh — tax or no tax — had very little to offer.

Only one man vowed to send ships to the troubled colony. King Philip of Spain had grown increasingly exasperated by the threat that Ralegh's men posed to Spanish shipping, and was alarmed by the vague rumours that the colony had been moved to Chesapeake Bay. When his advisors said that this proved the Roanoke experiment had been a failure, Philip's response was testy. "The fact that he [Ralegh] has changed its site is no indication of a decision to abandon it," he said, "but rather to change its position."

The king was so troubled by Ralegh's colony that he continued to plan a search-and-destroy mission throughout the Armada campaign. When the sea war interrupted the flow of messages between El Escorial and the New World, the governor of Spain's Florida outpost decided to equip a vessel to root out and slaughter all of the English colonists.

The commander of this mission, Vicente Gonzalez, was so convinced that Ralegh's colonists had moved to Chesapeake Bay—even though he had no concrete information—that he sailed past the Outer Banks without even stopping. His search only began in earnest when his vessel entered the bay and began coasting the shoreline. His men delighted in the "very high land," and all agreed that it was the perfect site for a colony. But although they conducted an exhaustive search, not a single lace-ruffed Englishman was sighted.

After a few days of disappointment, there was a sudden flurry of excitement. Gonzalez managed to coax a few Indians on board his vessel and quiz them about the possible site of an English colony. It was not the easiest of conversations, for neither side understood the other, but Gonzalez felt sure that he had caught the gist of their meaning. "The English colony," he wrote, "according to what the Indians have said, is established . . . northwards on a river." He added that the river "passed through to the other sea [the Pacific]." Since dozens of rivers poured their waters into Chesapeake Bay, and the Indians could tell him no more, Gonzalez reluctantly conceded that such vague information would make it almost impossible to locate the colony. Disappointed and annoyed, he abandoned all hopes of slaughtering Ralegh's colonists and turned his ship southwards, heading back to Florida.

As he steered his course along the white sand dunes of the Outer Banks, the breeze suddenly stiffened and "they were forced to dismast the ship and to bring her to the shore by means of oars." Gonzalez was unsure of his exact location, but his description of the shoreline and the shallowness of the water indicate that he had arrived at Port Ferdinando, one of the inlets into Pamlico Sound that had been named by Simon Fernandez in honour of himself. "The view towards the north gave on to a great part of the bay and revealed a large arm in the north-west curve which was heavily wooded." Unbeknown to Gonzalez and his men, they were less than ten miles from Roanoke, and almost within sight of Ralph Lane's fort.

It was the accidental discovery of a slipway on the Outer Banks that awakened the Spaniard's suspicions. He landed a party on the sand dunes, where the men soon found "a number of wells made with English casks, and other debris." Gonzalez was intrigued and noted that "a considerable number of people had been here," yet there were no obvious signs of life and his men showed no desire to row across to Roanoke. With high tide fast approaching, he edged his vessel over the sandy bar and set sail for St. Augustine. He had no idea that he was two miles from the "Citee of Ralegh," and therefore just missed discovering whether White's colonists were still living on the island.

The information provided by Gonzalez—such as it was—caused serious alarm in Spain. The Council of the Indies ordered the preparation of a major expedition, including four warships and a battalion of soldiers, which was to "attempt the destruction of the enemy's fort and settlement." It was then to establish "a fort capable of holding 300 infantrymen as a garrison, under a governor, with orders that, when an opportunity arose, he or his lieutenant should penetrate into the interior." This would have proved a formidable challenge to any future attempts by the English to settle a colony. But an unexpected crisis meant that the fleet never set sail. White's men and women—if they were still alive—had escaped at least one of the many threats to their existence.

John White finally set sail for Roanoke at the end of March 1590, by which time an alarming two years, six months, and twenty-four days had passed since he had last seen his daughter and granddaughter. There had been no news in all that time, and White had no idea whether the settlers were still on the island.

Although shipping was still subject to "a restraint and stay," Ralegh talked the queen into allowing his ships to sail. White himself was to travel in the *Hopewell*, while the supplies were to be carried in the *Moonlight*. When Captain Cocke saw the quantity of possessions that White hoped to take to America, he could scarcely believe his eyes. He refused to carry more than the absolute minimum, and even forbade him from taking "a boy to attend upon me, although I made great sute and earnest intreatie." White threatened to complain to Ralegh, but with the ships "being then all in readinesse to goe to the sea, [they] would have bene departed before I could have made my retorne." Faced with a choice between seeing his daughter and losing his possessions, White nobly plumped for the former.

The tedium of the sea voyage was frequently enlivened by piratical skirmishes and, on one occasion, a full-scale battle. After a lengthy bout of privateering in the Caribbean—and more than five months after leaving England—Cocke at last led his fleet northwards towards the Outer Banks. Progress was slow, for the weather seemed determined to frustrate their efforts. "The wind scanted," wrote an impatient White, "and from thence forward we had very fowle weather with much raine, thundering and great spouts, which fell round about us nigh unto our ships." On August 3, the sun broke through the clouds just long enough for Cocke to take a quadrant reading and deduce that they were nearing the Outer Banks. The lookout claimed he could see "low sandie ilands, . . . but the weather continued so exceeding foule that we could not come to an anker bye the coast."

For five days the seas raged, and it was not until the second week of August that "the storme ceased and we had very great likelihood of faire weather." The ships paused briefly to replenish their water supplies, then inched northwards along the wooded shores of the

Outer Banks until they at last reached Port Ferdinando. White was now in familiar territory. He excitedly clambered up the mainmast for a better view of the coast, and was overjoyed by what he saw: "At our first comming to anker on this shore, we saw a great smoke rise in the Ile of Roanoke, neere the place where I left our colony in the yeere 1587." This was a sight that he had long dreamed about, for smoke was the normal means of signalling to a ship, and it "put us in good hope that some of the colony were there expecting my returne out of England."

He was by now itching to get ashore, but it was already growing dark and Cocke wisely cautioned that it was too late to man the ship's rowing boats. White spent the night in fretful excitement. At the crack of dawn he helped to organise the landing party—two boats led by Captains Cocke and Spicer. He was so anxious to inform the settlers of his arrival that he "commanded our master gunner to make readie two minions and a falkon well loden, and to shoot them off with reasonable space betweene every shot." This was to announce their impending arrival to the colonists on Roanoke.

The ships lay several miles offshore, and rowing across to the Outer Banks was backbreaking work. When they had covered more than a mile "[and] were halfe-way betweene our ships and the shore," the men noticed a second plume of smoke rising from a nearby chain of sand dunes on the Outer Banks. Both White and Cocke assumed that they were being signalled by Roanoke lookouts, and possibly warned of danger; "we therefore thought good to goe to that second smoke first." This involved considerably more exertion, for the surf that washed the sandbanks carried a powerful undertow, and it was only as the men reached the shore that they realised the current had pulled them off course. The smoke signal was some distance away—"much further from the harbour where we landed then we supposed," wrote White, "so that we were very sore tired before wee came to the smoke."

The weary sailors trudged along the foreshore until they at last reached the fire. To their intense disappointment, "we found no man nor signe that any had been there lately." The fire had not been lit as a signal after all, but seemed to have been started by a lightning strike. White had dragged the men here for nothing.

Only now did the mariners realise how exhausted they were. The August sun had been beating down on them for hours and the men were hot and parched. To their dismay, they discovered there was "no fresh water in all this way to drinke," and they had to stagger back to their boats without quenching their thirst. It was now too late in the day to head for Roanoke, "so we deferred our going to Roanoke until the next morning, and caused some of those saylers to digge in those sandie hilles for fresh water whereof we found very sufficient." After a brief rest, "wee returned aboord with our boates and our whole company in safety." It was dark by the time all the men were back on board the ships.

White woke at dawn in the hope of making an early start, only to discover that Captain Spicer had already been up for some hours and "had sent his boat ashore for fresh water." This caused an unfortunate delay, and "it was ten of the clocke aforenoone before we put from our ships." The journey from ship to shore was always dangerous, but the risks had increased considerably with the arrival of a stiff northwesterly. Powerful currents at the entrance to Pamlico Sound created choppy water and threatened to capsize even quite stable craft. The men decided to head first to the Outer Banks and, after regrouping, continue across the lagoon towards Roanoke.

Spicer had accompanied the first trip to the shore that morning and must have cautioned White about the dangers, but the governor was not to be dissuaded. He insisted on heading for land in the capable company of Captain Cocke and a party of thirteen men. Spicer reluctantly agreed to follow once the water casks had been unloaded.

The sailors quickly realised that the boat was not built for such conditions. "[We] passed the breach," wrote White, "but not without some danger of sinking, for we had a sea brake into our boat which filled us halfe full of water." White furiously bailed out the flood and, "by the will of God and carefull styrage [steerage] of Captaine Cocke, we came safe ashore, saving onely that our furniture, victuals, match and powder were much wet and spoyled." The men had been extremely lucky, for the wind was blowing "direct into the harbour—so great a gale that the sea brake extremely on the barre and the tide went very forcibly at the entrance."

As they unloaded their sodden possessions onto the Outer Banks, they caught sight of Captain Spicer and his crew nearing the shore, weaving an erratic course through increasingly treacherous waters. The fearless steersman seemed barely in control, and was constantly exposing the boat to the breaking waves. Even to White, who was not a sailor, this bordered on the foolhardy. "Captaine Spicer came to the entrance of the breach with his mast standing up," he wrote, "and was halfe passed over but, by the rash and undiscreet styrage of Ralph Skinner, his master's mate, a very dangerous sea brake into their boate and overset them quite." The waves had flipped the little craft upside down, trapping several of the men underwater.

White and Cocke could scarcely bring themselves to watch the unfolding tragedy, for they knew that it would take superhuman strength to right the boat. "The men kept the boat," he wrote, "some in it and some hanging on it, but the next sea set the boat on ground"—a shoal—"where it beat so that some of them were forced to let goe their hold." The half-drowned men tried to wade ashore, "but the sea still beat them downe so that they could neither stand nor swimme, and the boat twise or thrise was turned the keele upward." A few of the men held on, including Captain Spicer and Master Skinner, who "hung until they sunke and [were] seene no more."

It was now, at this moment of tragedy, that Captain Cocke showed his true colours. Without a thought for his own safety, he pushed his boat back out into the water and tried to rescue the few survivors flailing around in the surf. "Four [men] that could swimme a little kept themselves in deeper water and were saved by Captain Cocke's meanes, who so soone as he saw their oversetting, stripped himselfe, and foure other that could swimme very well, and with all haste possible, rowed unto them." But it was too late to save many of the crew. "Seven of the chiefest were drowned," wrote White, "whose names were Edward Spicer, Ralph Skinner, Edward Kelly, Thomas Bevis, Hance the Surgion, Edward Kelbourne, Robert Coleman."

The accident struck the fear of God into the sailors who had seen the men drown, and "did so much discomfort the saylers that they were all of one mind not to goe any further to seeke the planters [on Roanoke]." White begged them to continue and, after several hours of persuasion, they reluctantly agreed.

The tragedy having used up precious hours of daylight, it was soon dark: "before we could get to the place where our planters were left," wrote White, "it was so exceeding darke that we over-shot the place a quarter of a mile." But he did not despair, for he was at last nearing his goal, and was further encouraged when he made out signs of life on the shoreline. "We espied towards the north end of the iland, ye light of a great fire thorow the woods, to the which we presently rowed." Night had fallen quickly, but White urged the men to row on through the blackness, straining his eyes to make out the settlement. He was anxious to land, even at such a late hour, but wiser counsel prevailed. Cocke warned that the men would be defenceless against an Indian ambush. As they were still some distance from the village, they decided to overnight in the boat.

"We let fall our grapnel neere the shore," just beyond the range of Indian arrows. After the men had eaten the food salvaged from the watery bottom of the craft, they attempted to alert the colonists to their presence. "[We] sounded with a trumpet a call," wrote White, "and afterwardes many familiar English tunes of songs, and called to them friendly, but we had no answere." They were still too far from the settlement, and the wind was carrying their greetings away from the island.

The men passed a fitful night on the boat, reliving the terrible events of the day. As soon as dawn lightened the sky, they raised the grapnel and rowed ashore. "We therefore landed at day-breake," wrote White, "and, comming to the fire, we found the grasse and sundry rotten trees burning about the place." It rapidly dawned on him that all was not right. The previous night's fire—like the smoke signal on the Outer Banks—had not been lit by the colonists.

White was now seriously concerned. Although he and his men were still two miles from the settlement, there was no sign of life, nor was there any reason to believe that the colonists were still living on Roanoke. "From hence we went thorow the woods," wrote White, "and from thence we returned by the water side, round about the north point of the iland, untill we came to the place where I left our colony in the yeere 1586."

The men realised how wise they had been not to come ashore the previous night, for "in all this way we saw in the sand the print of the savages feet." This was alarming, but White did not despair. He immediately set the men to work, searching the shoreline around the natural harbour for any sign that might have been left behind by the lost colonists. He instructed them to pay particular attention when they came to examine the forest, for the settlers had assured him that they would carve their destination onto the trunk of a lofty tree.

The woodland search took time; the undergrowth was dense and tangled, yet it was not long before one of the men raised an excited cry. "As we entred up the sandy banke," wrote White, "upon a tree, in the very browe thereof, were curiously carved these faire Romane letters CRO." He fell to his knees and gave thanks, for these three letters convinced him that the colonists were still alive. Although the rest of his men were perplexed by this mysterious word, White assured them that he was now able "to signifie the place where I

"We sounded with a trumpet a call," wrote John White, "and afterwardes many familiar tunes of songes . . . but we had no answere."

should find the planters seated"—Croatoan Island. Yet there was something peculiar about the way the letters had been carved. Although there was no cross cut alongside—the warning of danger—they appeared to have been hastily hacked into the tree and left half-finished, perhaps under pressure of an ambush. White ordered the men to look for more signs, but with no success, and they soon left the harbour and headed instead for the main settlement.

The breathless tone of White's journal reveals that he was in a state of nervous excitement. But his return to the village where he had said his farewell to Eleanor, his daughter, and Virginia, his granddaughter, also filled him with apprehension. He already knew that he would not find his family in the settlement, but was aware that the state of the dwellings and storehouses would hold many clues as to when and where they had moved.

As the men approached the village, they realised that it had been abandoned for some time, for the communal buildings had collapsed and "the houses [were] taken downe." White's own house was a ruin, while that of his daughter and son-in-law was a wreckage of broken timber. Yet the place was still "very strongly enclosed with a high palisado of great trees, with cortynes and flankers very fort-like."

After a cursory glance at the dwellings, White's eye was drawn to "one of the chiefe trees or postes at the right side of the entrance, [which] had the barke taken off and, five foote from the ground, in fayre capitall letters, was graven CROATOAN without any crosse or signe of distresse." Here at last was the message that White had so hoped to find. It was clearly engraved into the tree, and showed no signs of having been carved in a hurry. The lost colonists had not fled in panic: they were safe after all.

He remained deeply puzzled as to why they would have chosen to move to Croatoan. Although it was Manteo's homeland, it was a tiny island with poor defences and very little fertile ground. White had expected them to move nearer to Chesapeake Bay, if they moved at all, and the more his men searched the derelict village the deeper the mystery became. "We entred the palisado [the stockade] where we found many barres or iron, two pigges of lead, foure yron fowlers, iron sacker-shotte, and such like heavie things, throwen here and there, almost overgrowen with grasse and weedes." Many of the heavier guns were remnants of Ralph Lane's colony and would have been difficult to transport in anything other than a large pinnace, but it was strange that the colonists had left bars of iron and pigs of lead, since these were necessary to make shot for their muskets.

"Wee went along by the water side towards the poynt of the creeke to see if we could find any of their botes or pinnisse," writes White, "but we could perceive no signe of them." Some of the mariners had remained in the village to conduct a more thorough search. They soon located a number of items, and ran to the shore to notify White. "[They] tolde us that they had found where divers chests had bene hidden, and long sithence digged up againe and broken up, and much of the goods in them spoyled and scattered about, but nothing left of such things as the savages knew any use of, undefaced." The lost colonists had been true to their word in looking after White's possessions, for they had buried all of his trunks in a vain attempt to prevent them from being looted.

"Captaine Cocke and I went to the place which was in the ende of an olde trench," he writes, "wheere wee found five chests that had been carefully hidden of [by] the planters." These had clearly been dug up by the Indians, smashed open, and stripped of everything of value. "Three were my owne," wrote White, "and about the place many of my things spoyled and broken, and my bookes torne from the covers, the frames of some of my pictures and mappes rotten and spoyled with rayne, and my armour almost eaten through with rust." He did not blame the colonists for the loss of his possessions, for he knew they had been looted by the Indians. "This could bee no other but the deede of the savages," he wrote, "[who] watched the departure of our men to Croatoan, and assoone as they were departed, digged up every place where they suspected any thing to be buried." His only consolation was that his daughter and granddaughter were in safe hands, for Croatoan was "the place where Manteo was borne, and the savages of the iland our friends."

There was no time for further exploration as it was getting late and the weather was fast deteriorating. Cocke ordered the men to row back to the *Hopewell*, "for the weather beganne to overcast, and very likely that a foule and stormie night would ensue." It was a long, hard journey back to the ship, and the men arrived in the nick of time, for "the winde and seas were so greatly risen that wee doubted our cables and anchors would scarcely holde untill morning."

The men passed an uncomfortable night, but the wind dropped slightly in the morning, "and it was agreed by the captaine and myselfe . . . to wey anchor and goe for the place at Croatoan." No sooner had they set out on their journey than the wind rose once again and the *Hopewell* began to be driven toward the shore. The ship's crew began a desperate battle with the sea. "If it had not chanced that wee had fallen into a chanell of deeper water," writes White, "we could never have got cleare of the poynt."

Captain Cocke was growing increasingly alarmed at the dangers of the coastline, especially since he had lost three of his anchors and only had one left. As the weather "grew to be fouler and fouler," he called White into his cabin and announced that he considered it too dangerous to remain any longer in these waters. He proposed that they head for the Caribbean, and return to Croatoan to search for the lost colonists the following spring. White reluctantly agreed with Cocke, but the party was soon to find that even this unsatisfactory plan was thwarted by the wind. The little *Hopewell* was blown thousands of miles across the Atlantic, unable to halt her eastward voyage until she took refuge at the Azores. Captain Cocke was by now so disheartened that he decided to abandon any attempt at sailing back to Virginia. Tired of ill luck at sea, he "framed our due course for England."

It was a weary and dejected White who stepped ashore at Plymouth. He knew that he would never again cross the Atlantic, for his patience and stamina were at an end. All he had were memories, hopes, and dreams of what might have been. In a letter to Richard Hakluyt, he wrote a weary valediction that signalled the end of his ties with America. With a heavy heart, he handed over responsibility for the colonists "to the merciful help of the Almighty, whom I most humbly beseech to helpe and comfort them."

Governor White had done all he could.

12

One Bess for Another

John White was broken by his experiences in Virginia. His attempt to govern a colony had proved a catastrophe, and the bitterest aspect of the failure was that it was due to his own inadequacies as leader. He had disappointed Ralegh, but he had also disappointed himself.

There was almost too much to mourn. He had lost all his personal possessions and, worse still, he had lost his family. Weary, dejected, and physically debilitated by hardship, he moved himself to a quiet farmstead in Ireland and devoted long hours to thinking about "the evils and unfortunate events." He retained a flicker of hope that somewhere in the vast forests of America his daughter and granddaughter were still alive, but he was pessimistic about ever seeing them again. He concluded that his governorship had ended "unfortunately," adding that it was "as luckelesse to many, as sinister to myselfe."

It was the end of a dream that had begun with high hopes. Three and a half years earlier, he had set sail with great optimism, his gleaming new coat of arms signifying his status as governor of Virginia. His enthusiasm had encouraged men, women, and children to sign up for his colony, and its success seemed at last to be within reach. Now it was time to count the costs—not just of his own failed colony, but of everything that had gone wrong since the initial triumph of 1584. Scores of English lives had been lost—hundreds, if the 1587 colonists were dead—and most had met with gruesome or unpleasant ends. If it was not typhoid or the flux, contracted in the sickly waters of the Caribbean, then it was the arrow and club of a hostile Indian.

The setbacks had been the result of human failings, miscalculations, and sheer incompetence. The grounding of the *Tiger* in 1585 had ruined the chances of Ralph Lane's colony; the settlers' brutal treatment of the Indians had been an act of incalculable folly. Only when it was too late did the English realise that their colony was doomed to fail without the active support of the native tribesmen.

John White was not alone in abandoning any plans of returning to America. One by one, all the leading lights were dropping out of the picture—unwilling or unable to sacrifice themselves in this most adventurous of projects. Ralph Lane, like White, had settled in Ireland, where he was appointed "muster-master of the garrisons." He fought with considerable bravery against the rebels, and was rewarded with a knighthood in 1593. Energetic to the last, he nevertheless expressed no desire to return to Virginia. He died in Ireland in 1603, by which time he was well into his sixties.

Simon Fernandez ended his connections with Ralegh soon after the 1587 fiasco, perhaps because he was held responsible for what had happened. He never again sailed across the Atlantic, although he did help in the fight against the Spanish Armada and served in at least one further action against Spain. He is last heard of in 1590 when he accompanied an English war fleet to the Azores. He probably died on this expedition, since he disappears from the records.

Sir Richard Grenville's exit from the Roanoke story was altogether more spectacular. Throughout his life he had been fired by an uncontrollable energy. Had he kept his mind focussed on America, there is little doubt that he could have overseen the successful establishment of a colony. But his hatred of Spain drew him south rather than west, and in the spring of 1591 he set off as second-in-command of a fleet in search of King Philip's treasure ship. When his superior, Lord Howard, sighted fifty-three enemy vessels, he took fright and ordered his ships to flee. Grenville was disgusted at such cowardice and "utterly refused to turne from the enimie, alledging that he would rather chose to dye then to dishonour himselfe."

The fight that followed was the crowning moment of an extraordinary career; it would quickly enter the annals of British history, largely because of Sir Walter's gripping account of the battle. Grenville had never been one to doubt his own abilities, but to pitch one vessel against fifty-three suggested a deluded degree of self-confidence. Yet the loyalty of his crew is proof enough of his inspirational leadership, for the soldiers fought for hour after hour, until "all the powder of the *Revenge*, to the last barrell, was now spent, all her pikes broken, fortie of her best men slaine, and the most part of the rest hurt." So horrendous was the destruction that the ship was awash with human parts, "being marvellous unsaverie, filled with bloud and bodies of deade and wounded men like a slaughter house." The ship itself was a wreck. "[It] had sixe foote water in hold; three shot under water ... and was besides so crusht and brused as she could never be removed out of the place." Sir Richard continued to rally his men until his body was so riddled with shot that he was scarcely able to speak. In his hour of death, his demonic nature asserted itself in truly horrific fashion. He vowed to blow his ship to smithereens, sacrificing his men to prevent the Spanish from capturing them. This proved too much for his crew, which refused to carry out his orders. Grenville died in agony, screaming that they were "traitors and dogs."

Only two of the original adventurers retained any interest in America: Thomas Harriot and Sir Walter Ralegh himself. But it was to be some years before their gazes would again be focussed on the western horizon, for both were deeply involved in other projects. Harriot had resumed his love affair with algebra; Ralegh had rediscovered his interest in women.

He had fallen in love with one of the queen's maids of honour—an act of considerable folly that was never likely to find favour with Her Majesty. When, two years previously, his rival at court, the Earl of Essex, had secretly married without the queen's permission, Elizabeth had been so infuriated that she banished Essex from the court. And when her maid eloped with another favourite, the queen gave her such a thrashing that she broke the poor girl's finger.

It is not hard to see why Ralegh was so attracted to Bess Throckmorton. She was quick-thinking, passionate, and independent of mind—qualities born of her troubled upbringing. Her father, Queen Elizabeth's first ambassador to Paris, had died when she was six and the money left for her care was quickly lost through poor investment. When her mother also died, young Bess was left with some bed hangings, an armful of clothes, and very few prospects. It was her courtier brother, Arthur, who saved the day by using his charm to secure Bess a position as one of the queen's maids of the Privy Chamber. In November 1584, she joined the inner circle of vestals who served and worshipped the queen.

Bess was very different from the other "witches" of the Chamber, and Sir Walter quickly found himself delighted by her frank honesty. He was now thirty-six years old and growing weary of his sterile relationship with the untouchable virgin. His new Bess was sensual and bright-eyed, with a physical attractiveness quite different from the queen's chaste beauty. Ralegh revelled in the voluptuous pleasures of her body:

> . . . *a violet breath and lips of jelly*
> *Her hair not black nor over-bright,*
> *And of the softest down her belly.*

His love for her soon developed into a passion, and he wrote fiery poems about "sweet embraces, such delights, as will shorten tedious nights." Their trysts were snatched in the brief moments when they could escape the queen, and they covered their tracks with skill. It was many months before Elizabeth's curtain-twitching gossipers learned the best piece of scandal in years: that Bess was pregnant and the couple were secretly married.

Different people reacted in different ways. Arthur, Walter's brother-in-law, was so worried about being ruined by the affair that he rushed to the nearest tailor and bought the queen a waistcoat for £9 and two beautiful ruffs, hoping that such costly gifts would assuage her wrath. Ralegh's instinct was to flee the country, and he was about to step aboard a flotilla of privateers when he was forbidden from doing so by his still-unknowing queen. Bess herself tried to pretend nothing untoward had happened; when her downy belly grew so large that it became hard to conceal her pregnancy, she mumbled excuses to the queen about having to absent herself from the court. In February 1592, Arthur noted in his diary that "my sister came hither to lie here."

The baby was born at the end of March and given the name Damerei in honour of Ralegh's distant Plantagenet forebears. Three weeks later, Bess returned to the court and resumed her position as maid of the Privy Chamber, acting as if nothing had happened. No one spoke of the matter—although word soon spread—and the court held its breath and awaited the queen's response.

When she learned the news, Elizabeth's reaction was strange. There was no public outburst and no wild emotion. For more than three months after Bess's return, she said nothing. When Walter at last approached her over a private matter, she might have expected him to offer his sincere apologies. Quite the contrary: he boldly asked for her signature on the lease of Sherborne Castle. The queen obliged, giving him the West Country estate he so craved, perhaps in the hope that her generosity might lead him to beg for forgiveness.

She was playing a game of cat and mouse, signalling that her inward fury would be assuaged by an abject apology. But Ralegh refused to respond. Too proud, too arrogant, too used to manipulating the queen, he was unable to admit his failing. "Sir Walter

Ralegh . . . hath been too inward with one of Her Majesty's maids," chuckled one courtier. "All think the Tower will be his dwelling." They were right. In the first week of August 1592, Walter and Bess were locked up—and Elizabeth went on a royal tour. It was anyone's guess how long they would be imprisoned.

Bess was distraught and immediately put quill to parchment, writing to the queen with her characteristically eccentric spelling. "I am dayly put in hope of my delivery," she wrote. "I assure you trewly I never desiared nor never wolde desiar my lebbarti without the good likeking ne advising of Sir W R."

Ralegh's letters were more mawkish. "My heart was never broken till this day," he wrote, "that I hear the queen goes away so far off . . . and am now left behind her, in a dark prison all alone." This was not strictly true, for his beloved Bess was imprisoned with him, along with a small army of servants, but Ralegh never fought shy of hyperbole. He wrote ever more extravagant letters about his jailer-queen: "[I] was wont to behold her riding like Alexander, hunting like Diana, walking like Venus, the gentle wind blowing her fair hair about her pure cheeks, like a nymph; sometime sitting in the shade like a goddess, sometime singing like an angel, sometime playing like Orpheus."

It was neither Bess's pleas nor Ralegh's flattery that won them their release. It was the arrival in Dartmouth of the richest prize ship ever captured during Queen Elizabeth's reign. The cavernous holds of the *Madre de Dios* were packed with 540 tons of sweet-smelling nutmeg, mace, and cloves, as well as pearls, amber, and musk. Within hours, hundreds of hawkers and profiteers had pitched up at the port to haggle over booty smuggled ashore by sailors. The queen was livid, for she claimed a large percentage as her own, and dispatched Robert Cecil to stop the plunder. But her hunchbacked courtier was unable to control the unruly mariners; he wrote despairingly that "fowler ways, desperater ways, nor more obstinate people did I never meet with." He estimated that the queen had already lost £20,000, a figure that was increasing daily. So huge was the scale of the disaster the she was urged to send someone who could wield authority over these truculent thieves. Sir John Hawkins declared there was only one man up to the task. He called for "the especial man," Sir Walter Ralegh, to be released immediately from the Tower after spending just five weeks behind bars.

The queen obliged with scarcely a murmur, commanding her prisoner to recover her booty. Ralegh seized the moment and vowed to have his revenge on all the merchants who were robbing the queen of her spoils. "If I meet any of them coming up," he railed, "if it be upon the wildest heath in all the way, I mean to strip them as naked as ever they were born. For it is infinite [amounts of booty] that Her Majesty has been robbed, and that of the most rare things." He neglected to mention that he, like the queen, had invested a huge sum in the privateering expedition and had a pressing concern to recover his own share of the loot.

Cecil was astonished at the effect of Ralegh's presence on the corrupt seadogs. His own arrival had singularly failed to make any impression, but Ralegh commanded total respect in the West Country. "I assure you," wrote an envious Cecil, "all the mariners come to him with such shouts and joy as I never saw a man more troubled to quiet them in my life."

Working with ruthless efficiency to track down the queen's treasure, Ralegh did sterling work, recovering a large part of the spoils. But he was all too aware of the cloud that continued to hang over him, causing Cecil to remark that "his heart is broken . . . whensoever he is saluted with congratulations for his liberty, he doth answer; 'No, I am still the Queen of England's poor captive.' "

If he hoped to be rewarded for his efforts, he was in for a rude shock. When the queen came to divide the spoils, she stripped Ralegh of his share and plunged him into debt. His investments in the venture had been huge; now he was left with a net loss. She was a great deal more generous with herself: she had ventured two ships and just £1,800; her payback for this small investment was a staggering £80,000. "If God hath sent it for my ransom," wrote Walter, "I hope Her Majesty, of her abundant goodness, will accept it."

The queen was indeed better disposed towards Ralegh. After briefly remanding him to the Tower, she released both him and Bess in time for Christmas 1592. He was still in disgrace and would remain so for five years, but he was at least a free man.

For the first time in years, Ralegh found himself in straightened circumstances. The few privateering missions in which he invested never seemed to reap the dividends of previous years, and one expedition to the Caribbean cost him so much in victuals, customs, and the customary percentage for the lord admiral that Ralegh wrote contemptuously that "wee might have gotten more to have sent them a fishinge." His American projects had swallowed much of his wealth—Hakluyt said that the 1587 colony alone cost more than £30,000—and his estates were providing him with only a trickle of income in these lean and difficult times.

The little money left at his disposal was now spent on his new home, Sherborne Castle. The castle was picturesque in a mildewed sort of way, but hardly the sort of place in which Sir Walter wished to live with his wife and family. He tore down much of the building and began work on a replacement property, an elegant manor with a profusion of chimneys and heraldic beasts that jutted like gargoyles from its hexagonal towers. The gardens were no less splendid; he took special delight in planting rare shrubs and flowers brought back from distant lands.

Ralegh had not forgotten White's colonists, but his interest in their fate did not resurface until some sixteen months after his release from the Tower. He was shaken into action by some disturbing news. In April 1594, Ananias Dare, John White's son-in-law, was proclaimed legally dead by virtue of an old rule that loss of contact for seven years implied death. His estate was placed into the hands of a relative, who was to hold it in trust until Ananias's illegitimate son turned eighteen. This news seriously alarmed Ralegh. His legal title to Virginia was dependent upon his having settled a permanent colony within seven years. Only by maintaining that the 1587 colonists were still alive could Ralegh retain his title.

The Dare case was hotly debated in London and sparked off a flurry of rumours about the whereabouts of the lost colonists. The herbalist John Gerard—a member of the syndicate that bought the rights to trade with the colonists from Ralegh in 1589—hedged his bets, arguing they were certainly alive, "if neither untimely death by murdering, or pestilence, corrupt aire, bloodie flixes, or some other mortall sickness hath not destroied them." George Abbot, future archbishop of Canterbury, used a confusing double negative to express his pessimistic view that "the possession of this Virginia is not discontinued, and the country at the present left to the olde inhabitants."

When Ralegh did, at last, bestir himself, his prime concern was to line his coffers, and his colonial eye was drawn at first to the treasure-rich land of Guiana in South America. Ralegh always had a streak of fantasy coursing though his veins, and his quest for the golden wealth of El Dorado was a manifestation of it. But gold was not his only goal; he also intended to call at Roanoke himself—his one and only attempt to go there in person—to land supplies "for the relief of those English which [he] had planted in Virginia."

The mission failed in every respect: Ralegh neither found the legendary El Dorado nor did he dig up any nuggets of gold. When he headed for Roanoke, "extremity of weather forst me from the said coast." Ralegh returned to England even poorer than before, and none the wiser as to the fate of his colonists.

On his return, his five-year period of disgrace was brought to an end when the queen recalled him to London to resume his position as Captain of her Guard. Ralegh was alarmed to see how time had withered her features; her face was thin and haggard, her teeth were brown, and she wore an extraordinary red wig that accentuated the sickly pallor of her skin. Although her wit was as sharp as ever, she was a pale shadow of the coquette that he had once worshipped. But Ralegh, too, was no longer a youth. The hardships in Guiana had turned his hair a silver-grey, while action in the Azores had left his left leg shattered, and he now walked with a pronounced limp. But he had retained his silken charm; he soon "rid abroad with the queen, and had private conference with her." Elizabeth delighted in his company and forgave Ralegh for his sins. He was at last back in favour with the queen.

His reconciliation with Elizabeth coincided with a renewed interest in Roanoke. In about 1599 he sent the first of several expeditions to the Outer Banks to search for the lost colonists. Little is known of the first two voyages—except that they failed to reach Roanoke—while the third was said to have suffered from "extremitie of weather and losse of some principal ground tackle." In 1602 Ralegh began preparations for a fourth expedition, commanded by Captains Samuel Mace and Bartholemew Gilbert. They were given one order, and it could not have been clearer: they were "to seeke out the people for Sir Walter Ralegh, left neere those parts in the yeere 1587."

Mace had been in command of the previous expedition. Before setting sail, he had made contact with Harriot for advice on what supplies the colonists—who had been left to their own devices for fourteen years—might be needing. Harriot took an extremely optimistic view of the resourcefulness of the men and women left behind by White, believing that they would have been able to make clothes, nails, and pots and pans. Aware that the manufacture of tools would have caused them the greatest difficulty, he advised Mace to take five dozen hatchets, twenty mattocks, twenty iron shovels, 600 knives, and lead powder and shot. He also supplied him with a short list of Algonkian words so that the English search parties would be able to communicate with the Indians.

The fourth expedition set sail with high hopes of success, "but the wind blew so sore, and the sea was so high" that the ships were soon separated by Atlantic storms. Bartholemew Gilbert's vessel was

When Ralegh set sail for Guiana, he vowed to call at Roanoke "for the relief of those English which he had planted."

driven towards Chesapeake Bay, where the men dropped anchor and jumped ashore. It was a bad decision, for "the Indians set upon them and one or two of them fell downe wounded." Only a few men made it back to England.

The other vessel's course was more mysterious. For months, Samuel Mace seems to have steered through storms and swirling sea mists, never entirely sure as to his position on the map. He arrived back in London at some point during the summer of 1603, and rushed straight to Durham House to inform Sir Walter Ralegh of the deeds and discoveries of his voyage.

13

A Miracle Among Savages

On the evening of March 26, 1603, a small group of men could be seen gathered at the window of Ralegh's study in Durham House. They were sobbing into their lace ruffs, distraught at the extraordinary scene that was being played out on the river below. A melancholy procession of torch-lit barges was slowly progressing down the Thames, and the cargo of this cortege was the embalmed corpse of the Virgin Queen, the *weroanza* of Virginia. Elizabeth I was dead and a golden age had come to an end. By dawn the next day, her lead coffin was lying in state at Whitehall Palace, nestled on a bed of black velvet and adorned with outlandish bunches of ostrich plumes. It lent an exotic touch to an otherwise doleful scene. Even in death, Elizabeth was flamboyant.

The outburst of national grief that followed her passing was so infectious that some wondered if the nation would ever recover. Londoners wept openly whenever the queen's name was mentioned, while the court, deprived of its glittering centrepiece, bewailed the loss of its celestial Astrea. Nature herself was afflicted with grief. According to William Camden, the fish in the Thames were so distraught at the sight of the death barge that they "wept out their eyes of pearle."

It was more than a month before the queen was actually buried.

On April 28, the lead coffin was carried in procession to Westminster Abbey. The four horses were draped in black velvet and the funeral bier, which carried the coffin, was surmounted by a life-sized wax effigy of the queen dressed in her robes of state and clutching an orb and sceptre. Following behind were thousands of noblemen, courtiers, heralds, and officials—all weeping quietly. Many of these were young men, the offspring of the late queen's long-dead favourites, but at the rear of the procession was an aged, limping, but still handsome courtier. Sir Walter Ralegh was leading the Gentleman Pensioners in their mourning, their gilded halberds pointing at the ground in token of their grief. All knew that this was the end of an era: "her hearse (as it was borne) seemed to be an island swimming in water, for round it there rained showers of tears." So wrote one onlooker; another—John Stowe—later recalled "such a general sighing, groaning and weeping as the like hath not seen or known in the memory of man."

Elizabeth's successor was King James VI of Scotland, an uncharismatic monarch who could scarcely have compared less favourably with his illustrious predecessor. James had no truck with flamboyant dress and manners and cared little for the gilded pleasantries of polite society. He was so malcoordinated at table that it was said to be possible to identify every meal he had eaten for seven years by studying the scraps of dried food stuck to his clothes. He had a phobia of water, both as a drink and as a means of cleanliness, and although he occasionally "rubbed his fingers' ends slightly with the wet end of a napkin," he rarely washed. As a result, he itched insufferably and frequently scratched his sweaty skin. When he was nervous, he had the alarming habit of fiddling with his codpiece.

He delighted in coarse jests and bawdy innuendo, as had the late queen, yet he lacked the witty sophistication of Elizabeth. When the Elizabethan courtiers flocked to meet him and pressed too closely, he warned that if they came any nearer, "I will pull down my breeches and they shall also see my arse." It was an unpleasant threat and the courtiers quickly retreated.

Ralegh led the Gentleman Pensioners at the queen's funeral. All knew it was the end of an era, and "it rained showers of tears."

Such a man was unlikely to find favour with Ralegh, and their first meeting was not a success. Sir Walter rode out to Northamptonshire to greet his new king, only to find himself dismissed with a curt jest: "Oh my soul, mon, I have heard rawly of thee." Everything about Ralegh offended the king, right down to his wearing an earring—one of James's pet hates. The king also abhorred tobacco and despised Sir Walter for introducing it to the court, arguing that England's precious reserves of silver were being wasted in lining the pockets of Spain's tobacco merchants, who had been quick to build to tobacco industry to supply the growing number of pipe enthusiasts.

Shortly after acceding to the throne, King James sat down to write *A Counterblaste to Tobacco*, in which he denounced smoking as the "toy" that was ruining the country, and argued—with extraordinary prescience—that it made "a kitchin of the inward parts of man, soiling and infecting them with an unctious and oily kinde of soote." He accused Ralegh of introducing "this savage custome," and at the same time took the opportunity to denounce him for having brought "savages" to England. "The poore wilde barbarous men died," wrote the king, "but that vile, barbarous custome is yet alive, yea, in fresh

King James I cared little for courtly life. He rarely washed, itched insufferably, and fiddled with his codpiece when nervous

vigor." He added that "it seemes a miracle to me, how a custom springing from so vile a ground, and brought by a father so generally hated"—Ralegh—"should be welcomed on so slender a warrant." Less than a year after his coronation, King James had imposed a massive new tax on the importation of tobacco, raising it from twopence per pound to "the somme of six shillings and eighte pence uppon everye pound waight thereof."

Ralegh's first meeting with the king was an ominous beginning to a relationship that was already doomed. Unbeknown to Ralegh, King James's mind had been poisoned by ambitious courtiers anxious to secure their own advancement by blackening his name. One of these was Lord Henry Howard, who wrote a string of secret letters to the king in which he described Ralegh as "the greatest Lucifer that hath lived in our age" and as one who "in pride exceedeth all men alive." Such insults, taken seriously by the nervous Scottish monarch, quickly turned him against the darling of the Elizabethan court. When the secretary of state, Robert Cecil, learned of the king's hatred, he dropped his old friend with unseemly haste. He then proceeded to fan the flames by blackening Ralegh's name with Machiavellian adroitness, hinting that he was dangerous, treacherous, and an atheist.

Ralegh's undoing came even more quickly than his spectacular rise. Two months after acceding to the throne, King James called in all royal monopolies. At one stroke, Ralegh lost the chief source of his income. A fortnight later he was deprived of his position as Captain of the Guard, and in June he was ordered by the king to vacate Durham House. This was a bitter blow. Ralegh had spent a fortune on turning this rotting mansion into a home and scientific laboratory, as well as the nerve centre of his New World enterprise. King James brushed aside Ralegh's remonstrances with disdain and ordered him to leave within two weeks. There was to be no compensation.

His fall from grace was soon to take a far more sinister turn. In July 1603 he was quizzed about his involvement in an alleged treasonable conspiracy against the king. After failing to convince his enemies on the Privy Council of his innocence, he was promptly confined to the Tower with a charge of treason hanging over his head. "All my good turns [are] forgotten," he wrote in a letter to Bess, "all my services, hazards and expenses for my country—plantings, discoveries, fights, councils and whatsoever else—malice hath now covered over." He was so anxious about his forthcoming trial, and so nervous about being found guilty of treason, that he reacted with indifference to the news of Samuel Mace's return from Virginia.

Samuel Mace could not have chosen a worse time to arrive back in London. Not only was his master in jail, but the city itself was "most grievously infected with a terrible plague" and the entire court had moved to the countryside. The affairs of state were in paralysis "by reason of the great infection . . . [and it] being very dangerous at such tymes to draw any multitude of people together."

Mace could find no one interested in listening to his story. Thomas Harriot had gone into hiding, concerned that his association with Sir Walter would implicate him in the accusations of treason. The city chroniclers—who would normally have sought out a newly returned captain—had disappeared with the court.

It was an unfortunate end to an exciting adventure, and it meant that Mace's voyage to Virginia was destined to become one of the great mysteries of the Roanoke story. There is no account of his landfall in America, nor is there a detailed record of the news he brought back about the lost colonists. Only a few snippets of information have survived, but they collectively suggest that Mace had unearthed some tantalising news about White's settlers.

He also seems to have brought back some Indians from Virginia, for a group of them were lodged at Cecil House on the Strand, just a stone's throw from Ralegh's old home. The colonial enthusiast Sir Walter Cope was staying in the house at the time and arranged for the visitors to demonstrate their skills at handling a dugout canoe.

According to the Cecil House account book, the Indians were rewarded with the princely sum of five shillings. They were then guided ashore and entertained at Cecil House by one of Lord Cecil's servants.

What happened next is unclear, for no one lodged in Cecil House saw fit to record the conversations that took place behind that grandiose facade. It is quite possible that Cope had acquired sufficient knowledge of Algonkian from Harriot to coax some information about the lost colonists from the Indians. Or Mace himself may have learned something from tribesmen on the shores of Chesapeake Bay. Although details are unlikely ever to come to light, one thing is certain: in the dying days of that plague-ridden summer of 1603, someone, somewhere, had turned up evidence to suggest that Ralegh's colonists were still alive.

The seafarer George Waymouth was one of those who had learned news of their survival. In his 1604 treatise about America, *The Jewell of Artes*, he asserted that a small number of men and women had lived through their seventeen-year ordeal, although he conceded that Virginia was "but weakly planted with the English" and that these survivors were in extreme danger. "[They are] weakly defended from the invasions of the heathen," he wrote, "amongst whom they dwell [and are] subject unto manifolde perills and dangers." Waymouth presented his treatise to the king on two occasions, urging him to dispatch building materials so that the settlers might construct a fortified town. His treatise clearly assumed that King James also knew of the lost colonists, and served as a polite reminder to His Majesty that he had subjects on the far side of the Atlantic for whom he was responsible.

Waymouth was not the only man to have heard that the lost colonists were still alive. Rumour of their survival had begun circulating in taverns and stews and was soon so widespread that their ordeal was being referred to in London's playhouses and written up in ballads and broadsheets. When *Eastward Hoe* was performed to a packed playhouse in 1605, the audience laughed cruelly at jokes about White's lost colonists. "A whole country of English is there, man," says Captain Seagull, "bred of those that were left there in '79 [he means 1587]. They have married with the Indians, and make 'em bring forth as beautiful faces as any we have in England; and therefore the Indians are so in love with 'em that all the treasure they have, they lay at their feet."

Languishing in prison awaiting trial, Ralegh was powerless to send a ship to Virginia. He had been stripped of his rights to America, and responsibility for the lost colonists—as well as for continued colonisation—had reverted to the king. But James was simply not interested in a land that was inhabited by "savages." Although Captain Waymouth repeatedly tried to persuade him to renew England's colonial projects, the king refused to listen. In his eyes, Virginia was "vile," and too long a time spent in the company of "savages" would turn even the most civilised Englishman into a barbarian. "Shall we . . . abase ourselves so far as to imitate these beastly Indians, slaves to the Spaniards, refuse to the world, and as yet aliens from the holy covernant of God?" Using sarcasm to underscore his point, he suggested that enthusiasts for colonisation should stick feathers in their hair and walk around stark naked. King James was not the man to search for the lost colonists, nor did he have any intention of masterminding any new plan to colonise America. He had more important goals, one of which was to destroy Sir Walter Ralegh.

Sir Walter was brought to trial in November 1603. He had no clear knowledge of the charges against him until they were read out in court, and since he was accused of treason, he was forbidden any representation. There was no cross-examination of the prosecution, no investigation of the evidence. Indeed, the court had already decided upon Ralegh's guilt; it was merely a question of proving it in as short a time as possible.

Ralegh categorically denied the charges and launched into an impassioned defence of his own conduct. "Your words cannot condemn me," he told the bullying attorney general. "My innocency is my defence. *Prove* against me any one thing of the many that you have broke, and I will confess all." He defended himself with considerable skill against a torrent of abuse, innuendo, and false witnesses, but nothing he could say was going to persuade the sham court of his innocence. Although no evidence was produced to substantiate the charges, the jury reached its verdict in minutes. Ralegh was found guilty of treason—a crime that had only one punishment: "You shall be drawn on a hurdle through the open streets to the place of your execution," declared Lord Chief Justice Popham, "there to be hanged and cut down alive, and your body shall be opened, your heart and bowels plucked out, and your privy members cut off and thrown into the fire before your eyes. Then your head to be stricken off from your body and your body shall be divided into four quarters, to be disposed of at the king's pleasure." Popham paused for a moment before adding, "And God have mercy on your soul."

The trial and verdict had a most unfortunate consequence for King James. For years, Ralegh had been an object of hatred and ridicule among the poor and needy. Now, those very same people took pity on the underdog and made him the man of the hour, celebrated as a champion of truth and justice. "Never was a man so hated and so popular in so short a time," declared one, while a Scottish friend of King James's warned that "when he saw Sir Walter Ralegh first, he was so led with the common hatred that he would have gone a hundred miles to see him hanged, [but] he would, 'ere they parted, have gone a thousand to save his life." King James mulled over this unexpected development and, after fiddling with his codpiece, heeded the popular sentiment. Ralegh was granted a reprieve on the day of his execution and was sent back to the Tower—a convicted traitor stripped of his rights. "Name, blood, gentility or estate I have none," he wrote in despair. He was living on borrowed time.

Life in the Tower proved surprisingly comfortable. Sir Walter had two servants to attend his needs and a third to bring him fresh ale. Bess moved in as well, along with their second son Wat

(Damerei had died in infancy), and Thomas Harriot was a regular visitor. Ralegh continued to harbour dreams of sending a new fleet to Virginia; shortly before his imprisonment, he had written a letter to Robert Cecil in which he predicted that "I shal yet live to see it an Inglishe nation." Yet even he must have been dismayed to learn that the man who picked up his broken colonial baton was none other than Sir John Popham, the Lord Chief Justice, who had presided over his trial. Popham's role was to act as chief organiser of the new enterprise—much like Sir Walter—but his motivations were not quite so noble as those of Ralegh and Harriot. He harboured no dreams of civilising the "savages" and spreading the gospel through a "barbarian" land. He had recently completed the draft of an act of Parliament which made banishment "into such parts beyond the seas" the punishment for vagrancy, and many courtiers muttered that his only interest in the new colony was as a human waste pit—a land that could be "stockt and planted out of all the gaoles of England."

Popham's plans took some time to formulate. It was not until the spring of 1606 that this "huge, heavie and ugly man" declared himself "affectionately bent to the plantation of Virginia" and began to summon "gentlemen merchants &c unto him." Royal involvement was to be minimal, for King James did not care one jot for the land of the Virgin Queen. On one of the few occasions he brought up the subject of Virginia, it was to ask Lord Southampton if it was true that the skies there were filled with flying squirrels. Southampton confirmed James's query, later confiding to a friend that "you know so well how he is affected to these toys."

The new project for Virginia was rooted in the triumphs and failures of the past. To those involved, it represented the last great Elizabethan adventure—a burst of energy and enthusiasm that belonged to a waning age. The commanders, colonists, and sailors were fired by the same dynamic recklessness that had fuelled the likes of Grenville and Lane; even the maps and charts they loaded into their ships were those prepared by Ralegh's men two decades earlier.

Even the new Virginia Company, set up to establish "a colonie of sondrie of our people into that parte of America," was dominated by Ralegh's men. One of the leading grantees was none other than his old friend Richard Hakluyt, whose monumental anthology of exploration, *The Principall Navigations*, had helped reawaken enthusiasm for the New World. It contained all of the journals and diaries from the Roanoke enterprise, including those of Ralph Lane, John White, and Thomas Harriot, as well as ships' logs, letters, and charters concerning America. It was priceless information for the new organisation, for it gathered together everything that was known about "the great and ample country of Virginia."

When Ralegh had sent his colonists to sea in 1585, he had been aided by Queen Elizabeth I, who loaned him a ship, weaponry, and gunpowder. King James showed no inclination to follow suit, and the Virginia Company was therefore obliged to cut costs by acquiring older and cheaper equipment when it came to assemble an expedition. The armour, swords, and bucklers were Elizabethan castoffs, obsolete military equipment that was little use in the set piece battles now common in Europe. The tents and textiles supplied to the new colonists were faded and worn and had cloth seals marked with the late queen's insignia. Even the coined money belonged to the Elizabethan age: the shillings, sixpences, and half-groats carried by the settlers all bore the portrait of the late queen.

Talk of a new colonising expedition spread like wildfire through the back streets of London, and preparations for the voyage gathered apace. By learning from the mistakes of Ralegh's abortive colony, the new organisation was able to assemble the proper tools and victuals with lightning speed. Hakluyt's presence in the Virginia Company proved especially useful, for it was he who had prepared the lists of workmen, tools, and goods that were considered necessary for the first Roanoke project in 1585. The dockside at Wapping was soon alive with the bustle of supplies being packed, bottled, and prepared for loading.

Even the fleet was assembled without too much difficulty. The

Virginia merchants hired three ships—the 120-ton *Susan Constant*, the smaller *Godspeed*, and the diminutive *Discovery*. The only threat to the speedy progress came when the crew of the *Susan Constant*, who had been "tiplinge and drinkinge" for much of the day, lost control of their ship and allowed her to slam into another vessel.

With everything going more or less according to plan, the Virginia grantees began casting about for a suitable commander to lead their expedition. Mindful of the disasters that had afflicted the Roanoke voyages, they plumped for the solidly dependable Christopher Newport, a swashbuckling, one-armed Elizabethan adventurer who had accompanied John White's Roanoke rescue mission in 1590 and was one of the most experienced seamen of the golden age. He was known as "Captain Newport of the one hand," but his disability did not deter him from launching himself into his new employment with gusto. He was given "sole charge and command" until the expedition reached Virginia: then, and only then, he would open the sealed packet that named the president and council of the new colony.

There were some 104 settlers on the three ships, of whom half were "gentlemen" and the rest labourers. There were no women in this first fleet, and the lack of farmers or husbandmen suggests that no one had learned the painful lessons from Roanoke. It would not be long before the colonists were bemoaning the fact that they lacked "some skillfull man to husband, sett, plant and dresse vynes, sugar-canes, olives, rapes, hemp, flax, lycoris, pruyns . . ."

The fleet sailed from London shortly before Christmas 1606 and made speedy progress towards the Caribbean. From here it followed the now familiar route along the Virginian coastline. The fleet's destination was Chesapeake Bay—Hakluyt had seen to that—and the first priority of the settlers was to establish a fortified village in a strategic location. There was to be no search for John White's lost colonists in the early months, for it would require all their effort to establish themselves on foreign soil, but they had not been forgotten. Many in London were curious about their fate, and there was much discussion as to whether they could have survived almost twenty years in the wilderness without a single supply ship from England. Few gave any credence to White's suggestion that all the colonists had moved themselves to Croatoan. The consensus was that the majority had relocated their settlement to somewhere close to the southern shores of Chesapeake Bay, which, as all who had studied the Roanoke enterprise knew, was fertile, friendly, and "not to be excelled by any other whatsoever."

No one was keener to learn whether the lost colonists were still alive than the merchants of the Virginia Company, who were only too aware that they would be a source of invaluable information about the land and its "savages." But they also knew that the first priority of the new settlers—and the reason why they had set sail—was to establish themselves in Virginia and build dwellings and storehouses. The search for White's men and women was likely to be a large-scale undertaking, for more than sixty miles of land separated Chesapeake Bay from the northern end of Pamlico Sound, almost all of it uncharted forest inhabited by bears and "wolfish dogges." To search such a huge expanse of wilderness would require a considerable number of heavily armed colonists, especially if they were going to be marching through potentially hostile territory. It was a task that would have to be carried out at the earliest opportunity, that was certain, but not in the first days of the colony.

At the end of April, some four months after setting sail, the sailors and colonists awoke to a wonderful sight: "faire meddowes and goodly trees," wrote one, "with such fresh waters running through the woods as I was almost ravished at the first sight thereof." This came as no surprise, for Harriot himself had waxed lyrical about these shores during his winter visit in 1586. He had also written of the friendliness of the Indians in these parts, and the settlers eagerly rowed ashore in the expectation of a warm welcome. Many on board had read the journals of Lane and White—skillfully edited by Hakluyt—and had swallowed the fiction of the jovial savage. They soon discovered that these particular natives wanted neither friendship nor trinkets or beads. "There came the savages, creeping upon all foure, from the hills like beares, with their bowes in their mouthes, charged us very desperately in the faces." The English landing party was stunned by the ferocity of the attack and was very nearly driven into the water by the hail of arrows. It was only when the Indians had "felt the sharpnesse of our shot" that they slunk back into the forest. It quickly dawned on the colonists that their arrival in the New World was not going to be greeted with quite the welcome that Harriot had led them to expect. It was some years before they learned that his *A Briefe and True Report* had not exaggerated the friendliness of the Chesapeake Indians, and that this unprovoked ambush had a strange and sinister explanation.

Captain Newport now announced that the time had come to open the sealed packet containing the names of the president and council. There was considerable excitement as he unfurled the document, for there were many hopefuls among the fifty or so gentlemen, but most were disappointed. Instead of a thirteen-man council, Newport's list contained only seven names, and many of the obvious choices were missing. The appointment of Edward Maria Wingfield to the presidency was begrudgingly accepted, since he had helped to establish the Virginia Company, but most of his seven deputies were virtual unknowns. The only person of any talent on the council was Captain John Smith, an adventurer whose flamboyant exploits had already raised many an eyebrow in London. He bragged of having been a pirate and mercenary, and even claimed to have slaughtered several of the Ottoman sultan's wrestlers in hand-to-hand combat. He was eventually captured and sold as a slave, and it was only when he murdered his Turkish captor with a threshing bat that he managed to escape back to England.

Smith was a colourful man in almost every respect. His large head was crowned with a shock of red hair, and his face was so covered in beard and whiskers that he looked more like an animal than a man. Every inch the Elizabethan adventurer, he was destined to tower over his gentlemen colleagues.

Once Newport had named the council, he turned his attentions to the second of his orders from London: to find a site for England's new colony in "the strongest, most wholesome and fertile place." After weeks of exploration and reconnoitring, he announced that he had selected the perfect spot—a low-lying island in the James River, a site that bore an uncanny resemblance to Roanoke. Unfortunately, Newport lacked the military eye of Ralph Lane; his island stronghold soon revealed itself to be a potential death trap. It could easily be attacked from the river, the marshy soil was far from "wholesome," and the surrounding swamps were a perfect breeding ground for malarial mosquitoes. Worse still, the settlers were obliged to use the river as their water source, drawing water from a site just a few feet away from their sewage outfall.

At first, few saw the drawbacks to this waterlogged island, and even John Smith declared it to be "a verie fit place for the erecting of a great cittie." That "cittie"—in reality a collection of rotting tents—was named Jamestown in honour of a king who had little interest in America and even less concern for the settlers. It was a cruel blow to Ralegh, whose "cittie of Ralegh"—situated just 100 miles to the south—now lay in ruins.

Scarcely had the colonists landed than a hundred "savages" pitched up "in a very warlike manner . . . to execute their villany." An attack was only prevented by a flash of swords and a volley of grapeshot. Alarmed by the hostility of the Indians and realising that canvas tents provided little protection against needle-sharp arrows, the settlers cut down "the boughs of trees" and "cast [them] together in the forme of a halfe moon."

A week spent landing supplies left the irrepressible Captain Newport sorely in need of adventure. He now proposed an exploratory expedition up the murky waters of the James, in search of the ore and minerals that Thomas Harriot had singularly failed to find. Twenty-one jaunty gentlemen accompanied him in the hope of high adventure. They had not gone far when they chanced upon a canoe rowed by eight Indian warriors. These Indians responded to the English salute with beaming smiles and, far from showing hostility, provided the men with a sketch map of the river. When they invited the English to their settlement, Newport found the welcome almost too effusive. The chieftain gave him a crown—a singularly inappropriate gift—and Newport responded by handing over "gyftes of dyvers sortes, as penny knyves, sheeres, belles, beades, glasse toyes &c." Then, after more smiles and japes, "we satt merye, banquetting with them, seeing their daunces and taking tobacco."

Newport's expedition had been under way for almost a week when one of his party, George Percy, began to grow suspicious. He spied an Indian tribesman who, along with the usual panoply of bows and spears, was carrying "pieces of yron to cleave a man in sunder." This set the alarm bells ringing: the Indians did not possess the necessary skills to smelt iron, and these chunks of metal could only have come from a European. There was no evidence that they had come from one of White's colonists, nor did Percy see fit to ask the Indian how he had acquired such potentially dangerous objects, but he was sufficiently intrigued to make a note of it in his journal.

It was not the only oddity noticed by Percy's sharp eyes. At one village, he caught a glimpse of "a savage boy, about the age of ten yeeres, which had a head of haire of a perfect yellow and a reasonable white skinne, which is a miracle amongst savages." This time Percy was genuinely taken aback and leaped to his feet to question the lad, but the white-skinned "savage boy" had slipped away silently into the forest.

The English party soon learned something of the various tribes that lived on Chesapeake Bay. The situation was very different from what Ralph Lane had experienced in Pamlico Sound. Here they were allied to a mighty *weroance*, the "emperor" Powhatan, who kept an iron grip on his land by a mixture of daring and political guile. "Cruell he hath bene, and quarrellous," wrote one, "[in order] to stryke a terrour and awe into them of his power and condition."

He was said to be hostile to all foreigners, and most unlikely to take kindly to a contingent of English soldiers settling on his land. Yet his lesser chieftains proved delightful company. One went so far as to call Newport his *"wingpoh chemuze"*—a term of endearment that the captain later discovered meant "canoe companion." Another was so delighted with the English "beere, aquavite and sack" that he drank himself into a stupor. Only on the following morning did he realise that there was a price to be paid for drunkenness. As he nursed his sore head, he blamed his "greefe" on Newport's "hott drynkes."

There were inevitable moments of misunderstanding, especially when Newport decided it was time to claim the land officially for King James. "He sett up a crosse with this inscriptyon, Jacobus Rex, 1607, and his owne name belowe." To the colonists, it was a moment of deep significance, a sign that they had rooted themselves in the soil of the New World. "At the erecting hereof, we prayed for our kyng and our owne prosperous success in this his actyon, and proclaimed him kyng with a greate showte."

Many of the Indians were bemused by the incident of the cross and "began to admire," not realising that they had just witnessed the formal annexation of their homeland. But other onlookers were less impressed and asked Newport to explain what it meant. The captain sensed the hostility and attempted to defuse the situation. With a twinkle in his eye, he explained "that the two armes of the crosse signified Kyng Powhattan and himself." This sparked a lively debate along the shores of the James, and many of the Indians "murmured at our planting in the countrie." They were only calmed by the intervention of their tribal elders, who told their suspicious tribesmen, "Why should you bee offended with them, as long as they hurt you not, nor take any thing away by force. They take but a little waste ground, which doth you nor any of us any good."

Soon after leading the exploratory party back to Jamestown, the energetic Newport suddenly announced his intention of returning

Captain John Smith looked extraordinary. He had bright red hair and his face was so covered in whiskers that he was more like an animal than a man

to England, having fulfilled his role of shipping the colonists to America. On June 21, 1607, all of the settlers and sailors were given communion. Shortly after, Newport weighed anchor and departed, promising to return with supplies within twenty weeks.

His departure coincided with the colonists' first message from the shadowy emperor, Powhatan, whose spies had been keeping a close eye on the English settlement. Powhatan's mistrust of the white man was born of long experience. He had known all about Ralegh's adventures on Roanoke in the 1580s and could even recall an earlier attempt at North American colonisation—when Spanish Jesuits had landed in Chesapeake Bay. What gave him such disquiet about this new influx were the prophecies of his superstitious elders, who informed him that "from the Chesapeake Bay, a nation should arise, which should dissolve and give end to his empier." Their warning had a disturbing postscript: they told Powhatan that the white man's first two attempts would fail, but "the third time, they themselves [the Indians] should fall into their subjection and under their conquest."

Powhatan was alarmed by such predictions, but he decided to bide his time, sending his envoy to Jamestown with the message that he offered only friendship. To prove his goodwill, he said he would ensure that all mischief-making on the part of the Indians would cease immediately. This message temporarily heartened the colonists, but they soon found they had other, more pressing concerns. So long as Newport's ships had lain at anchor on the river, "our allowance was somewhat bettered by a daily proportion of bisket which the sailers would pilfer to sell, give or exchange with us, for mony, saxefras [sassafras], furrs or love. But when they departed, there remained neither taverne, beere-house nor place of relief but the common kettle." This common kettle—the communal cooking pot—was far from appetising. "[It] was halfe a pinte of wheat and as much barly boyled with water for a man a day, and this having fryed some 26 weeks in the ship's hold, contained as many wormes as graines." Although the bullish John Smith was happy to munch his way through worm-infested barley, the gentlemen colonists were disgusted with the fare. None was more distraught than the illustrious George Percy, the sharp-eyed brother of the Earl of Northumberland, who moaned that Newport had left "verie bare and scanty victuals" and did not take kindly to a diet he considered fit only for animals.

It was not long before men began to go hungry and fall sick. "It fortuned that within tenne daies," wrote Percy, "scarse ten amongst us could either goe, or well stand, such extreame weaknes and sicknes oppressed us." The sultry heat and the clouds of mosquitoes took their toll on the weary colonists. Men began to drop like flies, and scarcely a day passed without at least one of the colonists being shuffled into a grave. "The sixt of August there died John Asbie of the bloudie flixe. The ninth day died George Flowre of the swelling. The tenth day died William Bruster, gentleman, of a wound given by the savages." The death rate appalled the colonists, for each man was terrified that he would be the next to die. Some, like Jerome Alikock, "died of a wound"; others "died suddenly" and without warning. Their ignorance in burying the men in shallow graves only increased the mortality rate. "The fifteenth day there died Edward Browne and Stephen Galthrope. The sixteenth day their died Thomas Gower, gentleman. The seventeenth day their died Thomas Mounslie. The eighteenth day there died Robert Pennington and John Martine, gentlemen. The nineteenth day died Drue Piggase, gentleman." On August 22, the sickness claimed its first council member, the Elizabethan privateer Bartholomew Gosnold, a friend of Sir Walter Ralegh. "He was honourably buried, having all the ordnance in the fort shot off with many vollies of small shot."

The sickness hit indiscriminately, regardless of rank or status. No one knew what caused it and no one could put a name to it. George Percy was horrified by what he witnessed, and left a graphic account of the suffering experienced by the settlers. "Our men were destroyed with cruell diseases, as swellings, fluxes, burning fevers, and by warres, and some departed suddenly, but for the most part they died of meere famine. There never were Englishmen left in a forreigne countrey in such miserie as wee were, lying on the bare cold ground what weather soever came warded all the next day, which brought our men to bee most feeble wretches."

The common kettle was now almost empty, and "our food was but a small can of barlie, sod in water, to five men a day." Worse still was the water: "Our drinke [was] cold water taken out of the river, which was at a floud [tide] verie salt [and] at a low tide full of slime and filth, which was the destruction of many of our men." Most were too sick to move, while those that had not yet succumbed to typhoid or dysentery were brought low from hunger. "Our men, night and day, groaning in every corner of the fort, most pittifull to heare." Even the robust John Smith was brought low, although his sickness did not stop him from cracking a cruel jest: "Had we beene as free from all sinnes," he wrote, "we might have bin canonized for saints."

In such a grim atmosphere, men began to look for scapegoats. The colony's president, Wingfield, was the obvious target. Never popular, he was now accused of "ingrossing . . . otemeale, sacke, oil, aquavitae, beefe, egs or what not." Wingfield denied any wrongdoing and vigorously defended his distribution of victuals. "I did allwayes give every men his allowance faithfully," he said, and dismissed allegations of secretly hoarding food. But he found himself wrong-footed when accused of roasting squirrels for his own private consumption. "I never had but one squirell roosted," he stuttered, "whereof I gave part to Master Ratcliff then sick; yet was that squirell given me." The argument was lost: Wingfield was deposed and Captain John Ratcliffe elected to replace him.

The change of leadership did nothing to halt the deaths. Fifty men had now died and still the sickness continued. The men were utterly at a loss to explain the cause of the disaster. They had studied the accounts of Ralph Lane and Thomas Harriot and were all too familiar with Lane's infamous boast that America was so wholesome that "but foure of our whole company . . . died all the yeere." Such words seemed cruel to the survivors, whose chief occupation was digging graves for the dying, "many times three or foure in a night, in the morning their bodies trailed out of their cabines like dogges to be buried."

The forty survivors were surprised that the local Indians, led by the bellicose Chief Pasapegh, had not mounted an assault, for there was no one left to defend the palisade, and few had enough strength even to fire a musket. "If it had not pleased God to have put a terrour in the savages hearts," wrote Percy, "we had all perished by those vild and cruell pagans."

When several Indians did approach the settlement, the English were astonished to see that they were carrying not bows and arrows but baskets of bread, fish, and meat. The explanation for this unexpected windfall was simple: now that the harvest was gathered, the natives had surplus food to trade with the English. "[It] was the setting up of our feeble men," wrote Percy, "otherwise wee had all perished." The influx of food happened to coincide with a break in the sultry weather, which brought an abrupt end to the sickness and death. Even Smith was grateful. "God," he wrote, "so changed the hearts of the salvages that they brought such plenty of their fruits and provision as no man wanted."

The fresh food had an instant effect. The common kettle was soon bubbling with meat stews. Within three weeks, "the president had reared upp twenty men able to worke." John Smith seized the moment: appointed chief merchant (or supply officer), he selected a team of the fittest men and led a series of food-collecting expeditions into the unknown interior of the country. His bravado soon reaped dividends—he found himself trading trinkets for venison, oysters, and grain. The cooler weather had also brought unexpected supplies of fresh food, for "the rivers became so covered with swans, geese, duckes and cranes, that we daily feasted with good bread, Virginia pease, pumpions and putchamins, fish, fowle and divers sorts of wild beasts as fat as we could eat them; so that none but our Tuftaffaty humourists [cranks] desired to goe for England."

As Christmas approached, the colonists gave thanks that they had survived their ordeal. With a new feeling of optimism in Jamestown, they now decided to send John Smith on a mission to meet Powhatan to trade for grain. The famine had made them realise—as it had the settlers on Roanoke—that their fate ultimately lay in the hands of the Indians. They also knew that if anyone was going to give them information about the mysterious fate of White's lost colonists, it would be the emperor Powhatan.

14

The King's Dearest Daughter

John Smith set off to meet Powhatan in early December. He selected nine companions, six of them oarsmen, and borrowed the colony's small barge, which had a shallow draught and was well suited for exploration.

As the men rowed up the Chickahominy River, whose confluence with the James lay some five miles from Jamestown, the tortuous channel grew narrow and the tree branches hung so low over the water that Smith had to hack them down with his sword. Soon the water became so shallow that even the barge kept scraping the bottom, and Smith was forced to divide his party. He and two others bartered for a canoe and two Indian guides and continued upstream into the "vast and wild wilderness," while the others rowed the barge back to a little bay with instructions to await Smith's return. He strictly commanded that "none should goe a shore till his returne."

Scarcely had he bid the men farewell than one of their number, George Cassen, slipped into the water and waded ashore. It was a foolish mistake, for he was immediately taken hostage by a group of Indians who demanded to know the purpose of their mission. Cassen refused to tell them—another mistake, for the Indians decided to teach their insolent captive a lesson. Cassen was seized, stripped naked, and bound hand and foot with thick ropes. Next, the

Indians prepared a huge fire, which the shivering Englishman knew was not being lit to keep him warm. When the blaze was roaring, Cassen was "tyed to a tree and, with muscle-shells or reedes, the executioner cutteth of his joyntes one after another, ever casting what is cut off into the fier." He screamed for mercy, but the heedless Indians continued with their clinical torture. They disjointed and removed his fingers and toes and, after scraping off the flesh, kept the little white bones as keepsakes. Next, they moved to his upper body, using "shells and reedes to case the skyn from his head and face, after which they rippe up his belly [and] teare out his bowells." Poor Cassen was still alive when they scooped up the burning coals, arranged them around their victim, "and so burne him with the tree and all." He was sacrificed, wrote one of the English, "to the devill."

Smith knew none of this, for he had made good progress on his journey to meet Powhatan and was soon almost twenty miles from where he had left the barge. The channel here was marshy and clogged with reeds, and the exhausted party decided to rest for a few hours, tying their canoe to the bank and gingerly stepping ashore. Smith immediately set off to explore with one of his Indian guides, leaving his two companions, Jehu Robinson and Thomas Emry, to keep a watchful eye on the boat. He cautioned them to guard their muskets and to "discharge a peece . . . at the first sight of any Indian."

Smith had not gone far when he realised that something was seriously wrong. "Within a quarter of an houre, I heard a loud cry and a hollowing of Indians, but no warning peece." He acted quickly, convinced that he and his companions were caught in an ambush. He seized his Indian guide "and bound his arme fast to my hand in a garter with my pistoll ready bent to be revenged on him." But the Indians had the advantage of surprise, and by the time that Smith was ready to defend himself, he found that he was already surrounded.

The ensuing attack was fast and furious. "I was struck with an arrow on the right thigh," he recalled, and although this bounced harmlessly off his buff jerkin, he soon found himself "beset with 200

Indians." He pulled out his French wheel-lock pistol and began firing at his attackers. "Three or four times I had discharged my pistoll," he writes, "[but they] invirond me, each drawing their bowe." He was still using his Indian guide as a human shield, and the poor fellow was so terrified of being killed that he screamed at his attackers, begging them to stop firing. His words had a miraculous effect, for the tribesmen suddenly laid down their weapons and began to negotiate with this wild-looking Englishman. "They demaunded my armes, the rest they saide were slaine, onely me they would reserve."

If the situation was looking grim for Smith, it had turned murderous back at the canoe. Robinson and Emry were lounging in the long grass when they were suddenly beset by the Indians. Robinson sat up, only to find himself floored by more than twenty arrows. He slumped back into the grass and bled to death. Thomas Emry, too, was killed, although the manner of his death remains unknown.

Meanwhile, Smith was determined to save himself. He seized his gun, leaped to his feet, and began to run for his life, hoping to reach the canoe before they could kill him. Unfortunately, he "stept fast into the quagmire" and sank to his knees in cold, oozing mud. The more he struggled, the more he sank, and he was soon up to his belly in the icy bog and cursing his bulky frame. It would be only a matter of minutes before he was sucked under, and he knew that his only hope of survival was to be pulled free by the Indians. "I resolved to trie their mercies," he writes. "My armes I caste from me, till which none durst approch me." His ploy worked; the forlorn Smith was pulled, wet and weaponless, out of the stinking bog.

The leader of these men, who happened to be the half-brother of Powhatan, was a terrifying warrior who was not accustomed to show mercy. Yet he was unsure what to make of Smith. He was alarmed by his extraordinary hairy features, which gave Smith time to think of a mystifying ploy that came straight from the pages of Thomas Harriot. Remembering that Harriot had bewitched the Indians with his "mathematicall instruments," Smith reached inside his dripping doublet and plucked out an ivory compass whose needle pointed in the same direction—towards Smith—whichever way it was turned. "Much they marvelled at the playing of the fly and needle, which they could see so plainely and yet not touch it because of the glasse that covered them." Smith realised he had hit upon a marvellous trick that held the Indians in awe. He proceeded to lecture them on "the roundnesse of the earthe; and skies, the spheare of the sunne, moone and starres . . . [and] they all stood amazed with admiration."

Smith's wizardry had saved his life, at least for the moment, and he was marched to a nearby village where the elders prepared him an extravagant supper: "a quarter of venison and some ten pounds of bread." Scarcely had he finished supper than breakfast arrived: "three great platters of fine bread [and] more venison then ten men could devour." Although he was concerned that he was being fattened for slaughter, he tucked into this unexpected feast while continuing to enquire about the land and its resources.

The answer to one of his questions made him sit bolt upright in astonishment. Smith had been quizzing the chieftain about the different tribes, only to be told that there was one faraway village—west of the Chowan River—where there were "certaine men cloathed, at a place called Ocanahonan; cloathed like me." This was exciting news. The Indians used the word *cloathed* of whites or Europeans—people who were not like themselves. Here was evidence, albeit vague, that there were white men living to the south of Chesapeake Bay. There was no certainty that these were John White's lost colonists, for the chieftain could have been referring to the survivors of a shipwreck, or even to the haggard remnants of the fifteen-strong band left behind by Sir Richard Grenville in 1586. But it was a tantalising addition to the riddle of the lost colonists, and one that was certain to cause excitement in London. Smith begged for more information, but the chief could shed no more light on these men and quickly dropped the subject. It would be some months before Smith could investigate further.

A few days after Christmas, he was marched overland to meet the

Captain Smith valiantly fought off two hundred Indians, and was only captured when he fell into a bog. The Indians were jubilant, for Smith was a valuable hostage

elusive emperor Powhatan and his royal court. After a wearisome slog, he eventually reached the forest settlement and was escorted with some ceremony into the imperial palace. The building was nothing to write home about; constructed from branches and twigs, it was little more than a large wooden shack. It was dark inside and it took some moments for Smith to grow accustomed to the gloom. But when his eyes finally adjusted, he was confronted by an alarming sight: "more than two hundred of those grim courtiers stood wondering at him as [if] he had beene a monster." He could have been forgiven for thinking the same about them, for their heads were painted bright red and their hair was decked with feathers. But Smith wisely kept his counsel and tried to work out which one was Powhatan.

Eventually he spotted the emperor at the far end of the room, "proudly lying uppon a bedstead a foote high, upon tenne or twelve mattes richly hung with manie chaynes of great pearles about his necke." In his journal, Smith depicted him as the embodiment of oriental splendour, dripping with jewels and attended by a selection of the choicest ladies from his harem. "At his heade sat a woman, at his feete another, on each side sitting uppon a matte uppon the ground were raunged his chiefe men . . . and behinde them as many young women, each a great chaine of white beades over their shoulders . . . [He had] such a grave and majesticall countenance, as drove me into admiration to see such state in a naked salvage."

Powhatan was polite and good-humoured. He handed over "great platters of sundrie victuals" before turning to the subject that was uppermost in his mind—the reason why the troublesome English had settled in his land.

Smith concocted a story on the spot, describing how they had been blown by storms into Chesapeake Bay and been forced to build a temporary settlement. Realising that Powhatan was less than happy with their presence on his shores, he stressed the story of their accidental arrival. He was itching to ask about the lost colonists,

Feared and respected, Powhatan looked every inch the emperor. Smith was filled with admiration "to see such a state in a naked salvage."

aware that this powerful ruler must surely know whether they had survived all these years in Virginia, but he knew that to raise the subject now would suggest a greater interest in colonisation than he cared to reveal. Instead, he fobbed Powhatan off with a story of how all of the English served under Captain Newport, "whom I intituled the *meworames*, which they call 'King of the Waters.' " He assured the emperor that they would leave as soon as this "king" returned to take them away.

Powhatan was "not a little feared" when he was informed of the might of England, and even more concerned by Smith's apparently supernatural powers. But he was so shaken by the doom-laden prophecies of his elders that he decided that Smith would be safer dead than alive. This, of course, posed another dilemma—choosing the best way to kill the redheaded sorcerer. Powhatan's favourite methods were to flay alive, "broyle to death," or "beat out their braynes;" after his elders had "held a long consultation" they finally plumped for the latter. "Two great stones were brought before Powhatan. Then, as many as could, layd hands on him [Smith], dragged him to them, and thereon laid his head, and being ready with their clubs to beate out his braines."

They were just about to crack open his skull when "Pocahontas, the King's dearest daughter, when no intreaty could prevaile, got his [Smith's] head in her armes and laid her owne upon his to save him from death." It was the first in a series of bravura actions on the part of Pocahontas that were to captivate and delight the readers of Smith's journal. Within less than a generation, her name had become familiar right across England, not as a real person but as an almost mythical character of fable and legend.

Powhatan could scarcely believe his eyes. Interpreting his daughter's intervention as a sign from the gods, he immediately ordered that Smith's life be spared. Instead of being beaten to death, the Englishman found himself adopted by the emperor and made a *weroance* in his own right. The only condition was that he was to "goe to Jamestowne to send him two great gunnes and a gryndstone, for which he would give him the Country of Capahowosick, and for ever esteeme him as his sonne."

It was a shrewd political move on the part of Powhatan, who had proved himself far more skilled in his dealings with the colonists than had the chieftains around Roanoke. Smith returned to Jamestown with no option but to carry out the wishes of his new "father," supplying him with weapons, tools, and machinery. To the immense annoyance of the English, Powhatan had seized the initiative.

Sir Walter Ralegh had been in the Tower for more than four years when John Smith met Powhatan, and there were no signs that he would ever be released. He was held at the king's mercy, and could only be freed if James himself desired it. This looked as unlikely in 1608 as it had when he was first incarcerated.

Ralegh was fortunate in sharing his prison with his friend the Earl of Northumberland, the "wizard earl," who had been implicated in the Gunpowder Plot, a Catholic conspiracy to blow up the king and Parliament. Unable to shake off the false accusations, Northumberland had been thrown in jail. He lavished considerable sums on making the men's captivity as comfortable and enjoyable as possible. He constructed a bowling green, levelled the Tower walkways with gravel, and had canvas awnings constructed over the paths to provide shade from the midday sun. He even had new windows knocked into the walls of his dingy private quarters.

Ralegh, meanwhile, had been doing his own building works. He had converted one of the Tower's derelict outhouses into a scientific workshop, and the two men spent much of their time distilling exotic liqueurs to quaff in the long evenings. Their favourite tipple was *spiritus dulcis*, a sweet eau-de-vie flavoured with "sugarcandie," "sacke," and "spirits of roses."

But the two men did not spend all their time drinking strong spirits. Ralegh's interest in colonisation was undiminished, and he and Northumberland were able to continue with their studies even in the confines of the Tower. For the earl had moved a part of his remarkable library into the prison, and continued to order and receive books that were of interest. He also commissioned two pairs of new globes, as well as brass spheres, clocks, watches, and compasses.

The two men kept abreast of developments in Virginia through the sporadic letters sent back to England by George Percy, Northum-

King Powhatan comauds C. Smith to be flayne, his daughter Pokahontas beggs his life has thankfullnesß and how he subiected 39 of their kings. reade § history.

printed by James Reeve

Powhatan decided Smith was safer dead than alive. He ordered his tribesmen to get "ready with their clubs to beate out his braines."

berland's brother, who had sailed with Captain Newport in 1606.
Young George had probably been talked into sailing to Virginia by
Thomas Harriot, with whom he lived at Syon House, and perhaps
by Ralegh himself. The information that he revealed about the
fledgling colony—first brought back to England with Newport's
returning fleet—was of the greatest importance for Ralegh, since he
was acting as an unofficial advisor to the Virginia Company, com-

piling documents and memoranda on how best the merchants should proceed.

Sir Walter was longing to step back into the forefront of American colonisation, and even wrote to the queen begging her to intercede with the king on his behalf. "I long since presumed to offer your majestie my service in Virginia," he wrote, "with a shorte repetition of the comoditie, honor and safetye which the king's majestie might reape by that plantacion." He added that "I doe still hombly beseech your majestie that I may rather die in serving the kinge and my countrey then to perrish here." The queen listened to his appeals with sympathy but was unable to act. Sir Walter's role within the Virginia Company remained under wraps, for the merchants knew that King James would be extremely annoyed to learn of his involvement. But not everyone remained ignorant of Ralegh's work; one of his letters fell into the hands of the Spanish ambassador to England, Don Pedro de Zuniga, who was trying desperately to unearth information about the Jamestown settlement. "I have a paper written by Vater Rales [Walter Ralegh]," he wrote to his king. "[He] is a prisoner in the Tower, and is the one who discovered that land, and whom people here consider a great man." He adds that "those of the council of Virginia guide themselves by it. It is here [in London] being translated, because it is his original, and when that is finished, we will compare it with the chart which they have made."

The exact nature of the advice offered by Sir Walter is unclear, for the letter has unfortunately been lost. But something of its content can be gleaned from Ralegh's remarkable essay on colonisation, in which he drew on his vast experience of the New World to suggest the most effective way of establishing and sustaining a colony. He declared that butchering the native population was a solution that benefited no one; Lane and Grenville had proved this in 1585, as had the Spanish in their overseas possessions. Nor was it right to settle on Indian land for the sole purpose of exploitation: "No Christian prince, under the pretence of Christianity . . . may attempt the invasion of any free people not under their vassaladge." He argued, instead, that the English should try to educate the Indians in matters of law and religion—"instructe them in liberall arts of civility"—and help them to "renounce their impietyes." Then, without too much difficulty, they could be "united to the crown of England" as grateful and loyal tributaries—a policy that would bring "riches with honour, conquest without blood." This had already been achieved in a minor way in 1586 when the chieftain Okisko had met Ralph Lane on Roanoke and declared his submission to *Weroanza* Elizabeth, promising "that from that time forwarde, hee and his successours were to acknowledge her majestie their onely soveraigne." Ralegh's idea was to build on this success; it was a bold yet simple plan that was derived, in part, from his dealings with Manteo. It was also prophetic: in one short essay, Ralegh had sketched out a blueprint for the future British Empire.

His argument soon found itself echoed in the Virginia Company's propaganda. "Our coming thither is to plant ourselves in their countrie," wrote Robert Johnson, "yet not to supplant and roote them out, but to bring them from their base condition to a farre better." And it was not long before the London merchants began working on plans to reduce the native chieftains of Virginia to the status of tribute kings, loyal and obedient to their English overlords. In the summer of 1608, they dispatched Christopher Newport back to America with orders to make Powhatan a subject king under the overlordship of *Weroance* James I. They acknowledged that this would not be easy, but believed that Newport was the man for the job. He was supplied with a cheap copper crown, scarlet robes, and a royal washbasin and pitcher. For a coronation present, the merchants bought a king-sized bed.

Newport arrived in Jamestown to find that much had changed. Captain Smith had replaced his corrupt predecessor as president and had immediately restarted work on the settlement, repairing the storehouses and renewing military drilling. He had also formulated his own views on how the colony should be run. When he learned of

Captain Newport's orders to crown Powhatan, he expressed his doubts in a letter to London. "For the coronation of Powhatan," he wrote, "I know not; but this give me leave to tell you: I feare they [the orders from London] will be the confusion of us all ere we heare from you againe." He suggested instead that the emperor be invited to Jamestown to "receive his presents," and added that any thoughts of a coronation should be quietly dropped.

Newport agreed with the first suggestion but overruled the second. Orders were orders, and London wanted Powhatan crowned. But he had no personal desire to break this news to the chieftain and told Smith that it was his task, as president, to inform the emperor of these developments.

Smith and his men arrived at Powhatan's village to find the chieftain out hunting. They were greeted by young Pocahontas, who offered to entertain them while a messenger was sent to summon her father. The spectacle she organised was one they were to remember for some time. "Thirtie young women came naked out of the woods, onely covered behind and before with a few greene leaves, their bodies all painted, some of one colour, some of another." The men were at first suspicious, for such women had proved all too adept at flaying men alive, but Pocahontas reappeared and told Smith "to kill her if any hurt were intended." Far from planning an ambush, she had arranged for the women to entertain the Englishmen with "hellish shouts and cryes . . . singing and dauncing . . . [and] infernall passions."

Powhatan arrived on the following day and Smith was immediately granted an audience. After the customary courtesies, he relayed the message that the emperor was to come to Jamestown to receive his presents from England. Incensed by Smith's impertinence, Powhatan refused to comply. "If your king have sent me presents," he said, "[then] I also am a king and this is my land. Eight dayes I will stay to receive them. Your father [Newport] is [to] come to me, not I to him." Faced with such an obstinate reaction, Smith declined to tell Powhatan that they also wished to crown him.

It was now clear that the presents and coronation garb would have to be brought from Jamestown. After a hasty exchange of messages, a large English expedition led by Newport slowly marched its way to the imperial village, while the bed and the other gifts were transported by boat.

There was a joyous little reunion when all the English had arrived. A team of men were instructed to unpack the bed and assemble it in Powhatan's longhouse. That done, everyone sat down to a hearty feast. What the English knew — but Powhatan did not — was that "the next day was appointed for his coronation."

It was with some trepidation that Newport and Smith awoke the following morning to carry out their orders. Neither of the men had attended a coronation, and they were unfamiliar with the procedure. When King James had been crowned, he had marched triumphantly into Westminster Abbey, had received the sacrament, had taken the coronation oath, and after receiving the orb and sceptre had seated himself on the throne in preparation to be crowned. If either of the men had known of this final stage, they could have made life much easier. As it was, they were forced to improvise.

"The presents were brought him," writes Smith, "his bason and ewer, bed and furniture set up, his scarlet cloke and apparell with much ado put on him, being perswaded by Namantack [his servant] they would not hurt him." Stage one had been accomplished without much difficulty: Powhatan had donned his robes and was ready to be crowned. But now came the tricky part in the proceedings. If the English had followed the usual custom, Powhatan would by now be seated on a makeshift throne. Unfortunately, he was still wandering around and showed no signs of stooping to receive his crown. "A foule trouble there was to make him kneele to receive his crowne," wrote Smith, "he neither knowing the majesty nor meaning of a crowne, nor bending of the knee, endured so many perswasions, examples and instructions, as tyred them all." They begged him to sit, cajoled him, and reasoned with him, but Powhatan refused to be dictated to. Newport and Smith realised it was time for more direct action. "At last, by leaning hard on his shoulders, he a little stooped and, three having the crowne in their hands, put it on his head." Powhatan was at last crowned as ordered by London—the first and last coronation ever staged on North American soil.

It was now time to celebrate in true English fashion. "The boats were prepared with such a volley of shot that the king start up in a horrible feare till he saw all was well." Smith rushed to his side to reassure him. After overcoming his initial suspicions, Powhatan became suddenly fond of his cheap crown and robes. "Remembring himselfe, to congratulate their kindnesse, he gave his old shooes and his mantell to Captaine Newport." With a loud cry of "Long live the King," which Powhatan must surely have thought was referring to him, the Englishmen threw their caps into the air.

Powhatan was now a vassal king, theoretically subservient to *Weroance* James I and, in English eyes, obliged to do exactly as he was told. But just as Smith had feared, the coronation only served to increase his sense of his own importance. When Newport demanded guides to lead him upstream into enemy territory, he obstinately refused. Nor did he intend to supply his "overlords" with much-needed food. The extent of his largesse was seven or eight bushels of grain. Newport was annoyed but not too dejected. He returned to Jamestown content that he had fulfilled the first item on the Virginia Company's list of instructions.

The second was to prove even more difficult. The merchants had ordered him to search for and find "any of them sent by Sir Walter Ralegh"—the lost colonists of 1587. The London merchants knew that their discovery would be a great boon to the Jamestown settlers, for White's men and women would have had more than twenty years of experience in the New World and would be able to supply the new colonists with priceless information about the land and its resources. They would be able to speak fluent Algonkian, and would possibly have intermarried with the Indians. But they would also be utterly changed by their experiences. Virginia Dare—John White's granddaughter—would be twenty-one years old and possibly married to a native Indian. If so, there is every likelihood that she would have given birth to children whose outlook would have far more in common with the forest Indians than with their English mother, who herself had never seen England. Many of the original female colonists might well have given birth to one or two children, swelling the original numbers, and even if a few of the settlers had died each year, the group would have remained much the same size as it had been in 1587. All would have learned how to survive in a hostile land, and many would be fast losing all vestiges of their Englishness. Their Elizabethan clothes would have worn out long ago and they would now be dressed in skins and furs. Even their English would be rusty; although they would, perhaps, still use it to speak to one another, their lingua franca would quite probably be Algonkian.

Smith had been so intrigued by the rumoured existence of white men living to the south of Chesapeake Bay that he had long vowed to send out search parties as soon as it was feasible. This had proved impossible in the immediate aftermath of his capture by Powhatan, but once he was back at Jamestown he began planning an overland expedition to look for the lost colonists. His task was made considerably easier when, in 1608, he struck up friendship with the previously hostile Paspahegh tribe. Chief Wowinchopunk declared his support for Smith's proposal to search for the English colonists and offered to accompany two of the Jamestown settlers on a trek through the thickly forested shores to the south of the bay. Their goal was the mysterious village of Ocanahonan, which no Indian could point to on a map, but which most agreed was on either the Roanoke or Chowan rivers—both of which had been explored by Lane, White, and Harriot.

The details of the expedition were never set down on paper, but John Smith gives some inkling of what happened, and a sketch map of the land around Jamestown allows for a partial reconstruction of their long march. The adventurous chieftain and the two explorers, penetrating deep into the wilderness, seem to have reached the thickly wooded banks of the Roanoke River. From here they turned inland and marched even further into the interior until their aching feet brought them into contact with a string of little villages. At every new settlement they asked for information until they eventually had some success. One tribe informed them that at a village called Pak-erikanick "remain the four men clothed that came from Roonock [Roanoke] to Okanahowan."

For some undisclosed reason, the men did not push further inland towards this village, perhaps because their Indian guide refused to accompany them. Instead, the men headed straight back to Jamestown to break the exciting news to Smith, and a report of their mission was immediately dispatched to England.

Newport's instructions were not just to locate John White's colonists, but to persuade "one of the lost company" to return to England. Smith did his best to oblige. In the winter of 1608 he "desired guides to Chowanoke" from another chieftain and sent a second search party out into the wilderness. "To performe this journey was sent Michael Sicklemore, a very honest, valient and painefull soldier; with him two guides and directions howe to search for the lost company of Sir Walter Rawley." Sicklemore set off into the wilderness as instructed, but his hardship was all to no avail. "[He] returned from Chawwonoke but found little hope and less certaintie of them [that] were left by Sir Walter Ralegh. The river he saw was not great, the people few, the countrey most overgrowne with pynes." Another party was dispatched to the territory of the Mangoak tribe, but despite a valiant effort by Nathaniel Powell and Anas Todhill, "nothing could they learne but they were all dead." Yet rumours persisted about the survival of the lost colony, and the Indians repeatedly spoke of a tribe to the southwest of Chesapeake Bay whose "people have howses built with stone walls, and one story above another, so taught them by those English."

Smith was intrigued by the conflicting reports and would certainly have widened the search had there not been a pressing need to find more food. Newport had brought with him a new influx of colonists, among them the first women, bringing the total number to about two hundred. Filling so many bellies was not easy, especially since most settlers were afflicted by the same disease—laziness—that had wrecked the chances of the Roanoke colony. They complained continuously, and when they were ordered to chop trees, "the axes so oft blistered their tender fingers that commonly every third blow had a lowd oath to drowne the eccho."

Smith considered a pint of grain a day essential to keep his colonists alive. This meant bartering with the Indians for 200 pints a day or about twenty-two bushels a week. While this was possible in the autumn, when food was plentiful, it became a great deal more difficult in the winter and spring. Clashes with the Indians had soured relations, and there had been several incidents in which crops had been taken from them by force. Newport had managed to secure additional supplies by trading his weapons, but when he sailed for England, Smith called a halt to this foolish policy. Powhatan was so furious that he vowed to starve the colonists to death.

It was not long before food ran short and Smith was forced to take immediate action to avert catastrophe. Shortly before Christmas 1608, he set off to confront Powhatan with the demand that he resume food supplies to the English colony.

It was a bitterly cold winter, and the men had to smash their way through the ice-littered water of the Chickahominy River. They arrived at Powhatan's settlement after nearly two weeks of exertion, only to find "the river was frozen neare halfe a myle from the shore." Smith was forced to hack at the thick ice with his oar until he and his party reached the semifrozen swamp. They could go no further in the boat; the only alternative was to slip into the waist-deep water and wade to the shore.

Smith "by his owne example . . . taught them to march neere middle deepe, a flight shot through this muddy frozen oase." One of his men, Master Russell, "being somewhat ill and exceeding heavie, so overtoyled himselfe as the rest had much adoe (ere he got ashore) to regaine life into his dead benumbred spirits." The bedraggled little party were desperately hoping for a warm welcome from Powhatan, but the emperor's speech—recorded by Smith in his journal—proved quite as frosty as the weather.

"Captaine Smith," he said, "some doubt I have of your comming hither, that makes me not so kindly seeke to relieve you as I would: for many doe informe me your comming hither is not for trade but to invade my people and possesse my country." Smith did his best to feign indignation, assuring Powhatan that he had no such intention. But his protestations were undermined by his refusal to hand over his weapons, and led Powhatan to launch wearily into a lecture on the benefits of cooperation. "Thinke you I am so simple," he said, "not to know it is better to eate good meate, lye well and sleepe quietly with my women and children; laugh and be merry with you . . . than be forced to flie from all, to lie cold in the woods, feede upon acornes, rootes and such trash?" He added that he was heartily sick of having to keep watch over the English, and repeated his demand that Smith hand over his weapons, assuring him that this would lead to permanent friendship. But Smith refused to cooperate on the grounds that it was not Powhatan's place to give orders.

"Powhatan," he said, "you must know [that just] as I have but one God, I honour but one king; and I live not here as your subject but as your friend, to pleasure you with what I can." In one short conversation, the two men had reached the crux of the problem—who was ruler of Virginia? Powhatan said it was him. John Smith said it was King James.

Powhatan was by now so sick of the English that he apparently decided to "have the head of Captaine Smith," ordering his kinsmen to slaughter the redbeard and all his men. He knew that without Smith at the helm, Jamestown could not survive.

The murders were to take place that very night while the Englishmen's boat was still stuck fast in the frozen mud. They were to be attacked while they slept, and put to the sword by Powhatan's "grim devils." But the emperor was to find himself outwitted in a way he could never have forseen. "For Pocahontas, his dearest jewell and daughter, in the darke night came through the irksome woods and told our captaine . . . [that] Powhatan and all the power he could make would after come kill us all." After informing Smith of the exact plan of attack, "shee wished us presently to be gone . . . with the teares running downe her cheekes, shee said shee durst not be seene . . . for if Powhatan should know it, she were but dead."

Smith could scarcely believe his good fortune: for the second time in a year, this precocious little girl of about twelve years of age had saved his life. Like Manteo two decades previously, she found her-

C: Smith takes the King of Paspahegh prisoner: A° 1609.

Smith was not a big man, but his fiery nature impressed the Indians. Even Powhatan had a sneaking admiration for his dealings with lesser chieftains

self captivated by the English settlers and their magical array of tools and instruments and wished to learn more about their strange ways. On this occasion, her action brought about the swift escape of Smith and his men. They fled to the boat and managed to smash their way out of the icy water, staggering back to Jamestown alive but hungry.

Unaware of the duplicitous role being played by his daughter, Powhatan sent her to Jamestown on several occasions to relay messages to the colonists. In the rare times when relations between English and Indians were peaceful, she was a regular visitor to the settlement and brought gifts of grain, turkeys, and bread. "Every once in foure or five dayes, Pocahontas with her attendants brought him [Smith] so much provision, that saved many of their lives, that els for all this had starved with hunger." Her visits were popular with many of the younger colonists, who particularly enjoyed watching her perform cartwheels—naked—around the settlement. She was "a well featured but wanton young girle," wrote the colony's secretary, "[who] sometymes resorting to our fort [would] gett the boyes forth with her into the markett place and make them wheele, falling on their handes [and] turning their heeles upwardes, whome she would follow and wheele so herselfe naked as she was, all the fort over."

As she matured, her intuitive intelligence came to the fore, and she "much exceedeth any of the rest of his people." Smith was impressed, and concluded that "for wit and spirit, [she was] the only nonpariel of his country."

By December 1608 her visits had come to a halt and the gifts of food from Powhatan had also dried up. Winter was always a testing time in Virginia, and as the snow fell on Jamestown with wearisome monotony, the colony stumbled from disaster to catastrophe. Two Dutchmen among the colonists were so convinced that Jamestown was doomed that they switched their allegiance to Powhatan, crowning their treachery by stealing hatchets, swords, and muskets. Soon after, eleven men set sail on a food-gathering expedition, but "so violent was the wind [in] that extreame frozen time" that their skiff was flipped upside down in the James River. All eleven men perished.

But the biggest blow of all came when the colonists came to clean out their storehouse. "In searching our casked corne, we found it halfe rotten, and the rest so consumed with so many thousands of rats . . . as we knew not how to keepe that little we had." Smith was only able to keep his settlers alive by sending rotating teams of men into the wilderness to forage on acorns, berries, and anything they were able to kill.

At long last, in June 1609, a supply ship arrived from England bearing good news. King James's lack of interest in his New World territories was such that he had removed the Virginia Company from direct control by the crown. It was now placed in private stewardship—under licence—and the distinguished Lord De La Warr had been named as governor general for life. Overnight, there was new blood in the enterprise. Preparations were under way for a huge supply fleet bringing fresh hands and a lieutenant governor, the experienced old warhorse, Sir Thomas Gates.

Good news was always accompanied by bad in Virginia, and this occasion was to prove no exception. The mighty fleet had indeed set sail as planned, but as it ploughed its way across the Atlantic, it sailed into the teeth of a hurricane. The *Sea Venture*, the flagship, was dashed against the infamous reefs of the Bermudas. The seven other vessels fared only slightly better. After makeshift repairs to their splintered timbers, they limped into Jamestown bringing scant supplies, "unruly" crews, and another 400 mouths to feed—including women and children. This would have been difficult in any circumstances, but it was made impossible by rival factions arguing over whether Smith's term as president had been brought to an end by virtue of the new charter. The great survivor was preparing to defend himself when he found himself overtaken by events. One afternoon, he had the misfortune to fall asleep in a boat while wearing his flask of gunpowder. Somehow, this came into contact with a lighted match and the powder was instantly ignited. "[It] tore the flesh from his body and thighes, nine or ten inches square, in a most pittifull manner; but to quench the tormenting fire, frying him in his cloaths, he leaped overboord into the deepe river where ere they could recover him, he was neere drowned." No one could say if it was an accident or a botched murder attempt, but the terrible burn broke Smith's indomitable spirit. He resigned the presidency and, physically debilitated, elected to sail home on the first ship to return to England. His reign had come to an end.

His replacement was George Percy, brother of the Duke of Northumberland, who was still languishing in the Tower of London with his old friend Sir Walter Ralegh. Percy was an "ambityous, unworthy and vayneglorious fellowe," according to Smith, and was epileptic and asthmatic as well. He was also obsessed with his appearance and devoted a great part of his time attending to his dress and his diet. In a letter to his brother, he expressed some regret at having spent more than £432 since arriving in America, but explained that it was imperative for a man in his position to "keepe a continuall and dayly table for gentlemen of fashion about me." He enclosed an order for £6 18s. of gold lace and a flamboyant Dutch beaver hat. If Percy was to be a colonial governor, he was going to look the part.

Feeding his colonists over the winter was to prove a great deal more difficult than dressing in splendour. Five hundred mouths required more than fifty bushels of grain a week—and that was just for subsistence. Since Powhatan refused to release any food, Percy was obliged to continue Smith's practice of dispatching small groups into the countryside to fend for themselves. Several of these expeditions ended in catastrophe. When Lieutenant Sicklemore and his men failed to return from one food-raiding expedition, a search party was sent to investigate and found them all "slayne, with their mowthes stopped full of breade, beinge donn as it seamethe in contempte."

Food supplies soon grew perilously low—"a poore alowanse of halfe a cann of meale for a man a day." Percy decided to take a gamble, sending Captain Ratcliffe and thirty men to negotiate with "the subtell owlde foxe," Powhatan. But the emperor, in no mood for clemency, turned on them with a fury. Only one, Jeffrey Shortridge, lived to tell the tale of how the men were slaughtered in now familiar fashion, with special horror reserved for Ratcliffe. "[He] surprysed Capte Ratcliffe alyve, who he caused to be bownd unto a tree naked with a fyer before [him] and by women his fleshe was skraped from his bones with mussel shelles and, before his face, throwne into the fyer."

With no possibility of food from Powhatan, the Jamestown colonists faced the bleakest of winters—far worse than anything they had so far experienced. They were surrounded by hostile tribes and too terrified to leave the relative safety of their settlement. Many were desperately sick, poisoned by the foul water, while those that still had their strength knew that only the fit and the fortunate would survive the lean winter months.

"Now all of us att Jamestowne beginneinge to feele that sharpe pricke of hunger," wrote Percy, "which noe man [can] trewly descrybe butt he which hath tasted the bitternesse therof." Several men were executed for stealing the last remnants of supplies, and then, "haveinge fedd uponn horses and other beastes as long as they lasted, we weare gladd to make shifte with vermine, [such] as doggs, catts, ratts and myce." Next to be eaten were "bootes, shoes or any other leather"; once those had been devoured, the starving men "weare inforced to searche the woodes and to feede upon serpens and snakes, and to digge the earthe for wylde and unknowne rootes."

Many of the weakest men were picked off by the Indians, while the survivors were driven so crazy with hunger that they did "things which seame incredible; as to digge up dead corpses outt of graves and to eate them; and some have licked upp the bloode which hathe fallen from their weake fellowes." Some of the corpses were "boyled"; others were "stewed with roots and herbs." None tasted very wholesome.

It was not long before half of the colonists had died. Many others were so deranged that they fled into the woods and were never seen again. The "starveinge tyme" drove men to ever more hideous acts: "And amongste the reste, this was the most lamentable: thatt one of our colline murdered his wyfe, ripped the childe outt of her woambe and threw itt into the river and after chopped the mother in pieces and salted her for his foode." The crime was not discovered until "he had eaten parte thereof."

Percy professed himself so shocked by this "crewell and inhumane fact" that he immediately tortured the man, hanging him "by the thumbes, with weightes att his feete." Once he had extracted a confession, "I adjudged him to be executed." This story eventually made it back to England, where it quickly caught the public imagination. Eating one's wife brought a whole new dimension to wedlock, and men began lively debates about how best to cook a spouse—all of them overlaid with a rich vein of black humour. "Now whether shee was better roasted, boyled or carbonado'd [grilled] I know not," said one, "but of such a dish as powdered [salted] wife, I never heard of."

As winter drew to a close, the colony faced oblivion. Some 440 men and women had starved to death or been "trecherously slayne," and the sixty skeletal survivors were just clinging to life. They were at the point of total despair when a sharp-eyed lookout noticed a blur of sails on the horizon: "we espyed towe pinnesses comeinge into the baye." The men soon realised that these boats were carrying the colony's lieutenant governor, Sir Thomas Gates, who had miraculously survived the shipwreck in Bermuda. He and his enterprising men had built two new ships and sailed them to Jamestown, arriving a year late.

They soon wished they had stayed in the storm-tossed mid-Atlantic. "The nextt tyde, [they] wente upp to Jamestowne where they mighte reade a lecture of miserie in our people's faces and perceve the skarsety of victewalles." It was not exactly the welcome they had hoped would greet their arrival. The "starving time" had left the survivors "so maugre and leane thatt itt was lamentable to behowlde them." Many had been driven mad "throwe extreme hunger . . . [and were] so leane thatt they looked lyke anotamies, cryeinge owtt, 'We are starved! We are starved!' "

Gates was shocked by what he found. "Entering the towne, it appeared raither as the ruins of some auncient [for]tification than that any people living might now inhabit it." He quickly realised that the place had been hit by a catastrophe of such magnitude that it was hard to see how it could recover. "We found the pallisadoes torne downe, the ports open, the gates from off the hinges, and emptie houses (which owners' death had taken from them) rent up and burnt." Gates had expected to arrive at a colony in good spirits, having been only recently refreshed by a new work force. Instead, the newcomers were dead and the rest were starving.

As he wandered through the half-derelict settlement, he knew there was nothing he could do. He had no supplies and meagre food, and had only added to the colony's woes by bringing an extra 148 mouths to feed. With heavy heart, he concluded that Jamestown was doomed to fail. Ralegh had been right all along: without the support of the native tribes, a colony was unable to sustain itself. If the settlers had been more hardworking, more determined, they might have succeeded in their enterprise. But they had been let down by their commanders, who, with the notable exception of John Smith, had failed to bring discipline and order to the unruly colonists in their charge.

The crunch came at the tail end of May. "It was resolved oppon by Sir Thomas Gates and the whole collonie with all spede to retourne for England." The curtain had fallen for the last time. America was being abandoned by the English.

Greeting the decision with enthusiasm, the sick and starving began preparing themselves for the voyage. "Moste of our men weare sett to worke, some to make pitche and tar for trimminge of our shippes; others to bake breade . . . so thatt [in] a small space of tyme, fower pinnasses weare fitted and made reddy." They were to sail to the Newfoundland Banks, where they could fish for cod and, with luck, find sturdier vessels to carry them home.

Shortly before boarding the ships, the colonists showed what they thought of Jamestown by preparing brands to set fire to their shacks. Sir Thomas stopped them in the nick of time: had he "nott laboured with our men, they had sett the towne on fyer."

There were no tears shed as the colonists clambered aboard. They had suffered such extreme privations in Jamestown and witnessed such appalling cruelty that they were prepared to risk their lives in Gates's hand-built pinnaces. A beating drum summoned the survivors to their boats and a volley of shot was fired into the forest. It seemed a fitting farewell to a hostile land.

As the flotilla slipped downstream, Jamestown slowly receded from view and its wooden shelters soon merged into the landscape. "At noone, they fell to the Ile of Hogs and the next morning to Mulbery Point." They were on their way at last. Beyond lay the entrance to Chesapeake Bay and the wide Atlantic Ocean.

15

Mr. and Mrs. Rolfe Go to England

It was shortly after dawn when the departing colonists noticed a small longboat racing towards their pinnaces. From afar, it looked like an Indian canoe, but as it drew nearer the men were surprised to see that it was flying from its helm the flag of St. George. The vessel was English, and it brought the worst possible news for these melancholy men and women. A new fleet had arrived in Chesapeake Bay, and it was equipped with tools, victuals, and colonists. It was also carrying a formidable new governor, the Right Honourable Thomas West, the Lord De La Warr, a man of ferocious temperament.

His lordship blew his top when he learned that the settlers had abandoned Jamestown and were on their way back to England. He had no sympathy for the sufferings they had endured, and refused to listen to tales of their hardships. Ruddy-faced and shaking with anger, he chastised them "for many vanities, and their idlenesse, earnestly wishing that he might no more finde it so, least he should be compelled to draw the sword of justice to cut off such delinquents." The colonists were immediately landed and frog-marched straight back to Jamestown, where De La Warr vowed to whip them into order. He appointed a new council, instituted a harsh penal code, and insisted upon a great deal of pomp and ceremony whenever he was seen in public.

The colonists soon realised that this was a man to be obeyed. When De La Warr attended the newly repaired church on the first Sunday, they lined up in such numbers that they found it hard to march without tripping over one another. His lordship was accompanied by his captains, officers, and gentlemen, "with a guard of halberdiers in his lordship's livery, faire red cloakes, to the number of fifty, both on each side and behinde him." To protect his posterior from the chill, "a greene velvet chaire" was carried into the church; to provide comfort for his knees when praying, he had a velvet cushion placed on the rough earth floor. Yet these provided small comfort to a man used to luxury. As he toured his spartan quarters, he was perturbed to find none of the furnishings that adorned his house in England—"arras hangings, tapistry, and guilded Venetian cordoran, or more spruce household garniture."

Lord De La Warr was a cold, unsentimental man who had no interest in Ralegh's lost colonists, nor any desire to find them. Although he must have known that their presence would be a boon to the Jamestown settlers, now more than ever, he also knew that it would detract from the achievements resulting from his own rule and actions. He chose to ignore them completely in his first letter to the "subtle King Powhatan," calling instead for the immediate return of all the English weapons that had been acquired over the previous few years. He began his letter with the customary pleasantries, but his fiery nature quickly got the better of him. Writing in English, a language that several of the tribesmen could now understand, he reminded Powhatan that the Indians were subjects of King James, "the great *weroance*," and that he had "formerly vowed not only friendship but homage, receiving from his majestie therefore many gifts, and upon his knees a crowne and scepter with other ornaments." He also took the opportunity to inform him that these were "symbols of civill state and Christian soveraigntie" and that they obligated him "to offices of dutie to his majestie."

Powhatan must have been utterly perplexed by the letter. The symbolic nature of the coronation ceremony had passed right over his head, and although he was immensely fond of his crown, he had no idea that this cheap ring of copper had somehow removed his authority. Far from complying with his lordship's request, Powhatan sent an angry reply to Lord De La Warr, ordering him to "confine ourselves to Jamestowne . . . or otherwise he would give in command to his people to kill us, and doe unto us all mischiefe." He added that the English should not bother to send any more messengers "unlesse . . . they brought him a coach and three horses."

Lord De La Warr had never been treated with such impertinence and was "mutch incensed" by Powhatan's disobedience. Worse still, the neighbouring Indians were becoming increasingly bold in their attack on the English, and the countryside surrounding Jamestown was now so dangerous that it was no longer safe for the governor to send parties of men to pick the wild strawberries he liked to munch after dinner. He decided to take firm and immediate action. He captured an Indian—"a notable villain"—and had "his right hand stroke off" with a blade. He then sent the one-handed Indian to Powhatan with the message that unless the English weapons were returned immediately, he would deliver the same punishment to every Indian that he captured.

He did not bother to wait for a response from Powhatan. Troops of soldiers were straightaway sent to butcher hostile tribes and wreak as much carnage and destruction as they could. One of the murder squads was led by George Percy, who was sent to ambush two particularly truculent tribes, the Paspaheghs and the Chickahominies. Percy delighted in the command and took to the task with gusto. "We fell in upon them," he wrote, "putt some fiftene or sixtene to the sworde, and almoste all the rest to flyghte." The Paspahegh tribe's queen and children were taken captive, and the rest of the elders were beheaded. Percy then ordered his men "to burne their howses and to cutt downe their corne groweinge aboutt the towne."

The bloodthirsty soldiers fulfilled this with unseemly relish, then returned to Percy and begged that they be allowed to kill the queen and "putt the children to deathe." Percy spared the queen, but allowed the men to slaughter the children, "which was affected by throweinge them overboord and shoteinge owtt their braynes in the water. Yett for all this crewelty, the sowldiers weare nott well pleased and I had mutche to doe to save the quenes lyfe for thatt time."

When Percy arrived back at Jamestown, he found that Lord De La Warr was annoyed that the queen had been kept alive. He ordered "thatt we sholde see her dispatched," and when Percy asked how to kill her, De La Warr calmly replied that "the way he thowghte beste [was] to burne her." Even Percy baulked at such savagery: "I replyed thatt haveinge seene so mutche bloodshedd thatt day, now, in my cowld bloode, I desyred to see noe more." He added that "I did not howlde itt fitteinge [to burn her], but either by shott or sworde to geve her a quicker dispatche."

Percy's argument won the day; the task of executing her fell to Captain Davis, who "did take the quene with towe sowldiers ashoare and, in the woods, putt her to the sworde."

The new governor's policy of slaughter and destruction ran counter to everything that Ralegh had sought to promote over the previous two decades. He had urged colonists and colonial governors to avoid bloodshed, arguing that "no Christians may lawfully invade with hostility any heathenish people . . . to kill, spoile, and conquer them only upon pretence of their fidelity." Lord De La Warr heartily disagreed, and his firm hand rapidly succeeded in brutally subjecting the local Indians. Chieftains were put to the sword, hundreds of tribesmen were butchered, and entire villages razed to the ground. But before the English had time to celebrate, their governor suddenly fell ill. "I was welcomed by a hot and violent ague," he wrote, "[and] began to be distempered with other greevous sicknesses, which successively and severally assailed me." Each illness further weakened him, and reduced his body's ability to fight off the numerous diseases that were rife in Jamestown. "The flux surprised me . . . the cramp assaulted my weak body with strong paines; and afterwards the gout . . . [which] afflicted me in such sort that making my body through weaknesse unable to stirre, or to use any maner of exercise, drew upon me the disease called scurvy." His physician ordered him to leave Jamestown immediately—and De La Warr readily complied. In March 1611 he set sail for the Caribbean island of Nevis, "to try what help the heavenly providence would afford me by the benefit of the hot bathe."

If the colonists expected a respite from hard work and butchery, they were in for a rude shock. Just eight weeks after De La Warr's departure, a new fleet of vessels roared into Jamestown under the command of Sir Thomas Dale, a terrifying martinet whose long years spent rising through the military ranks had taught him that men would best obey through fear. He had been appointed as marshall of Jamestown, but in Lord De La Warr's absence he assumed the role of governor and prepared to impose his own special brand of discipline on the colonists. His first action on landing was to grab Christopher Newport by the beard and threaten to hang him for misleading London with reports of nonexistent prosperity in the colony. "Was it meant," he screamed, "that the people here in Virginia should feed upon trees?" Dale was truly shocked by what he saw, and blamed the colony's woes on the "disordered persons" who lived in Jamestown. They were "so prophane, so riotous, so full of mutenie" that he decided to teach them a lesson they would never forget. Within a week of his arrival, he issued a new legal code that made virtually every crime—from blasphemy to stealing an ear of corn—punishable by death. Even picking a flower from a neighbour's garden became a capital offence.

Quick executions were deemed far too humane for Jamestown's good-for-nothing settlers; Dale used his tortured imagination to dream up ever more hideous ways of dispatching dishonest colonists. "Some he apointed to be hanged, some burned, some to be broken upon wheles, others to be staked and some to be shott to deathe; all theis extreme and crewell tortures he used and inflicted upon them to terrefy the reste." Dale's punishments were so hideous that men began to look upon De La Warr's administration with something approaching nostalgia, and the only person who praised the new governor's harsh decrees was the colony's official chronicler, Ralph Hamor. "Dale hath not bin tyranous nor severe at all," he wrote, adding that "the feare of a cruell, painefull and unusuall death more restrains then death itselfe."

Once Jamestown's petty criminals had been disposed of, Sir Thomas set to work on those he had chosen to keep alive. Carpenters were ordered "to build cabins and cottages," and everyone else was sent to the fields to dig, weed, and plant grain. This took five days, after which time many of the men hoped they would be given a day or two of rest. But Dale was in no mood to be lenient and sent them straight back to work, ordering "the reparation of the falling church and so of the storehouse, a stable for our horses, a munition house, a powder house [and] a new well." Bricks were made, a quay was built, and a large barn constructed. No sooner was this finished than Dale penned a letter to his old friend Lord Salisbury, asking him "to furnish hither 2,000 men to be here by the beginning of next Aprill." He promised that "in the space of two yeares . . . [he would] render this whole countrie unto his majestie" by building a string of forts and settlements in the area of land between the James and York rivers.

The Indians watched Dale's progress with fear and trepidation, aware that the time would soon come when he would turn his wrath on them. They were absolutely right; Dale had brought from England "greatt store of armour [and] municyon" with which he intended to launch an all-out offensive against the Indians. His aim was "to so over-master the subtil mischievous Great Powhatan that I should leave him either no roome in his countrie to harbour in, or drawe him to a firme association with ourselves."

The armour was Dale's secret weapon. He had found a stockpile of Elizabethan weaponry in the Tower of London, where it was slowly gathering rust. Breastplates, pauldrons, gorgets, and greaves — none provided any protection against lead shot, but they formed an effective shield against the Indians' arrows and would enable his musketeers to get close to their targets before firing. Dale was itching to launch an offensive and soon had his men sufficiently trained to lead them into battle. Without provocation, he marched a band of his well-armed soldiers against the troublesome Nansemond tribe on the western shores of the Chesapeake, leading from the front with such foolhardy bravado that he almost got himself killed. An arrow landed "juste upon the edge or brimme of his headpiece, the which, if itt had fallen a thowght lower, mightt have shott him into the braynes."

The Indians, having never before seen men in complete suits of armour, were astonished that their arrows bounced off the metal without the slightest effect. "[They] did fall into their exorcismes, conjuracyons and charmes," wrote one soldier, "thereby to cawse raine to fall from the clowdes to extinguishe and putt owtt our men's matches and to wett and spoyle their powder." But the rain held off, and the Indians were killed or captured. The men revelled in their easy victory. "[They] cutt downe their corne, burned their howses and, besydes those which they had slayne, browghtt some of them prisoners to our foarte."

Sir Thomas Dale's brutally effective leadership had shaken Jamestown out of its torpor in a way that not even Lord De La Warr could have imagined. The tribes nearest to the settlement had been all but neutralised, and the threat of violence had subdued even the belligerent Powhatan—at least for the time being. But Dale still had one serious problem that needed to be tackled if Jamestown was ever to prosper. It was imperative that he find a long-term source of wealth for the colony—something that would justify the expense of the Virginia Company's supply ships.

The difficulty was to discover what that commodity might be. As long ago as 1586, Ralph Lane had concluded that no American colony could survive unless it generated more wealth than the cost of its upkeep. "The discovery of a good mine . . . or a passage to the south sea . . . and nothing else, can bring this country in request to be inhabited by our nation." Harriot had agreed with Lane's prognosis, although he had been rather more imaginative in his conclusions. In the absence of gold and silver, he concluded that tobacco was the only commodity that had the potential to reap massive cash dividends.

This had not been possible in the 1580s, for smoking was still very much a novelty. But much had changed in the intervening years. Pipe smoking had become a commonplace rather than a luxury, and despite King James's well-publicised aversion to smoking, more and more of his courtiers had followed Ralegh's example and taken up the custom of "drinking" tobacco. The popularity of the new pastime had led to a flurry of publications about the merits and drawbacks of smoking. Although no one went so far as to suggest it was bad for the health, a few critics hinted that it was addictive, and criticised its "wanton and excessive use." But a far greater number extolled its benefits. Roger Marbecke was one of the most vocal; he championed the cause of heavy smokers in his *Defence of Tabacco*, reviving the old argument that tobacco was an effective cure for the rheum and reminding the antipipe fraternity that "we are by nature subject to overmuch moisture and rheumatic matter." It was a line of reasoning that was eagerly adopted by the slop-bellied elite, for the logical conclusion to such an argument was that the more one ate, the more one needed to smoke, and the more one smoked, the more one could eat.

Increased demand had pushed prices sky-high. In 1600 tobacco was, according to John Aubrey, "sold for its weight in silver." He claimed to have heard "some of our old yeomen neighbours say that when they went to Malmesbury or Chippenham Market, they culled out their best shillings to lay in the scales against the tobacco." This should have been the best possible news for Jamestown, but there was one major drawback that even Harriot had neglected to mention. The tobacco that grew in Virginia was *Nico-*

tiana rustica, a sour-flavoured leaf that was "poore and weake and of a byting tast." It was so disgusting that even the most fanatical of smokers ended up spluttering into their beards after an evening puffing it in their pipes. By the time King James was on the throne, virtually all of the tobacco smoked in England was *Nicotiana tobacum*, a far superior plant, which came from the Spanish New World. The economic consequence of this was severe: tons of English silver ended up in the pockets of Spanish tobacco merchants, which added fuel to the fire of the critics who bemoaned the fact that "the treasure of this land is vented for smoke."

One man who agreed with this conclusion—but who was also an inveterate smoker—was John Rolfe, who had sailed for Virginia on the *Sea Venture*, the ship that was wrecked in the Bermudas in 1609. He was fortunate to rescue his sea chest from the surf, for among his doublets and ruffs he carried a tiny packet of seeds that he hoped to plant on reaching Jamestown. These were seeds of the fine-tasting *Nicotiana tobacum*, and Rolfe's aim was to cultivate enough plants to keep him in tobacco for the rest of his days. But he also kept one eye fixed on the possibility of making his fortune out of his experiment. The Rolfes were a canny clan, and John's father's epitaph might have equally served as his own: "he increased his property . . . by exporting and importing such things as England abounded in or needed."

Rolfe planted his seeds shortly after his arrival in Jamestown. Much to his surprise, they sprouted into healthy plants whose large leaves were soon ready to be picked and cured. There followed an agonising wait while the tobacco dried. After a few months, Rolfe asked fellow colonist Ralph Hamor to take part in the "experience and triall." No sooner had the two men lit their pipes than they realised that they were sampling a sublime smoking tobacco which was both smooth and strong and also had a lingering aftertaste. "No country under the sunne may, or doth, affoord more pleasant, sweet and strong tobacco then I have tasted there [in Jamestown]," wrote Hamor. He penned a letter to the London merchants informing them of the exciting news that it would not be long before Rolfe and his fellow colonists "will make and returne such tobacco this yeere that even England shall acknowledge the goodnesse thereof."

Rolfe himself was more cautious, yet he was quietly impressed by the success of his experiment and devoted his evening hours to curing his leaves. "Tobacco [is] verie commodyous," he wrote, "which thriveth so well that (no doubt) after a little more triall and experience in the curing thereof it will compare with the best in the West Indies."

This "triall" took almost two years, but by 1612 Rolfe was confident that his tobacco was a match for anything grown by the Spanish. He sent a small batch back to England and awaited the reaction of London's courtiers. Their response was extremely positive. They concurred with Rolfe's claim that his own leaves were as fine as those that came from Spain's merchants, and many predicted that his tobacco would prove the saving of Jamestown. "This commodity tobacco," wrote Ralegh's old friend Robert Harcourt, "will bring as great a benefit and profit to the undertakers as ever the Spaniards gained by the best and richest silver myne in all their Indies." He was absolutely right: large bales of tobacco were soon being shipped to England to satisfy the demand, and most colonists were growing "enough to buy clothes and such necessaries as are needfull for themselves and household." Soon they had earned enough money to warrant the Virginia Company's sending a ship "furnished with all manner of clothing, household stuff and such necessaries to establishe a magazin [shop] there." Tobacco had quickly become Jamestown's "principall commodytie"—and the colony had its first shop.

Dale was alarmed rather than pleased at the industriousness of Rolfe and his fellow colonists. He had put considerable effort into persuading them to till the land for planting much-needed food crops. Now, to his dismay, he discovered that the plants sprouting in the fields were not wheat or oats but tobacco. Since this was certain to lead to food shortages, he immediately issued another of his infamous decrees: "no farmer . . . shall plant anie tobacco unles he shall yerely manure, sett and mayntayne for himself and every manservaunt twoe acres of ground with corne." If the colonists obeyed this order, then "they may plant as much tobacco as they will." If not, then "all their tobacco shalbe forfeyte to the colony."

Dale had been right to worry about the lack of crops, for food once again ran short as soon as winter approached. To avoid a repetition of the "starving time," he sent Samuel Argall, one of his captains, on a food-bartering expedition to the Indians that lived on the Potomac River—tribes found to be friendly on previous visits.

Although food was Argall's principal objective, he also had a more ambitious project in mind—one that had been proposed by the merchants of the Virginia Company, probably on the advice of Sir Walter Ralegh. In the absence of any news of John White's lost colonists, they had sent instructions "to procure from them [the Indians] some of theire children, to be brought up in our language and manners." It was hoped that once these Indian youths spoke English, they would be able to reveal undisclosed secrets about their land. The merchants also suggested that a few priests be sent back to England in order that they might be converted to Christianity. Christianised Indians, it was believed, would be less warlike than pagan ones.

Captain Argall headed for the Potomac River and renewed his acquaintance with the local chieftain, Iapassus, who readily agreed to barter his grain for trinkets. Laden with more food than he could carry, the captain then turned to his second objective—cajoling an Indian into accompanying him back to Jamestown. He had no particular care as to the identity of this captive until he learned that a most enticing hostage was within his grasp. "Whilst I was in this businesse," he wrote, "I was told by certaine Indians, my friends, that the great Powhatan's daughter, Pocahontas, was [nearby]." This sent him into a flurry of excitement, for he knew that such a well-born captive would prove a valuable bargaining chip "for the ransoming of so many Englishmen as were with Powhatan, as also to get such armes and tooles as hee, and other Indians, had got by murther." Argall immediately began to hatch a plot, "resolving to possesse myselfe of her by any stratagem that I could use."

His plan was calculated, pragmatic, and altogether more cunning than the one being pursued by Sir Thomas Dale. The governor had attempted to check Powhatan's authority by murdering his subjects. Argall preferred to use guile to achieve the same result. He gave a sackload of trinkets to his "old friend" Chief Iapassus and asked him "how and by what meanes he might procure hir captive."

Iapassus was wary about becoming involved with such a dangerous scheme. Pocahontas, after all, was Powhatan's favourite daughter, and the emperor would be sure to revenge himself on the Potomac Indians if any harm befell her. But Captain Argall assured the chieftain that he would "use her with all faire and gentle entreaty." After much persuasion, Iapassus agreed to lend his support, suggesting that Argall use "his wife [as] an instrument" to coax young Pocahontas aboard the English vessel.

The plan was straightaway put into effect and everything went smoothly. Although Pocahontas was reluctant to visit the ship, the chieftain's wife assured her that there was nothing to fear. "So, forthwith, aboord they went, the best cheere that could be made." As Argall's three guests ate their meal, Iapassus casually asked if they could spend the night on the ship. Pocahontas was taken aback by such a strange request, but she did not wish to offend her host by objecting. "Supper ended [and] Pocahontas was lodged in the gunner's roome" while Iapassus and his wife slept nearby.

Pocahontas spent a fretful night on board, being "possesed with feare and desire of returne," and she woke at the crack of dawn and begged Iapassus to be gone. But the chieftain stalled for time, giving Argall the chance to break the news that she was now a hostage. Pocahontas was "exceeding pensive and discontented" when she realised that she had been the victim of trickery. She begged Iapassus to secure her release, but although he said he was "no les discontented that he should be the meanes of her captivity," he held out little hope of success.

Now that Argall had the "princess" under armed guard, he explained the reasons for his actions. He apologised for taking her hostage, but reminded her that her father was holding "eight of our English men" as well as "many swordes, peeces and other tooles." Pocahontas quickly realised that there was little use in resisting, and allowed herself to be taken to Jamestown. A messenger was immediately sent to Powhatan to inform him that "if he would send home the Englishmen . . . and also a great quantitie of corne, that then he should have his daughter restored; otherwise not."

The news "much grieved" Powhatan, but he stalled for time, dispatching seven English prisoners back to Jamestown and assuming that Pocahontas was worth more to the English alive than dead. In this he was correct; Sir Thomas Dale issued strict instructions that she was to be well treated, and also asked one of the settlement's young ministers to begin instructing her in the Christian faith. Such a policy had been proposed some years earlier by Ralegh, who held it "very reasonable and charitable to send preachers, safely guarded if need bee, to offer infidells the gladd tidings of the Gospell."

Several months passed without any new messages from Powhatan. He was sent a reminder that "it should be at his choice whether he would establish peace or continue enemies with us." Still there was no response. The emperor seemed to have retreated into the wilderness, abandoning his "dearest darling daughter" to her English captors.

By the spring of 1614, Dale had grown so impatient that he decided to take matters into his own hands. Anxious to meet Powhatan face to face, he selected 150 of his best men and "went up into his owne river where his cheifest habitations were, and carried with us his daughter, either to move them to fight for her . . . or to restore the residue of our demand."

Word of Dale's expedition spread like wildfire. The Indians made

Captain Argall bribed an Indian chief to help coax Pocahontas on board his ship. His actions were to prove the turning point in Jamestown's fortunes

"a great bravado ... demaunding the cause of our comming thither." The armour-clad English responded by shouting to the tribesmen that the purpose of their mission "was to deliver Pocahontas, whom purposely we had brought with us, and to receive our armes, men and corne." A few of the more nervous chieftains asked what would happen if Powhatan refused to strike a deal. Dale's answer was as uncompromising as ever, warning them he would "fight with them, burn their howses, take away their canoas, breake downe their fishing weares, and doe them what other damages we could."

He meant every word: when one tribe lifted their bows and fired on the governor's boat, Dale "went ashoare and burned in that verie place some forty houses and of the things we found therein made freeboote and pillage ... [and] hurt and killed five or sixe of these men." The Indians were so shocked at the ferocity of his attack that they told him "they themselves would be right glad of our love and would indeavour to helpe us to what we came for."

The English party continued upstream to the populous settlement of Matchcot, where they found 400 warriors, "well appointed with their bowes and arrowes," who dared the men to come ashore. The soldiers had no wish to look cowardly, "so ashoare we went, our best landing being up a high steepe hill." A tense standoff followed while the two enemies assessed each other's strengths and weaknesses. A clash seemed inevitable until Pocahontas stepped ashore to defuse the situation. She also passed on the message to the Indians that "if her father had loved her he would not value her lesse then old swordes, peeces or axes," and that unless Powhatan complied with Dale's request, "she should still dwell with the English men who loved her."

The Indians continued to taunt their English foes, telling them that "they were there ready to defend themselves if we pleased to assault them." But Dale refused to rise to the bait, for he was genuine in his desire to negotiate Pocahontas's release. He informed the chieftains that he intended to play by the rules, "assuring them till the next day, by noone, we would not molest, hurt nor detaine any of them, and then before we fought, our drum and trumpets should give them warning."

During this uneasy standoff, Dale received an important delegation: "Two of Powhatan's sonnes, being very desirous to see their sister, who was there present ashoore with us, came unto us; at the sight of whom, and her wellfare . . . they much rejoyced." They assured Dale that they were tired of the continual bloodshed and promised "that they would undoubtedly perswade their father to redeeme her and to conclude a firme peace forever with us." Shortly afterwards, Powhatan's brother also arrived at Dale's camp with much the same message. "[He] promised us his best indeavors to further our just requests."

It suddenly dawned on Dale that he was being presented with a unique opportunity to make peace with Powhatan. His visitors seemed genuine enough in their desire for an end to the hostilities, and Dale was in possession of the one person—Pocahontas—who could secure a truce. Aware that matters of war and peace could only be decided by the emperor, he selected two emissaries—Master Sparkes and John Rolfe—and sent them to Powhatan with orders to negotiate an end to almost eight years of conflict.

The events that followed are as bizarre as they are confusing. The fragmentary records that survive leave many gaps in the story, but there is enough information to piece together what was, even by Jamestown's standards, a quite extraordinary development. After Dale's two negotiators set off into the forest, the governor was given the astonishing news that John Rolfe was in love with Pocahontas and had secretly proposed to marry her.

This was no passing fancy. "Long before this time," recalled colonist Ralph Hamor, "Maister John Rolfe had bin in love with Pocahontas and she with him." Rolfe had managed to keep their affair a secret—no mean feat in the tiny settlement of Jamestown—and the first that the governor learned of the romance was now, "at the instant that we were in parlee with them [the Indians]."

Rolfe had asked his old friend Hamor to break the news while he was away, aware that Dale was likely to explode with rage. He had also composed a long letter—to be given to the governor once he was deep in the forest—in which he attempted to persuade him of the benefits of their getting married. "I freely subject myselfe to your grave and mature judgement," he wrote, "either perswadinge me to desist or encouraginge me to persist herein with a religious feare and godly care." He need have looked no further for support than the writings of Sir Walter Ralegh, who had long believed in the value of mixed marriages, arguing that Indian men should be shipped to England, civilised, and then sent back to be paired off with English colonists. "[After] being civilled and converted heere," he wrote, "upon there returne . . . they may be matched in marriage with English women."

Rolfe chose a more personal line of argument, explaining to Dale that he had fought long and hard to control his passion, and that "my hart and best thoughtes are, and have byn a long tyme, soe intangled and inthralled in soe intricate a laborinth that I was even awearied to unwynde myselfe thereout." He realised that marrying Pocahontas would be somewhat unconventional, and conceded that her "education hath byn rude, her manners barbarous [and] her generacion cursed." These were not his only concerns. He knew that "the vulgar sorte" would taunt him with the jibe that he only wished to marry her "to gorge myselfe" on her female body.

The young lover listed dozens of reasons why Pocahontas was an unsuitable partner, allowing himself the briefest of paragraphs to explain the benefits of the match: "for the good of the plantacion, the honour of our countrye, for the glorye of God, for myne owne salvacion and for the convertinge to the true knowledge of God and Jesus Christ an unbelievinge creature, namely Pocahontas."

Rolfe did not wait for Dale's response before making his move. In the course of the peace negotiations with Powhatan, he decided to risk the governor's wrath by asking for Pocahontas's hand in marriage. The details are again obscure, and the official account—written at a later date by Hamor—records only that "[news] of this pretended marriage came soone to Powhatan's knowledge." But there was no outburst or rash violence from the emperor, and no suggestion that he objected to the proposal. Indeed, Rolfe's desire to marry his daughter was "a thing acceptable to him," and he gave "his sudden consent thereunto."

Dale would have had good reason to punish John Rolfe for acting with such presumption, and in any normal circumstance he would have probably had him executed. But his tyrannical temper was softened by the idea of a marriage alliance with the Indians. He had mulled over Rolfe's letter and been unable to find any compelling reason why they should not be married, especially as Pocahontas had recently converted to Christianity. "[She] renounced publickly her countrey idolatry, openly confessed her Christian faith, [and] was, as she desired, baptised." To Rolfe's evident relief, the governor declared that he was "well approving of the match, [and] gave his consent." He did so, he said, "for the good of the plantacion."

The preparations for the wedding completely overshadowed the peace negotiations. This was not a time for the Indians and English to be fighting, and both sides immediately suspended hostilities— ostensibly so that they could plant their crops. A few of the more hawkish English troops felt they had been cheated of a fight, but most were relieved at the outcome and marched back to Jamestown to prepare the settlement for the first joyous celebration in years. The forthcoming wedding even softened the belligerent Powhatan; "[he] sent an olde uncle of hirs, named Opachisco, to give her as his deputy in the church, and two of his sonnes to see the mariage solemnized."

The wedding, which took place on April 5, 1614, was performed by the Reverend Richard Buck, a "painfull [diligent] preacher" who had the dubious distinction of being father to "the first idiot born in that plantation." The ceremony was an occasion of great joy, for both the English and the Indians, and was followed by the customary festivities. Dale was so delighted with the match that he allowed a rare glimpse of good humour into his writing. "Her father and friends gave approbation to it," he wrote, "and her uncle gave her to him in the church. She lives civilly and lovingly with him [Rolfe], and I trust will increase in goodness as the knowledge of God increaseth in her."

The marriage proved to be the turning point in the colony's fortunes. It prompted both Indian and English to draw back from the abyss of eternal warfare, and caused the two leaders to consider whether a lasting peace might better serve everyone's interests. Dale showed an uncharacteristic reluctance to lead his troop back on the offensive, while Powhatan's great age had exhausted his desire to fight. He had long ago realised that he had no hope of expelling the English from his land, and had no wish to spend his declining years watching his race slide into oblivion. He wrote a loving letter to Dale "desiring to be ever friends" and informing him that Pocahontas "should be [Dale's] childe, and ever dwell with [him]." He also returned all of the English "peeces, swords and tooles," which had for so long been a sticking point. Unbeknown to anyone, and unnoticed by Dale, this stash of weaponry included antiquated muskets and a brass mortar that predated the Jamestown settlement by almost twenty years.

Powhatan was anxious that the peace should apply not only to his own tribe but to those who fell under his indirect control. He now approached Dale and "named such of his people, and neighbouring kings, as he desired to be included and have the benefit of the peace." He also promised that if any "of his men stole from us, or killed our cattel, he woulde send them to us to bee punished as we thought fit."

This new truce was eagerly adopted by Powhatan's extended family and subject kings. The first to agree to peace was his warlike half-brother, Opechancanough. He visited Dale and told him that he "desired I would call him friend, and that he might call me so, saying he was a great captaine and did alwaies fight; that I was also a great captaine and therefore he loved mee." The chieftain excelled himself in his generosity, sending parcels of food and victuals to Sir Thomas, "and every eight or ten daies I have messages and presents from him, with many apparances that he much desireth to continue friendshippe."

Others quickly followed suit, and even the powerful Chickahominy tribe, for so long a thorn in the side of the English, decided that the time for hostility was over. They sent a message to Dale informing him that they "longed to be friends." When he put them to the test by asking them "if they would have King James to be their King," they readily assented, and with a great cry "pronounced themselves Englishmen." Indeed, they were so keen to prove their loyalty that they expressed their desire "to become not only trusty friends, but even King James's subjects and tributaries." After a hastily arranged vote, they changed their tribal name to *Tossantessas*—a distortion of the Indian word for *English*. Henceforth they were to be known as "new Englishmen."

The colonists were astonished by the turn of events brought about by Rolfe's marriage to Pocahontas. A long and extremely bloody chapter was at last coming to a close, and peace now seemed a real possibility. Ralph Hamor concluded his account by informing his readers that the surprise marriage had brought "friendly commerce and trade, not onely with Powhatan himselfe, but also with his subjects round about us." He saw no reason, he said, "why the collonie should not thrive a pace."

Even Sir Thomas Dale was cautiously optimistic. He listed the many dividends that he expected peace to bring: "our catell to increase without danger of destroying; our men at libertie to hunt freely for venison; to fish, to doe anything else or goe any whither without danger." Aware that Pocahontas was "the knot to binde this peace the stronger," he was even able to foresee a time when the Indians—"as we grow in familiaritie with them"—would become friends.

Dale resigned his post in the spring of 1616 and set sail for England, taking with him John Rolfe, Pocahontas—whose name had

Peace brought rich dividends for the English, and Sir Thomas Dale antici-
pated the time when the Indians, "as we grow in familiaritie with them,"
would become friends

been Christianised to Rebecca—and their infant son, Thomas. Their visit was a stroke of genius on the part of Dale, for not only did it afford the Virginia Company invaluable publicity for their colony, but it also offered tangible proof of the peace that now existed between the English and the Indians.

The timing could not have been better, for the pace of colonisation had slowed down over recent months, and political manoeuvrings had led to a number of adventurers' dropping out of the Company. Now, with a civilised savage in town, the London merchants were able to refute, once and for all, the charge that Virginia was a land peopled by barbarians.

Dale's vessel anchored at Plymouth and Mr. and Mrs. Rolfe continued on their journey by stagecoach. They were accompanied by a retinue of a dozen Indians—Pocahontas's "court"—led by her brother-in-law, Tomocomo, who had been given strict instructions by Powhatan to make a mental record of everything of interest. He was also ordered to count the population of England by cutting a notch into his "long sticke" every time he saw a new face. Poor Tomocomo tried to fulfil this latter request, but he had scarcely left Plymouth harbour before "his arithmetike fayled" and his stick had been whittled down to a handful of wood shavings. "He was," noted John Smith wryly, "quickly weary of that taske."

The journey to London was one of considerable discomfort, not made any easier by the fact that the merchants of the Virginia Company had given the party an extremely ungenerous allowance of just "fowre pound a weeke." Nor did they show any courtesy towards their distinguished visitors. Unlike Sir Walter Ralegh, who had taken Manteo first to Hampton Court and then to Durham House—his own home—the merchants hired cheap rooms in a tawdry alehouse. One company wag booked them into the Belle Sauvage Inn of Ludgate Hill, to the probable mirth of his colleagues. The owner of the tavern, Mr. Sauvage, quickly capitalised on the fame of his exotic guests and replaced his pub sign with a portrait of Pocahontas.

But if the Company was curiously indifferent to the presence of its guests, London itself was enchanted. The Indians caused a sensation in the streets and markets of the capital, and they found themselves feted wherever they went. The great and the good were particularly excited at the prospect of being entertained by a troop of genuine savages, and Tomocomo proved a good sport when it came to delighting his hosts. His party turn was "to sing and dance his diabolicall measures"—something that never failed to impress his audience. His war dances were even more impressive—"singing and clapping hands . . . shooting, hollowing, stamping with antike gesture, like to many devils." He also liked to "discourse of his countrey and religion," using Dale's "man" as his interpreter, and enjoyed giving lengthy monologues about the Indian god, Okee.

News of this soon reached the Lord Bishop of London, John King, who declared himself keen to meet this curious band of Indians. They were invited to his palace, where the bishop received them "with festivall state and pompe," according to the Reverend Samuel Purchas, "beyond what I have seene in his great hospitalitie afforded to other ladies." Pocahontas behaved with particular propriety and decorum. "[She] did not onely accustome herselfe to civilitie," wrote Purchas, "but still carried herselfe as the daughter of a king, and was accordingly respected, not onely by the Company, which allowed provision for herselfe and her sonne, but of divers particular persons of honor."

Tomocomo was less impressed by the niceties of polite society and launched into another lengthy monologue about Okee, bragging that the Indian god was a more tangible presence than the remote Christian deity. "[Okee] doth often appeare," he informed the horrified bishop, adding that the deity could be conjured from thin air by priests uttering "certaine words of a strange language." It made for a terrifying sight, for Okee wailed in "strange words and gestures" and made "awefull tokens of his presence."

When the bishop asked Tomocomo for a description of this bizarre phantom, the Indian explained that he looked very much like an Indian tribesman. "His apparition is in forme of a personable

Virginian," he said, "with a long blacke locke on the left side, hanging downe neere to the foot." These Virginian "love-locks" had become all the rage in London, having been first brought back to the capital by Sir Walter Ralegh's men more than thirty years previously. It was not a fashion that found favour with the Reverend Mr. Purchas. He declared them to be "sinister . . . Christians imitating savages, and they the devill."

The now ageing John Smith had known for some time of Pocahontas's arrival, yet it was several months before he headed to London, accompanied by a party of curious friends. More than seven years had passed since he had last seen Pocahontas, and the princess had changed from a girl into a married woman. His excitement at seeing her was soon checked by her frosty reception: "after a modest salutation, without any word, she turned about, obscured her face, as not seeming well contented; and in that humour . . . we all left her two or three houres." The reason for her strange behaviour bewildered Smith, and he sat outside her chamber puzzling over it. He was no less surprised when the door opened and she invited him back into the room, smiling as if nothing had happened. Smith never learned the cause of her ill humour, and the two of them chatted about old times and relived the many occasions on which Pocahontas had helped the English. At one point, Smith paused to ask her why she insisted on calling him "father."

"You did promise Powhatan [that] what was yours should bee his, and he the like to you," she explained. "You called him father, being in his land a stranger, and by the same reason so I must doe you."

Smith was disappointed to learn that the Indians had not yet been received at court, and he took it upon himself to write to King James I's wife, Anna, to inform her of all the kindnesses that "this tender Virgin" had performed for the English in Virginia, and to beg that she be received with all due pomp at the royal court. He reminded the queen that Pocahontas had saved the lives of dozens of Englishmen, and has also been "the instrument to preserve this colonie from death, famine and utter confusion." She was a living example of what could be achieved by the civilising influence of an English colony in Virginia, having rejected "her barbarous condition, [and] maried to an English gentleman with whom, at this present, she is in England, the first Christian ever of that nation, the first Virginian ever spake English, or had a childe in mariage by an Englishman."

The queen heeded Smith's advice and invited Pocahontas and her retinue to the most extravagant and bibulous festival of the year—the Twelfth Night revels. They were to attend the first performance of Ben Jonson's *Masque of Christmas*—written specially for the occasion—and would afterwards join the revellers in the Banqueting Hall, which had been redecorated in gold and silver. The planned entertainment was to be so lavish that one courtier predicted it would "increase his majesty's debt by two thousand pounds."

The queen arranged for her guests to be treated with kindness. They were "well placed at the masque" and were "graciously used." But King James was not quite so receptive as his sympathetic wife. His well-publicised phobia about Indians had in no way diminished over the years; he still considered them to be "barbarous," "beastly," and "vile." For all his misgivings about their presence at the festivities, he showed an uncharacteristic courtesy and even had the good grace to allow Pocahontas and her party to be presented to him. The bewildered Indians were passed along a long line of perfumed courtiers until they reached a dirty and rather dishevelled fifty-year-old with food in his beard and stains on his waistcoat. Overcome by the noise and bustle of the occasion, the significance of the moment escaped them. They had no idea that they had been introduced to the mighty King James, *weroance* of Virginia, and it was only when they were told to fall to their knees in homage that they realised he was someone of importance. When John Smith later asked Tomocomo what he thought of England's *weroance*, "he denied ever to have seene the king," wrote Smith, "till by circumstances he was satisfied he had." Even so, he was sorely disappointed that King James cut such an unimpressive figure and

Pocahontas arrived in London in 1616. She was given lodgings in the Belle
Sauvage Inn, whose owner capitalised on her fame by replacing his pub sign
with her portrait

was surprised that he had not been presented with gifts and trinkets.

"You gave Powhatan a white dog," he reminded Smith, "which Powhatan fed as himselfe, but your king gave me nothing, and I am better than your white dog." Smith nodded wearily, but did not have the heart to tell him that King James was so prejudiced against "savages" that Tomocomo was lucky not to have been thrown to the dogs.

Pocohontas's arrival in London coincided with some wholly unexpected news for King James's most famous prisoner, Sir Walter Ralegh, who was now in his sixty-fifth year. On March 19, 1616, the lieutenant of the Tower was handed a royal warrant that authorised his immediate release from prison. After thirteen years behind bars, Ralegh suddenly found himself a free man.

The news came as a bolt from the blue. For years he had been petitioning for his freedom, promising that as soon as he was out of jail he would return to Guiana and renew his search for the gold mines of El Dorado. "I am contented," he wrote to the Privy Council, "to venture all I have." He had written to Robert Cecil, begged the queen to intervene, and used his influence over the young Prince Henry to try to secure his release. All had expressed their sympathy, and Prince Henry had castigated the king for keeping Ralegh in prison, declaring that "none but my father would keep such a bird in a cage." But Ralegh's request to be released had been blocked on every occasion, and the lords of the council had sent other adventurers to Guiana in his place. Now—with royal finances in dire straits—the king had dramatically changed his mind and decided to give Ralegh the opportunity to prove his claims. He was to sail to South America and bring back the gold that could replenish King James's empty coffers.

Sir Walter's first act on being released was to take a long walk through the streets of London. "[He] goes up and down," wrote one, "seeing the sights and places built or bettered since his imprisonment." Much had changed during the long years he had been in the

Tower. The half-timbered Tudor city was fast being replaced by handsome stone structures—the Banqueting Hall, the New Exchange, and the imposing Northumberland House in Charing Cross. Even Durham House had been transformed: its mouldering facade had been reconstructed in finely hewn stone.

Changes were also apparent in Westminster Abbey, where one particularly magnificent tomb must certainly have arrested Ralegh's step. The monument to Queen Elizabeth I was now complete, an extravagance of marble that had been adorned by the greatest craftsmen of the age. Nicholas Hilliard had coloured the queen's cape, while John de Critz had tooled the chiselled inscription with gold. The Latin epitaph would have pleased Elizabeth, for it remembered her as "the mother of this her country, the nurse of religion and learning; for perfect skill of many languages, for glorious endowments, as well of mind as of body, a prince incomparable." But there was one notable omission in the long list of successes and achievements: there was no mention of Virginia, the land of the Virgin Queen. It was a sorry oversight, since it was Elizabeth who had been the first and original benefactor of the New World and the monarch who had made colonisation possible.

More than three decades after Ralegh had welcomed a trembling Manteo into Elizabeth's glittering court, he rode out to greet another Indian, the princess Pocahontas. Tradition relates that he met her in the gilded splendour of Syon House, home of the Earl of Northumberland, where the aged and now infirm Thomas Harriot was still in residence. But truth and legend have merged into one, and what really happened behind the walls of that great house remains a mystery. England's diligent antiquarians have searched high and low for any whisper of evidence, but they have been unable to unearth any details from Syon's dust-filled library. Yet they had no wish to allow the empty truth to get in the way of a good story. Softened by the romance of the tale, they allowed a rare streak of fantasy into their accounts, relating how the little party might have clambered into a carriage and trooped off to the Tower of London to entertain the wizard earl. Here, deep in the bowels of that ancient prison, Northumberland was said to have mended Pocahontas's mussel-shell earrings.

It was a fairy-tale end to an enchanting story, but it probably belongs to the realms of fiction. The truth about that ice-chill winter of 1616 will never be known, for the Great Fire of London swept through most of the records, and the only known fact is that the Indian princess did indeed move her lodgings to Brentford, the site of Syon House.

Yet it remains fitting that fact and legend have blended into one and that our last glance of Ralegh and Pocahontas is of them seated side by side in a boneshaker carriage, vanishing like ghosts into the mists of a frozen London.

The only certainty of that winter is that Ralegh was delighted by the joyous news that John Rolfe brought from Jamestown. The establishment of a settlement had been his goal for the greater part of thirty years—a seemingly impossible dream that he had pursued with great energy since the spring of 1584. He had lavished his fortune on the colonisation of the New World, and had assembled many of the brilliant minds of the Elizabethan age to help him in the project. He had inspired loyalty and courage, and pushed men to the limits of their endurance. He might have succeeded had his commanders not let him down and allowed his dream to founder on the marshy island of Roanoke, amid a flurry of arrows and the murderous screams of the Indians.

Now, three decades on, others had built upon his foundations. Inspired by men like Harriot and Lane, they had set sail for the New World with high hopes of success. Their triumph was Ralegh's triumph, and the silver-haired adventurer was enough of a realist to read the signs of their success. It was not to be found in the propaganda of the Virginia Company, and nor was it contained in the eternally optimistic letters of the governors. The truth was buried in a humdrum report brought back to England by John Rolfe. He brought news that Jamestown had 144 cattle, 216 goats, and "great

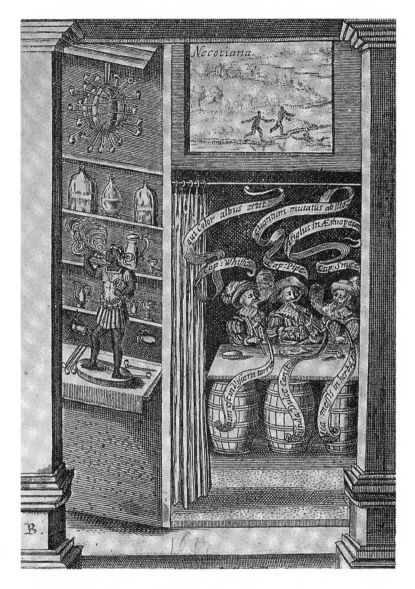

John Rolfe's tobacco was snapped up by London's merchants. "No country under the sunne doth affoord more pleasant, sweet and strong tobacco then I have tasted in Jamestown," wrote one

plentie" of chickens—a simple enough achievement, but one which was to guarantee the colony's future. Jamestown had become self-sufficient, the long-term goal of Ralegh's colonists all those years before. It also had a reason to exist. Tobacco was proving "verie commodyous," while the horizons of this vast continent were being unrolled with every year that passed. America was truly a land of opportunity, and Rolfe told an excited London that there was room "for many hundred thousands of inhabitans."

But the best news of all was the fact that the Indians and the English were at long last living in peace. It had come at a terrible price, but it had led to a "quiet enjoying" of the land. The suits of armour were packed into their crates, the gunpowder was placed in storage, and the muskets remained silent. With no more need for warfare or bloodshed, the search could once again begin for the lost colonists of Roanoke.

EPILOGUE

More than three decades had passed since there had been any news of the settlers left behind on Roanoke, and much had changed in the intervening years. England was now a great sea power, and was respected throughout Europe—a cause of celebration for all the captains and mariners who had challenged Spain's self-proclaimed rule over the oceans. But Queen Elizabeth's brilliant reign was fast fading into history—a glittering epoch that was already being spoken of as a golden age.

Yet two of the greatest Elizabethans, Sir Walter Ralegh and Thomas Harriot, were still alive. Stiff-jointed and withered by age, these doughty champions of American colonisation retained an immense pride in the role they had played in the establishment of a settlement over the seas. The lost colonists were the only reminder that not all had gone according to plan, that there had been much disaster and mishap on the way. They also provided a timely warning that Ralegh's bold and audacious experiment had two endings: one happy and one distinctly tragic.

John White's settlers were not the only ones to be lost on American soil. Three men had been left behind when Sir Francis Drake evacuated Ralph Lane's colonists in 1586. Sir Richard Grenville had deposited a further fifteen men on Roanoke as a holding party in the same year. Some of these had been killed, including Master Coffin and one of his deputies, but that still left a total of at least 123 English men, women, and children unaccounted for—lost in the unmapped wilderness of America. The fate of these unfortunate souls had long fired the imagination of a curious England, and there were many—even in 1618—who believed that some had survived their thirty-two-year ordeal.

Four centuries after they were "lost," their fate continues to fascinate and intrigue. Did White's settlers really move to Croatoan Island? Were they clubbed to death or starved into submission? Or did they settle and intermarry with the local Indian tribes?

Their disappearance has been the subject of endless speculation, and numerous theories have been advanced. Although many have seemed initially plausible, almost all have rested upon slender evidence that has later been proved false.

The most exciting "proof" of the survival of the lost colony surfaced in the latter part of the nineteenth century, when a North Carolinian enthusiast, Hamilton McMillan, claimed to have discovered the descendants of White's settlers. McMillan had become intrigued by a group of "red-bones," or mixed-blood Indians, living in the southeastern corner of the state. His research into their archaic language led to the hypothesis that they used an Elizabethan dialect similar to that spoken by White's colonists. This seemed plausible, and many were inclined to believe him. But when linguistic experts were called in to conduct a detailed investigation into McMillan's work, they found it to be blighted with errors. His English "red-bones" turned out to be nothing more than a figment of his own fantasy.

In the 1930s an exciting new piece of evidence came to light. A chiselled stone was unearthed which bore Eleanor Dare's initials, as well as a lengthy inscription written in Elizabethan English. This revealed the surprising news that the colonists had indeed moved their settlement—not to Croatoan Island, but to the banks of the Chowan River. At first, there was great excitement at the find, but disappointment set in when mistakes were found in the Elizabethan inscription. Soon after, scientific tests conclusively proved that the stone had been carved in the recent past.

The next theory, promulgated by Robert E. Betts in London's *Cornhill Magazine*, was that a Spanish military force had located and killed the lost colonists soon after White's departure. But this, too, was quickly disproved when new evidence was discovered in Spain's archives in Seville.

One by one the claims and theories fell apart, and the riddle of the lost colonists remained as mysterious and intriguing as ever. Too many theoreticians looked for evidence among the records of Ralegh's Roanoke enterprise, and neglected the diaries and journals kept by the early Jamestown settlers—the very men who actually went in search of the lost colonists. It was they who scoured the forests; they who quizzed the Indians; and they who were in the best position to establish the truth. Although their eyewitness accounts are not supported by concrete proof—only a spectacular archaeological discovery will be able to supply that—their findings are as compelling as they are exciting, and offer the only plausible hypothesis as to what happened to John White's lost colonists.

The first clues of their whereabouts were found by John White on his 1590 search-and-rescue mission. He determined that they no longer remained on Roanoke, but brought back little more than supposition as to where they might have gone. There was the word CROATOAN carved into a tree—suggesting that the colonists had headed to Manteo's island home—and there was White's perplexing statement that the colonists had previously told him of their intention to move "50 miles further up into the maine." Neither of these facts made much sense: Croatoan—the first option—was little more than a giant spit of sand, on which its native inhabitants found it hard to produce enough crops to feed themselves. When White had visited the island in 1587, their first concern was that his empty-bellied men would eat into their precious food stocks, "for that they had but little."

The second choice was only slightly more plausible. It would have been hard, though not impossible, for 107 colonists to transport themselves to another location without a much larger vessel than the pinnace that they had at their disposal. Not only did they need to be moved, there were also their personal belongings—which amounted to perhaps 120 large wooden sea chests—as well as a significant quantity of weaponry, tools, and general supplies. To transport such a stockpile of material would have taken three or four journeys, even allowing for the fact that the heavy weaponry had been left behind on Roanoke.

From 1590 until 1607, the colonists were both lost and abandoned. Although the 1603 expedition led by Samuel Mace appears to have brought back news of their survival—or at the very least some plausible rumours—he had no contact with them. The first hint that they might be alive, but in grave danger, came in the last week of April 1607, when Captain Christopher Newport sailed into Chesapeake Bay with the first batch of Jamestown colonists. His initial landfall was on the southern shores of the bay, where, he had been reliably informed, he would find the friendly Chesapeake tribe and their impressive settlement. Much to Newport's surprise, there was no sign of any settlement, nor were there any friendly tribesmen waiting to greet his men. Indeed, scarcely had they landed than they came under a vicious attack from a band of hostile Indians.

Newport continued along the shoreline, puzzled by the fact that although the land had been cleared for farming, there were no tribesmen to be seen. "We went on land and found the place five miles in compass without either bush or tree," wrote George Percy. They wandered through "excellent ground full of flowers . . . [and] came into a little plat of ground full of fine and beautifull strawberries," but "[in] all this march we could neither see savage nor towne." All they did see, rather ominously, were "great smoakes of fire" rising from the clearing in the forest—a fire that appeared to have been started deliberately.

Some months after Newport landed his men at Jamestown, he gleaned information about the tribes that lived on the shores of Chesapeake Bay. All of them, he was told, fell under the rule of Powhatan, except for the Chesapeake tribe. These "Chessipians" had steadfastly refused to submit to Powhatan's authority and were "perceived to be an enemy generally to all these kingdoms." Newport could learn nothing of the lost colonists, and was bewildered as to why the Chesapeake tribe had proved so hostile to his own men— soldiers and musketeers who might have been considered useful allies in their struggle against Powhatan. Nor was he privy to the startling news that John Smith would learn during his visit to Powhatan the following winter.

The purpose of Smith's visit was to acquire desperately needed food supplies, but he soon learned that the emperor had no intention of handing over any grain. Powhatan was by now heartily sick of the Jamestown colonists and had decided to demonstrate his powers of life and death over the Englishmen by revealing the truth about the lost colonists. After years of speculation and rumour, he told an astonished Smith that John White's settlers had survived for almost two decades on the southern shores of Chesapeake Bay, and that most of them—but not all—had been brutally murdered by his henchmen in the spring of 1607, just days before Newport's landfall in the bay. "The men, women and children of the first plantation at Roanoke were by practize and commaundement of Powhatan . . . miserably slaughtered without any offence given him."

Smith was stunned by what he heard. He had long doubted that White's lost colonists could have survived the harsh terrain of Chesapeake Bay—a conclusion reached from the terrible sufferings endured by his own band of settlers. Jamestown's colonists had only survived by the skin of their teeth, even though they had arrived in

America with plentiful victuals and supplies. Now, Smith was being told that White's hardy men and women had achieved something far more remarkable. Their deep well of resourcefulness had enabled them to survive for twenty years in the forest, scratching an existence from the shrubs and berries of the land, collecting crabs on the foreshore, and occasionally snaring rabbits and deer.

It was extremely doubtful that any of the Jamestown settlers could have held out for so long. White's lowborn artisans—brought up in the violent backstreets of London—had proved tougher than them all. Their success was perhaps due to their governor's secret ingredient, the presence of women. Widows, housewives, and young maidens: all knew how to till the land, plant seeds, and tend crops. It was they who had kept their menfolk and children in rude health.

White's lost colonists had defied all the odds. Cut off from the rest of the world, without ships, supplies, or company, they had nonetheless managed to keep themselves alive. How tragic it was that their hopes had been dashed by a single, brutal attack on a bright spring day in 1607. And what made it all the more terrible was the fact that it was their own fellow countrymen who had been the trigger for their demise. For the English were later able to put a date on the massacre, discovering that "the slaughter [occurred] at what tyme this, our colony, under the conduct of Captain Newport, landed within the Chesapeake Bay." Since the date of Newport's arrival is well documented, the massacre must have taken place between April 24 and 27, 1607.

It was the grim prophecies of Powhatan's priests that lay behind his bloody actions. "[They] told him how that from the Chesapeake Bay a nation should arise which should dissolve and give end to his empier, for which he destroyed and put to the sword all such who might lye under any doubtfull construccion of the said prophesie." The roll call of the dead included all of "the inhabitants, the weroances, and his subjects of that province," and had left the Chesapeake tribe "at this daie, and for this cause, extinct." The extent of the massacre—and the annihilation of the tribe—account for the hostile attack experienced by Newport and his men when they first landed on the southern shores of the bay. The warriors who ambushed them were not the Chesapeake Indians, as Newport had mistakenly thought, but tribesmen loyal to Powhatan—probably the very men who had just committed the massacre.

The date of the attack also explains the great plumes of smoke rising from the forest clearings. Powhatan's henchmen were destroying the dwellings of White's settlers, because they did not wish the English arrivals—sighted on the horizon by sharp-eyed lookouts—to discover their murderous deeds.

The onslaught, when it came, probably followed a depressingly familiar pattern. As long ago as 1587, Thomas Harriot had warned that the Indians' favourite method of fighting was "by sudden surprising one another, most commonly about the dawning of the day." The ambush must have come without any warning: a hail of arrows, a scream from the forest, and a ferocious and terrifying assault. The Indians would have formed themselves into small bands whose task was to single out the toughest of the English. These poor victims would have been seized and bound before the tribesmen "beat out their braynes" with wooden cudgels. Only when the strongest men had been slaughtered would they have turned their attentions to the weak, the sick, the women and children. Some, perhaps, were "broyled to death"—slowly burned on a bed of charcoal. Others would have been stripped and flayed alive. Only the fortunate would have been killed in the initial onslaught on the village.

Details of the attack were never recorded, but if archaeologists ever retrieve the skeletons of these lost, unfortunate Elizabethans, they are likely to find skulls and bones that have been crushed, fractured, and pierced with arrows. Powhatan's murderers were always ruthless, and many a colonist must have had his brains dashed out by the thick wooden clubs of the paint-daubed Indians.

The news that Powhatan broke to Captain Smith was both shocking and amazing, but what made it also tantalising was the fact that a few survivors had escaped the massacre. Smith realised that these battered survivors must surely be alive, somewhere in the limitless forest, living in terror of being captured by Powhatan's brutal henchmen. How they had escaped from the attack remained a mystery for the time being, for Powhatan declined to tell Smith exactly what had happened. He chose, instead, to show him "a musket barrel and a bronze mortar and certain pieces of iron which had been theirs." These were his trophies of war, a signal of his superiority over the English colonists, and he reminded Smith that he now had the weaponry that he had craved for so long.

Smith knew that news of the slaughter had to be kept secret, since it was certain to prove deeply embarrassing to King James. He, after all, was still celebrating the fact that he now had a vassal king in America. If news leaked out that Powhatan was actually a mass murderer, James would be the laughingstock of England. Smith therefore took the highly unusual precaution of sending his confidential report directly to the king, thereby circumnavigating the Virginia Company.

Powhatan had also intended his secret to remain undisclosed, for he had vowed to murder Smith that very night. But the unexpected intervention of Pocahontas caused his plans to misfire and Smith was able to escape—taking with him the news of the lost colony. But Smith remained true to his word about keeping silent, and it was more than a decade before he publicly revealed that "Powhatan confessed that hee had been at their slaughter and had divers utensils to show." Others among King James's courtly circle were less discreet: news of Smith's tragic discovery was soon leaked to the Virginia Company. When colonial secretary William Strachey was sent to Jamestown in 1609, he was sufficiently intrigued to spend time and effort piecing together all the evidence. His findings, along with the other evidence, allow for a tentative reconstruction of events that occurred between the departure of John White in 1587 and the great slaughter of 1607.

It seems certain that the colonists concluded that their best chance of survival was to split into two groups. One set—numbering, perhaps, ten or twelve men—headed for Croatoan Island to keep a lookout for the supply ships that were believed to be bringing Governor White back to America. Croatoan was an excellent place to keep watch, for its eastern coastline looked out over the Atlantic breakers and any vessel could be quickly contacted by the traditional method of fire and smoke. The main body of the colonists, meanwhile, moved to the southern shores of the Chesapeake, close to the settlement of Skicoac, where John White and Thomas Harriot had been given such a warm welcome in 1586.

It is impossible to put an exact date on when the colonists moved from Roanoke, but Governor White's journal reveals that it is likely to have occurred soon after he left for England. When he arrived back on the island in 1590, he had found the settlement "almost overgrowen with grasse and weedes"—an important piece of evidence. The houses had collapsed and his buried chests had been "long sithence digged up againe and broken up." Indeed, his most treasured possessions had clearly spent several seasons exposed to the elements, for his "pictures and mappes [were] rotten and spoyled with rain, and my armour almost eaten through with rust."

The colonists would certainly have wanted to establish their new settlement before the onset of winter, allowing themselves time to build their framework dwellings and clear some of the land. The presence of wives and children would have been an added stimulus for the men to prepare fields in readiness for spring. They must have been cordially welcomed by the Chesapeake tribe, who saw them as useful allies in their struggle against Powhatan, and for the next two decades the two communities appear to have lived in peace. "[For] twenty and od yeares [they] had peaceably lyved," wrote Strachey, "and intermixed with those savadges [the Chesapeakes] and were off his [Powhatan's] territory."

Two decades in America would have transformed the colonists— perhaps making them more Indian than English—and they would have almost certainly intermarried with the local tribeswomen. The writers of the 1605 play *Eastward Hoe* may not have been altogether fanciful when they claimed that "a whole country of English is there . . . they have married with the Indians and make them bring forth as beautiful faces as any have in England." White's men and women would have learned to hunt, trap, and fish—skills they did not possess when they had first arrived—and they would have given the Indians many benefits in return: smelting metal, the wheel, firearms, and the art of constructing two-storey dwellings. These formed the source of many of the rumours about the lost colonists that filtered back to Jamestown in the early years of the settlement.

It is intriguing to wonder who, among the 1587 settlers, was still alive in the year of the massacre. Virginia Dare would have been in her twentieth year and might have given birth to a number of children. Young "Harvie," known only by his surname, would have been a similar age, and perhaps espoused to an Indian girl. The older generation would be approaching their forties—old age—but it is quite likely that many of them would still have been in robust health. America's climate had already proved itself to be far more healthy than the damp, disease-ridden air of England.

As the years rolled on, the lost colonists would have become more and more accustomed to their new homeland. Many, perhaps, preferred life in America to England; food, after all, was plentiful, and hostility from the Indians was little more than a distant memory. Lulled into a false sense of security, they were caught completely off guard when Powhatan launched his attack—the single biggest massacre in the early history of the New World.

Strachey's research into that massacre—and John Smith's account of Powhatan's confession—might have closed the case once and for all. But not all of the lost colonists were butchered on that April day in 1607. A few swift-footed survivors fled for their lives into the surrounding forest, throwing themselves on the mercy of less hostile Indians. The sensational rumours that filtered back to England—that some of them were still alive—were indeed true.

The Virginia Company was the first to take seriously these shadowy stories. Its 1608 official pamphlet, A *true and sincere declaration*, revealed the exciting news that "some of our nation, planted by Sir Walter Ralegh, [are] yet alive, within fifty miles of our fort." The merchants were desperate to find these colonists, aware that they could "open up the womb and bowels of this country." They ordered a search party to be sent into the forests to track them down, and this diligent band—the first serious attempt to locate the lost colonists—came within a whisker of finding them. They only gave up when they found their path blocked by the Indians. Nevertheless, the evidence they produced was exciting. "Though denied by the savages speech with them, [they] found crosses and letters, the characters and assured testimonies of Christians cut in the barks of trees."

Within a year, the Company had received further news of their survival. It was able to assure Sir Thomas Gates of their exact location, informing him that at a village called Pakerikanick, close to the Chowan River, "you will find four of the English alive, left by Sir Walter Rawley, which escaped from the slaughter of Powhatan." They added that these men were captives, living "under the protection of a *weroance* called Gepanocon, by whose consent you will never recover them." He was said to be holding them against their will, because he had recently discovered a rich source of copper and needed the English expertise to help him forge it into utensils and weapons.

It was unfortunate that by the time Gates arrived in Jamestown, he was not in a position to go searching for the lost colonists. His ship had been wrecked in Bermuda and he landed at the settlement to find a pitiful band of half-starved men. Not only were the lost colonists left to their fate, but Jamestown itself was abandoned.

The diligent Strachey continued to hunt for more information about these survivors, with some success. He was assured by an amicable Indian, Machumps, that the rumours were true and that proof was to be found in the half-timbered and gabled dwellings built by the Indians, "so taught them by those English who escaped the slaughter." He said that the four survivors held captive by Gepanocon were not the only ones to have escaped the bloody massacre. "At Ritanoe," he said, "the *weroance* Eyanoco preserved seven of the English alive, fower men, twoo boys and one young maid, who escaped and fled up the river of Choanoke, to beat his copper, of which he hath certayn mynes at the said Ritanoe."

Although news of their survival had been confirmed by several different sources, there were few efforts made to recover the lost colonists in the years between 1609 and 1611. The tribes holding them hostage were too powerful, and the colonists in Jamestown were themselves in a desperate plight, stricken with famine and warfare. There was a renewed opportunity to resume the search under the regime of Sir Thomas Dale, but Dale was an unsentimental man who showed little interest in discovering the fate of John White's colonists. Besides, by 1612, the Jamestown settlers had learned a great deal about their surrounding landscape and the new colony was beginning to find its feet. There was no longer a pressing need to locate the survivors from 1587.

Nor was there any search along the Outer Banks for the small party of colonists who were believed to have settled on Croatoan, presumably with Lord Manteo. No ships visited these desolate shores for many years. Their story remained a mystery for almost a century—a band of missing adventurers who seemed to have vanished without trace, along with the three colonists and several hundred slaves left behind by Drake and the troops left on Roanoke by Grenville. Although there was an attempt to look for them in 1619, the search parties returned with little new information. In 1622, John Smith put what seemed to be a full stop to the story when he wrote that after thirty-five years, "we left seeking our colony, that was never any of them found, nor seen to this day."

These were almost the final words. But the tale of the lost colonists was to have an intriguing and thrilling postscript. In the year 1701, a sober-minded surveyor of the Carolinas, John Lawson, edged his ship towards the Outer Banks and dropped anchor at Croatoan Island. As he trudged across the sand dunes to the little settlement where Manteo had been born more than a century earlier, he was astonished to find himself greeted by a band of Indians who looked quite unlike any other tribe that inhabited this stretch of coastline. Their skin was pale and their hair was light brown. A curious Lawson struck up a conversation with the amiable elders, only to be told that "several of their ancestors were white people and could talk in a book [read] as we do, the truth of which is confirmed by gray eyes being found frequently amongst these Indians and no others." He added that "they value themselves extremely for their affinity to the English, and are ready to do them all friendly offices." After a lengthy investigation into the history of their tribe, Lawson, a skeptical individual, nevertheless concluded that "the English were forced to cohabit with them for relief and conversation and that in the process of time they conformed themselves to the manners of their Indian relations."

It was a remarkable discovery, for it revealed that the small group of White's colonists who had ensconced themselves on Croatoan had also survived their long years of abandonment. Isolated, helpless, and utterly dependent on Manteo's kinsmen, they had eventually tired of gazing forlornly at the horizon, hoping for a glimpse of the flag of St. George. England's promise of a relief ship had proved hollow, and these men realised that they were doomed to see out their days on a remote and desolate spit of sand—far from their families and loved ones. Abandoned by the Old World, they eventually sought solace in the New—seeking comfort with the Indians and forging ever closer ties until the idea of intermarriage was no longer as shocking as it must have seemed all those years before. Here, on Croatoan Island, the first fruits of their union were born—the mixed-blood descendants of Ralegh's failed experiment. Deprived of contact with England for almost a century, these children grew up knowing only that their fathers had come from a strange and faraway land.

Lawson's discovery was the final word on the lost colony. It was a haunting end to the story, and one that still echoes to this day on the wild, windswept Outer Banks. When, in 1998, an Elizabethan gold signet ring was unearthed in the sandy soil close to the site of Manteo's village, there was great excitement in the local community. Four centuries after John White's family and colonists set sail, a new generation of Americans remains captivated by the ghosts of Sir Walter Ralegh's brave, foolhardy, and ultimately doomed settlers.

Ralegh himself kept the lost colonists in his thoughts and prayers until his dying day. After a disastrous expedition to Guiana, in which his soldiers broke King James's express command to avoid conflict with the Spanish, Sir Walter limped home to face his execution. As he prepared to lay his head on the block on that grim October day in 1618, he positioned himself so that he was facing west, towards America, instead of the customary east. When an onlooker asked if he would not prefer to lie in the direction of the promised land, he gave a wry smile. "So the heart be right," he said, "it is not matter which way the head lieth."

A few seconds later, the executioner's axe sliced through the chill air and Ralegh's silver-haired head fell to the ground. It was held up to the crowd, but the axeman refused to utter the traditional words: "Behold, the head of a traitor." Instead, one of the onlookers called out a more appropriate epitaph: "We have not another such head to be cut off."

Fifteen years after the death of the Virgin Queen, and more than three decades after Manteo was first introduced to the court, the Elizabethan age had finally come to an end. It was Sir Walter Ralegh who had made possible its lasting and crowning achievement: the establishment of England's first permanent settlement on the far side of the Atlantic. It was the dawning of modern America.

BIBLIOGRAPHY

Elizabethan spelling has been retained for quotations wherever possible, but in a few instances only a modern transcription of the original text was available. Grammar and names have been standardised, and certain spellings have occasionally been adjusted to clarify the sense (e.g., *there* or *theyre* has been changed where appropriate to *their*).

Writings from the Sixteenth and Seventeenth Centuries

Aubrey, John. *Brief Lives*. 2 vols. Ed. Andrew Clark. Oxford, 1898.

Barbour, Philip L., ed. *The Complete Works of Captain John Smith*. 3 vols. University of North Carolina Press, 1986.
The Jamestown Voyages under the First Charter, 1606–9. 2 vols. Hakluyt Society, London, 1969.

Brown, Alexander. *The Genesis of the United States*. 2 vols. New York, 1890.

Bulow, G. von. "Journey through England and Scotland made by Lupold von Wedel in the years 1584 and 1585." *Transactions of the Royal Historical Society*, 2d series, vol. 9, 1895.

Calendar of State Papers, domestic, 1581–90, 1865; *Addenda, 1580–1655*, 1872; *colonial, America and West Indies, 1574–1660*, 1860; *Addenda, 1574–1674*, 1894.

Camden, William. *Remains Concerning Britain*. Toronto, 1984.

C[hute], A[nthony]. *Tabaco. The distinct and several opinions of the late and best phisitions that have written of the diverse natures and qualities thereof.* Printed by Adam Islip, 1595.

Elyot, Sir Thomas. *The castel of helth*. London, 1541.

Everaerts, Gilles. *Panacea; or the universal medicine: being a discovery of the . . . vertues of Tobacco*. 1659. Originally published in 1587 under the title *De herba Panacea, quam alii Tabacum, alii Petum aut Nicotianam vocant . . . brevis commentariolus.* Antwerp.

Frende, Gabriell, Practitioner in Astrologie and Phisicke. *An Almanacke and Prognostication for the yeere . . . 1585.* Watkins and Roberts, 1585.

Fuller, Thomas. *Worthies.* London, 1663.

Gilbert, Sir Humphrey. *Queen Elizabeth's Academy.* E.E.T.S., London, 1869. *The Voyages and Colonising Enterprises of Sir Humphrey Gilbert.* 2 vols. Ed. D. B. Quinn. Hakluyt Society, 2d series, vols. 83–84. London, 1940.

Greepe, Thomas. *The true and perfecte newes of the woorthy and valiaunt exploytes performed and doone by that valiant knight Syr Frauncis Drake.* 1587.

Hakluyt, Richard. *Divers Voyages.* Hakluyt Society, London, 1850. *The Principall Navigations, Voiages and Discoveries of the English Nation.* 1589. Reprinted in 1903–5 by Hakluyt Society in 12 vols.

Hamor, Ralphe. *A True Discourse of the Present Estate of Virginia.* 1616. Reprinted in the series *Theatrum Orbis Terrarum.* Da Capo Press, Amsterdam, 1971.

Harcourt, Robert. *A Relation of a Voyage to Guiana.* Hakluyt Society, London, 1928. (Originally published in 1613.)

Harriot, Thomas. *A Briefe and True Report of the New Found Land of Virginia.* New York, 1972. (A facsimile of vol. 1 of Theodor de Bry's 1590 English-language edition of *America,* published in Frankfurt.)

Harvey, John, Master of Artes and Student in Phisicke. *An almanacke or annuall calendar, with a prognostication for . . . 1585.* Watkins and Roberts, 1585.

Hilliard, Nicholas. *A Treatise Concerning the Arte of Limning.* 1598. Walpole Society, Oxford, 1912.

Holinshed, Raphaell. *Chronicles of England, Scotland, Ireland.* London, 1577.

Hulton, P., and Quinn, David B. *The American Drawings of John White.* Chapel Hill, N.C., 1964.

"Humfray Gylbert, knight, his charte." *Geographical Journal,* vol. 72, 1928.

James I. *A Treatise on Scottis Poesie; A Counterblaste to Tobacco.* Reprinted in *A Royal Rhetorician.* Ed. Robert S. Rait. 1900. (Original published in London in 1604.)

Keeler, Mary F., ed. *Sir Francis Drake's West Indian Voyage, 1585–86.* Hakluyt Society, London, 1981.

Las Casas, Bartolomé de. *The Spanishe Colonie.* Translated by M.M.S. W. Brome, London, 1583.

Laudonnière, René de. *A notable historie containing foure voyages made by certayne French captaynes unto Florida.* Translated by Richard Hakluyt. T. Dawson, 1587.

Lawson, John. *A New Voyage to Carolina.* London, 1709.

Lloyd, Euan, Student in Astronomie. *An Almanacke and Prognostication for . . . 1585. Wherein is . . . set forth the disposition of the ayre with other accidents that are like to happen this yeere.* Watkins and Roberts, 1585.

Marbecke, Roger. *Defence of Tabacco.* London, 1602.

Monades, Nicholas. *Joyfull Newes out of the Newe Founde Worlde.* 1577.

Moore, Philip. *A Fortie Yeres Almanacke . . . untill 1606.* London, 1570.

Naunton, Sir Robert. *Fragmenta regalia.* Ed. E. Arber. London, 1870. (A reprint of the posthumous edition of 1653.)

Percy, George. "Trewe Relacyon." *Tyler's Quarterly Historical and Genealogical Magazine,* vol. 3, 1922.

Platter, Thomas. *Thomas Platter's Travels in England.* London, 1599.

Porter, Thomas, Chirurgian. *An Almanacke or Prognostication for the Yeere of Christe, MDLXXXV.* Watkins and Roberts, 1585.

Purchas, Samuel. *Hakluytus posthumus or Purchas his pilgrimes.* 4 vols. 1625. Reprinted in 20 vols., Hakluyt Society, extra series, Glasgow, 1905–7. *Purchas his Pilgrimmage, or Relations of the World and the Religions.* London, 1613.

Quinn, David B. *New American World: A Documentary History of North America to 1612.* 5 vols. New York, 1979.
The New Found Land of Stephen Parmenius. Toronto, 1972.
The Roanoke Voyages, 1584–1590. 2 vols. Hakluyt Society, London, 1955.

Ralegh, Sir Walter. *The Discoverie of the large and bewtiful Empire of Guiana.* Ed. V. T. Harlow. London, 1928.
The Last Fight of the Revenge. Ed. E. Arber. London, 1886.
Poems. Ed. A. M. C. Latham. London, 1951.
Works. 8 vols. Oxford, 1829.

Smythe, Sir John. *Certain discourses . . . concerning the formes and effects of divers sorts of weapons.* London, 1590.

Stowe, John. *Survay of London.* London, 1598.

Strachey, William. *The Historie of Travaile into Virginia Britannia.* 1612. Hakluyt Society, London, 1849/1953.

Taylor, E. G. R. *The Writings and Correspondence of the two Richard Hakluyts.* 2 vols. Hakluyt Society, vols. 76–77, London, 1935.

Williamson, J. A. *The Cabot Voyages and Bristol Discovery Under Henry VIII.* Hakluyt Society, London, 1962.

Wright, I. A. *Further English Voyages to Spanish America.* Hakluyt Society, London, 1973.

Reference Works

Adams, R. G. "An Attempt to Identify John White." *American Historical Review,* vol. 41, 1935–36.

Adamson, J. H., and Folland, H. F. *Shepherd of the Ocean.* London, 1969.

Andrews, K. R. "Christopher Newport of Limehouse, Mariner." *William and Mary Quarterly,* 3d series, vol. 2, 1954.

Elizabethan Privateering. Cambridge, 1964.

"The Elizabethan Seamen." *Mariner's Mirror,* vol. 68, 1982.

Barbour, P. *Pocahontas and her World.* London, 1971.

The Three Worlds of Captain John Smith. Boston, 1964.

Batho, G. R. "Thomas Harriot and the Northumberland Household." *Durham Thomas Harriot Seminar,* no. 1, 1992.

Bevan, Bryan. *King James.* London, 1996.

Camden, Carroll. *The Elizabethan Woman.* London, 1952.

Coote, Stephen. *A Play of Passion: The Life of Sir Walter Ralegh.* London, 1993.

Corbett, Julian S. *Drake and the Tudor Navy.* 2 vols. London, 1899.

ed. "Papers relating to the navy in the Spanish war, 1586–7." *Navy Records Society,* vol. 11, 1898.

Cumming, W. P. "The Identity of John White, Governor of Virginia, and John White the Artist." *North Carolina Historical Review,* vol. 15, 1938.

Durant, David N. *Ralegh's Lost Colony.* London, 1981.

Edwards, Edward. *The Life of Sir Walter Ralegh.* 2 vols. London, 1868.

Forbes, Thomas Roger. *Chronicle from Aldgate.* New Haven and London, 1971.

Greaves, Richard L. *Society and Religion in Elizabethan England.* Minneapolis, 1981.

Greenblatt, S., ed. *New World Encounters.* University of California Press, 1993.

Humber, John L. *Backgrounds and Preparations for the Roanoke Voyages, 1584–1590.* North Carolina Dept. of Cultural Resources, 1986.

Hume, Ivor Noel. *From Roanoke to Jamestown.* New York, 1994.

Roanoke Island: America's First Science Center. 1994. (First published in the Spring 1994 issue of *Colonial Williamsburg,* the journal of the Colonial Williamsburg Foundation.)

Hume, M. A. S. *Sir Walter Raleigh.* London, 1847.

Kane, Robert J. "Anthony Chute, Thomas Nashe and the First English Work on Tobacco." *Review of English Studies,* vol. 7, 1931.

Kelso, William M. (and others). *Jamestown Rediscovery.* 5 vols. Association for the Preservation of Virginia Antiquities, 1995–99

Lacey, Robert. *Sir Walter Ralegh.* London, 1973.

Lewis, Clifford M., and Loomie, Albert J. *The Spanish Jesuit Mission in Virginia, 1570–72.* Chapel Hill, N.C., 1953.

Manning, C. "Sassafras and Syphilis." *New England Quarterly,* vol. 9, 1936.

Mattingly, G. *Defeat of the Spanish Armada.* London, 1959.

Merriman, R. B. *The Rise of the Spanish Empire.* 4 vols. New York, 1934.

Miller, Helen Hill. *Passage to America.* North Carolina Dept. of Cultural Resources, 1983.

Neale, J. E. *Queen Elizabeth.* London, 1934.

Nichols, John. *The Progresses and Public Processions of Queen Elizabeth.* 3 vols. London, 1788.

Pearson, L. E. *Elizabethans at Home.* Stanford, 1957.

Powell, William S. "Roanoke Colonists and Explorers: An Attempt at Identification." *North Carolina Historical Review,* vol. 34, 1957.

Quinn, David B. "Christopher Newport in 1590." *North Carolina Review,* vol. 29, 1952.

England and the Discovery of America, 1481–1620. London, 1974.

European Approaches to North America, 1450–1640. Aldershot, 1998.

The Failure of Raleigh's American Colonies. London, 1949.

The Lost Colonists: Their Fortune and Probable Fate. North Carolina Dept. of Cultural Resources, 1984.

"Preparations for the 1585 Virginia Voyage." *William and Mary Quarterly,* vol. 6, 1949.

Set Fair for Roanoke. Chapel Hill and London, 1985.

"Some Spanish Reactions to Elizabethan Colonial Enterprises." *Transactions of the Royal Historical Society,* 5th series, vol. 1, 1951.

"Thomas Harriot and the Problem of America." The 1990 Thomas Harriot Lecture. Published in 1992.

"Thomas Harriot and the Virginia Voyages of 1602." *William and Mary Quarterly,* 3d series, vol. 27, 1970.

"Virginians on the Thames in 1603." *Terra Incognitae,* vol. 2, 1970.

Roanoke Colonies Research Newsletter, vols. 3–6, Greenville, N.C., 1996–99.

Rowse, A. L. *The Elizabethans and America.* London, 1959.

Sir Richard Grenville of the Revenge. London, 1937.

Salmon, Vivian. "Thomas Harriot and the English Origins of Algonkian Linguistics." *Durham Thomas Harriot Seminar,* no. 8, 1993.

Shirley, John W. *The Scientific Experiments of Sir Walter Ralegh, the Wizard Earl and the Three Magi in the Tower, 1603–17.* Ambix, 1949.

Sir Walter Ralegh and the New World. North Carolina Dept. of Cultural Resources, 1985.

Thomas Harriot: A Biography. Oxford, 1983.

Stick, David. *Roanoke Island: The Beginnings of English America.* Chapel Hill, N.C., 1983.

Strathmann, Ernest A. *Sir Walter Ralegh: A Study in Elizabethan Skepticism.* New York, 1951.

Strong, Roy. *The Cult of Elizabeth.* London, 1977.

Taylor, E. G. R. "Instructions to a Colonial Surveyor in 1582." *Mariner's Mirror,* vol. 37, 1951.

"Master Hore's Voyage of 1536." *Geographical Journal,* vol. 77, 1931.

Trigger, Bruce G., ed. *The Northeast.* Vol. 15 of *Handbooks of the Indians of North America.* Gen. ed., William C. Sturtevant. Washington, D.C., 1978.

Unwin, Rayner S. *The Defeat of John Hawkins.* London, 1960.

Weir, Alison. *Elizabeth the Queen.* London, 1998.

Willard, M. Wallace. *Sir Walter Raleigh.* 1959.

Williams, Neville. *Elizabeth, Queen of England.* London, 1967.

Williams, Norman Lloyd. *Sir Walter Raleigh*. London, 1962.
Williamson, J. A. *Age of Drake*. London, 1938.
Willson, D. Harris. *King James VI and I*. London, 1956.
Winton, John. *Sir Walter Ralegh*. London, 1975.
Wright, I. A. "Spanish Policy towards Virginia, 1606–12." *American Historical Review*, 1920.
Youings, Joyce. *Ralegh's Country*. North Carolina Dept. of Cultural Resources, 1986.

INDEX

Abbot, George, 246
Agincourt, Battle of, 38
Algonkian language, 66–68, 118, 287, 288
Algonquins, 58
Alikock, Jerome, 269
Amadas, Philip, 45, 52–53, 55–57, 60, 81, 96, 106, 110
Angulo, Captain Rengifo de, 94–95
Anna, Queen of England, 323–24, 326
Aquascogoc (Indian village), 106, 195
Argall, Samuel, 310–13
Arundell, Captain John, 110
Asbie, John, 269
Assehurst, Thomas, 6
Aubrey, John, 45, 307

Babington, Anthony, 171
Bagot, Anthony, 203
Bark Bonner (ship), 150
Barlowe, Arthur, 53–54, 61, 68–69, 82, 96; friendship of Ralegh and, 45, 52, 53; Indians and, 56, 57, 59, 60, 62, 110
Baylye, Roger, 180

Bennett, Mark, 186
Berde, William, 186
Betts, Robert E., 333
Bevis, Thomas, 232
Brave (ship), 221
Brocke, John, 116
Brown, Richard, 21
Brown, William, 186
Browne, Edward, 269
Browne, Maurice, 16, 19, 23, 28, 32
Bruster, William, 269
Bry, Theodor de, 179
Buck, Richard, 317
Burghley, Lord, 200
Butler, Michael, 45
Buts, Thomas, 9, 10, 15
Buts, William, 9, 15

Cabot, John, 6
Camden, William, 21, 250
Carew, Robert, 202
Carleill, Christopher, 144–45, 147
Cassen, George, 273–74
Catholicism, 39, 86–87, 146, 171, 281

Cavendish, Thomas, 82, 92, 94, 102
Cecil, Robert, 243, 244, 254, 256, 259, 326
Champernowne, Katherine, 38
Chancerie, 9
Chesapeake tribe, 334, 336–37, 339
Chickahominy tribe, 302, 319
Church of England, 29
Clarke, John, 82, 94
Clement, William, 186
Cocke, Captain, 228–32, 236, 237
Coffin, Master, 170–71, 173, 175, 183, 191, 193–98, 205, 332
Coleman, Robert, 232
Columbus, Christopher, 6, 79
Constable, Marmaduke, 114
Cooper, Christopher, 180, 213
Cope, Walter, 255–56
Cornhill Magazine, 333
Council of the Indies, Spanish, 134, 227
Cox, Master, 32
Critz, John de, 327

Dale, Thomas, 304–6, 309–12, 314–22, 342
Dare, Ananias, 180, 235, 245–46
Dare, Eleanor, 180, 181, 187, 212, 214, 215, 228, 234–36, 238, 332
Dare, Virginia, 212, 214, 215, 228, 234, 236, 238, 287–88, 340
Dasamongueponke (Indian village), 195
Davis, Captain, 303
Dawbeny, Oliver, 11–14
De La Warr, Thomas West, Lord, 294, 300–6
Delight (ship), 26, 30, 32, 37
Dethick, William, 182
Discovery (ship), 261
Dorothy (ship), 82, 101
Drake, Bernard, 133–34

Drake, Francis, 133, 140–54, 193, 342; circumnavigation of globe by, 82, 143; in defence of England against Spanish Armada, 220; evacuation of Lane's colonists by, 152–54, 170, 186, 331; at Roanoke, 140, 149–51; sacking of Santo Domingo by, 143–47
Dudley, Robert, 40

Eastward Hoe (play), 256–57, 340
Elizabeth (ship), 82, 92–94, 96, 97
Elizabeth I, Queen of England, 152, 166, 246–47, 259, 331; Babington's estates granted to Ralegh by, 171; and Barlowe's expedition, 54; and conflict with Spain, 85, 131, 133–34, 142, 147, 219, 220, 223, 224; death of, 250–51, 344; Drake and, 142, 144; Essex and, 203–4, 241; 1587 progress of, 200–2; and Gilbert's expedition, 5, 16, 26, 28; Grenville's arrival at Roanoke reported to, 110, 112; Hakluyt's treatise on colonisation for, 71–72; impressment authority granted to Ralegh by, 88; Indians and, 63–64, 126, 128, 183, 210, 284; monument in Westminster Abbey to, 327; Ralegh as favourite of, 39–43, 64, 65, 71, 198–99; Ralegh in disgrace with, 241–45; Ralegh knighted by, 72–73; ship and gunpowder provided to Ralegh by, 76, 82, 260; transferral of Gilbert's grant to Ralegh by, 44–45, 51; Virginia named in honour of, 72, 146
Elizabeth Bonaventure (ship), 152, 153

Elyot, Hugh, 6
Elyot, Thomas, 162
Emry, Thomas, 274, 275
Ensenor, 126, 135
Eskimos, 178
Essex, Robert Devereux, Earl of,
    203–4, 241
Eyanoco, 342

Facy, Captain Arthur, 220, 221
Falcon (ship), 17
Fernandez, Simon, 81, 94, 96–98,
    180, 216, 227, 239; treachery
    against White by, 189, 191–93,
    212–13, 217
Fever, John, 116
Flowre, George, 269
Francis (ship), 149, 150
Frobisher, Martin, 178
Fuller, Thomas, 39
Fullwood, William, 180

Galthrope, Stephen, 269
Ganz, Joachim, 116, 156
Gates, Thomas, 294, 297–99, 341
Gentleman Pensioners, 251, 252
Gepanocon, 341, 342
Gerard, John, 246
Gerard, Thomas, 25
Gilbert, Adrian, 38
Gilbert, Captain Bartholemew, 247
Gilbert, Humfrey, 6, 7, 16–30,
    32–36, 38, 39, 71, 82; abortive
    1578 expedition of, 5, 17–18; death
    of, 34, 80; financing scheme of,
    24–25; Indians and, 25–26; and
    Ingrams's account of American
    trek, 20–23; loss of flagship of,
    32–33; map of North America
    acquired by, 5–6, 16, 19;
    transferral to Ralegh of American

grant of, 44–45, 51; voyage to
    America of, 26–28
Gilbert, John, 37, 38
Gilbert, Otho, 38
Glande, Darby, 114, 187
Glane, Elizabeth, 187
Godspeed (ship), 261
Golden Royal (ship), 133
Gonzalez, Vicente, 226, 227
Gosnold, Bartholomew, 269
Gostigo, John, 114
Gower, Thomas, 269
Granganimeo, 56, 58–59, 110
Great Fire of London (1666), 67,
    328
Grenville, Richard, 79–82, 84,
    101–3, 110, 113, 131, 140, 173,
    175, 180, 259, 276; death of, 240;
    Drake and, 220; financial support
    of Ralegh by, 76; first voyage to
    America of, 88–91; Indians and,
    106, 107, 110, 171, 283; loss of
    supplies by, 98–101; return to
    Roanoke of, 169–71, 186, 331–32,
    342; Spanish and, 85, 91–96,
    129–31, 141–42, 239–40
Grey, Lord, 39
Grocer's Company, 118
Gunpowder Plot, 281

Hakluyt, Richard, 10, 50, 87, 167,
    237, 260–62; advice on
    requirements for colony provided
    by, 77–78, 82–83; on expenditures
    for 1587 colony, 245; and Lane's
    return to England, 154–55; treatise
    encouraging royal financing of
    colony written by, 71–72; vision of
    colonisation of, 175
Hamor, Ralph, 305, 308, 315–17, 319
Hance (surgeon), 232
Harcourt, Robert, 309

Harriot, Thomas, 45–48, 72, 175, 177, 211, 240, 260, 264, 328, 337; account of experiences in America by, 157–60, 166, 167, 174, 270, 275; dietary recommendations of, 160, 162; eclipse of sun noted by, 89; encounters with Indians described by, 55, 104, 107, 117–18, 166, 262, 263; evacuated from Roanoke by Drake, 152, 153; exploration and mapping by White and, 120–21, 123, 176, 179, 288, 339; on Grenville's expedition to Pamlico Sound, 102; in Lane's colony, 113–15, 136, 140; Manteo and, 66–70, 82; navigation classes taught by, 47, 49, 51–52; in old age, 327, 331; Percy and, 282; during Ralegh's imprisonment in Tower, 259; and search for lost colonists, 247, 255, 256; tobacco production encouraged by, 163–64, 307; White's illustrations for writings of, 179
Hart, John, 66–67
Harvey, Dyonise, 180
Harvey, Thomas, 118, 120, 157
Harvie, Margery, 187
Hatton, Christopher, 40, 142
Hawkins, John, 20–21, 86, 164, 244
Hawkins, William, 8
Hayes, Edward, 27, 30, 33, 34, 36
Henry, Prince, 326
Henry VIII, King, 8–9, 15, 74
Hewet, Thomas, 186
Hilliard, Nicholas, 178, 327
Hopewell (ship), 228, 236–37
Hore, Richard, 7–9, 12–15, 31, 50–51
Howard, Lord Henry, 240, 254
Howe, George, 180, 206, 208–10
Hynde, John, 186

Iapassus, Chief, 310, 311
Ingrams, Davy, 20–24, 35, 49, 56, 86, 158
Innes of Court, 9
Inquisition, 87, 89

James I, King of England, 251–53, 259, 264, 266, 308, 319, 344; coronation of, 286; and lost colonists, 256, 257; and Pocahontas's visit to England, 323, 324; Powhatan as vassal king of, 284, 287, 291, 301, 326, 339; and Ralegh's trial and imprisonment, 257, 258, 281; tobacco use abhorred by, 252, 254, 307; Virginia Company and, 260, 283, 294
Jesuits, 268
Jews, 45
Johnson, Robert, 284
Jonson, Ben, 324

Kelbourne, Edward, 232
Kelly, Edward, 114, 232
Kendall, Abraham, 114
Keymes, Laurence, 45
King, John, 322
Knollys, Lettice, 40

Lane, Ralph, 81, 118, 129, 133, 157, 159, 176, 177, 180, 184, 194, 227, 259, 264, 265, 283, 284, 328; account of experiences in America by, 179, 260, 262, 270–71; in Caribbean, 91, 94, 141; departure from Roanoke of, 147–53, 168–70, 331; expedition up Roanoke River of, 123–25, 134, 288; exploration and mapping by Harriot and White for, 120–21; on financial realities of colonisation, 306–7; as governor of Roanoke colony, 112–15; on Grenville's expedition to Pamlico Sound, 102; and grounding of *Tiger*, 97, 239; Manteo as catalyst for colony of, 182; return to England of, 154–56; Stafford and, 188; tobacco use by, 165; weaponry left on Roanoke by, 235; Wingina and, 117, 122, 125–26, 135–40, 158, 207–9

Las Casas, Bartolomé de, 49–50

Lassie, James, 186

Lawrence, Margaret, 187

Lawson, John, 343–44

Leicester, Robert Dudley, Earl of, 142

Lion (ship), 82, 101, 188–93, 213, 216, 217

Lloyd, Euan, 74–75

Luttrell, John, 15

Mace, Captain Samuel, 247, 249, 255, 256, 334

Machumps, 341

Madre de Dios (ship), 243

Mangoak tribe, 289

Mannering, Jane, 187

Manteo, 61, 76, 88, 93, 99, 157, 158, 284, 292; arrival in England of, 62, 63, 321, 327; baptism of, 192, 210–12; on Grenville's Pamlico Sound expedition, 102, 103, 106; Harriot and, 66–70, 82; Harvey and, 118; and Lane's colony, 120, 123, 124, 135, 137, 139, 151; and lost colonists, 235, 236, 333, 342–44; meeting with Granganimeo arranged by, 110; named Lord of Roanoke by Ralegh, 182–83, 210; and White's colony, 194–95, 197, 207–10

Marbecke, Roger, 307

Martine, John, 269

Mary Rose (ship), 80

Masque of Christmas (Jonson), 324

Maximilian, Holy Roman Emperor, 80

McMillan, Hamilton, 332

Menatonon, 122–23, 126

Mendoza, Bernadino de, 85, 86, 142

Monades, Nicholas, 164–65

Monkie (ship), 218

Montgomerie, Compte de, 39

Moonlight (ship), 228

Mouslie, Thomas, 269

Namantack, 286

Newport, Captain Christopher, 261, 263–65, 268, 269, 279, 282; and crowning of Powhatan as vassal king, 284–87; Dale and, 304; and fate of lost colonists, 289, 334–37; first contact between Indians and, 265, 266; first women colonists brought to Jamestown by, 290

New Year's Gift (ship), 146

Nicholes, William, 186

Nicholls, John, 180

Northumberland, Earl of, 269, 281–82, 295, 327–28

Nugent, Edward, 114, 140

Ogle, Thomas, 142–43

Okisko, 128, 284

Opachisco, 317

Opechancanough, 318

Ovalle, Cristobal de, 144

Oxford University, 45–47, 114

Painter-Stainers company, 178

Parliament, 68, 114, 118, 259, 281

Pasapegh, Chief, 271
Paspahegh tribe, 288, 302–3
Payne, Rose, 187
Peckham, George, 25, 37, 55, 158
Pennington, Robert, 269
Percy, George, 265, 269, 271,
    281–82, 295, 297, 302–3, 334
Philip II, King of Spain, 72, 76, 85, 91,
    134, 225–26, 240; attack on England
    attempted by, 219, 224; Drake's
    mission against, 142, 143, 146;
    Inquisition established in America
    by, 86–87; seizure of English grain
    ships plotted by, 131–33
Philips, Miles, 86–88
Piggase, Drue, 269
Plat, James, 180
Pocahontas, 280, 285, 292–93,
    310–19, 321–28, 338
Pomeioc (Indian village), 103–5, 107
Popham, John, 258, 259
Porter, Thomas, 74
Potomac tribe, 311
Powell, Nathaniel, 289
Powhatan, 265–66, 268, 272–75, 288,
    310, 321, 323, 326, 339; crowned
    vassal king of James I, 284–87,
    301–2; Dale and, 305, 306, 311,
    312, 314–18; and fate of lost
    colonists, 335–38, 340, 341; food
    supplies refused to colonists by,
    290–93, 295–96; and Rolfe's
    marriage to Pocahontas, 316–18;
    Smith as captive of, 275, 278–82
Pratt, Roger, 180
Primrose (ship), 132–33
Privy Council, 199, 255, 326
Pugh, Hugh, 42
Purchas, Samuel, 322, 323

Ralegh, Carew, 39
Ralegh, Damerei, 242, 259

Ralegh, Walter, 10, 18, 87, 123, 133,
    153, 157, 163, 164, 192, 264, 269,
    309, 323, 330; during Armada
    campaign, 220, 222–24;
    Babington's estates bestowed on,
    171–72; background of, 38–39; as
    Captain of the Guard, 199–201,
    246; Chesapeake Bay considered as
    colony site by, 175–77; courtiers'
    attitude towards, 201–3; in
    disgrace, 241–45; Drake's aid to
    colonists of, 140, 142, 147, 148;
    and Elizabeth's death, 250–51; as
    Elizabeth's favourite, 39–43, 64,
    65, 71, 198–99; Essex as competitor
    for Elizabeth's affections with,
    203–4; and establishment of first
    Roanoke settlement, 101, 102, 112,
    131; expenditures for colonial
    ventures of, 225; and Gilbert's
    expedition, 23–25, 27, 38; Harriot's
    friendship with, 45–47;
    impressment powers granted to, 88;
    imprisonment in Tower of, 243–45,
    255, 258–59, 281, 283, 295,
    326–27; Indians and, 49–51, 61,
    63, 68, 70, 103, 128, 268, 298, 303,
    312, 316, 321, 327–28; James I's
    antipathy towards, 252, 254;
    knighting of, 72–73; and Lane's
    return to England, 155, 156; lost
    colonists of, 245–49, 256, 287, 289,
    301, 333, 341, 343–44; Manteo
    made Lord of Roanoke by, 182–83,
    210; marriage of, 240–43; in old
    age, 331; preparations for first
    colonial undertaking of, 75–79;
    reconnaissance mission for, 52–54,
    58, 60; recruiting of colonists by,
    185–86; selection of first expedition
    leaders by, 79, 81–82, 122; Spanish
    hostility to colonisation activities of,
    85–86, 134, 146–47, 225–26;

supply ship sent to Roanoke by,
  168–69; and tobacco use, 163, 164,
  166–68, 254, 307; transferral of
  Gilbert's American grant to, 44–45,
  51; treason charges against, 254–55,
  257–58; Virginia Company and,
  260, 282–84, 310; White chosen as
  leader of second colony by,
  177–80; and White's rescue
  mission, 228, 238; and White's
  return to England, 213–15, 218–20
Ralegh, Wat, 41, 258
Rastell, John, 7
Ratcliffe, Captain John, 270, 295–96
Raymond, George, 82, 101
Revenge (ship), 240
Robinson, Jehu, 274, 275
Roe (ship), 221
Roebuck (ship), 82, 94, 101, 113
Rolfe, John, 308–9, 315–19, 328–30
Rolfe, Thomas, 321
Rowse, Anthony, 114
Russell, Master, 291

Salisbury, Lord, 305
Sampson, John, 180
Sanderson, William, 77
Santa Cruz, Marques de, 142
Santa Maria (ship), 129–31
Sare, Richard, 116
Sea Venture (ship), 294, 308
Secotan (Indian village), 106–7, 111,
  195
Shortridge, Jeffrey, 296
Sicklemore, Lieutenant Michael,
  289, 295
Sidney, Philip, 25, 40, 204
Skinner, Ralph, 231, 232
Smith, Captain John, 263–64, 267,
  269–82, 290–92, 321, 326;
  captured by Indians, 275–78; and
  crowning of Powhatan as vassal

king, 285–87; and fate of lost
  colonists, 288–89, 335–38, 340,
  342; Pocahontas and, 280, 292–93,
  323; as president of Jamestown
  colony, 284–85, 294–95, 298
Smythe, Thomas, 16, 23
Southampton, Lord, 259
Spanish Armada, 219, 220, 222–24,
  239
Sparkes, Master, 315
Spendlove, John, 186
Spicer, Captain Edward, 216, 218,
  229–32
Squirrel (ship), 33, 34
Stafford, Captain Edward, 114, 135,
  140, 148–49, 188, 208
Steevens, Thomas, 180
Stowe, John, 251
Strachey, William, 338–41
Susan Constant (ship), 261
Swallow (ship), 28

Talbot (ship), 142
Tappan, Audry, 187
Tarleton (jester), 198–99
Thomas, John, 6
Throckmorton, Arthur, 241, 242
Throckmorton, Bess, 241–43, 245,
  255, 258
Tiger (ship), 76, 82, 83, 85, 88–93,
  95–98, 100, 103, 106, 107, 110,
  113, 120, 129–31, 180, 239
Todhill, Anas, 289
Tomocomo, 321, 322, 324, 326
Topan, Thomas, 187
Tossantessas tribe, 319
Trinity (ship), 9–11, 15
Twide, Richard, 21

Vaughan, John, 114
Viccars, Ambrose, 187

Viccars, Elizabeth, 187
Virginia Company, 260–62, 294,
306, 328; establishment of, 260,
263; and fate of lost colonists, 338,
341; Indians and, 284, 287, 310,
321, 322; Ralegh's role in, 282–83;
tobacco profits of, 309

Wade, Armigil, 9
Wade, William, 9
Walsingham, Francis, 16, 21, 22, 24,
76, 131
Wanchese, 61–63, 66–68, 88, 99,
102, 103, 135
Warren, Joan, 187
Warwick, Earl of, 200
Waymouth, Captain George, 256,
257
Wedel, Lupold von, 63, 64
Weekes, Master, 9
Wenter, William, 184
White, John, 82, 118, 152, 153,
176–80, 182–94, 205–21, 224, 257,
260; appointed governor of
Roanoke by Ralegh, 177, 179–80;
background of, 177–78; birth of
granddaughter of, 212; coat of
arms designed for, 182; and
disappearance of Coffin's party,
193–94, 197, 205; exploration and

mapping by Harriot and, 120–21,
123, 176, 179, 288, 339;
Fernandez's treachery against, 189,
191–93, 212–13, 217; on
Grenville's expedition to Pamlico
Sound, 102, 104; London
merchants and, 225; lost colonists
of, 232–37, 245, 247, 255, 257,
262, 272, 276, 287, 289, 331–44;
paintings of Indians by, 109, 119;
recruitment of prospective
colonists by, 183–88; relations
between Indians and colony of,
206–12; rescue mission to Roanoke
of, 227–33, 261; return to England
of, 213–19
William (ship), 9–12
Williams, Roger, 112
Wingfield, Edward Maria, 263, 270
Wingina, Chief, 69, 110, 116–17,
119, 121–22, 125–26, 176, 207–9;
ambush planned by, 135–38; death
of, 139–41, 158; English assisted in
food production by, 128; interest in
colonists' religion of, 117–18
Wood, Agnes, 187
Wowinchopunk, Chief, 288
Wright, John, 186

Zuniga, Don Pedro de, 283

CLUES

I CLU ES 0640413 C

FEB   2005

970.0049 Milton, Giles.
MIL
        Big Chief Elizabeth.

$24.00

DATE		

Discarded by
Millville Public Library

MILLVILLE PUBLIC LIBRARY
210 BUCK ST
MILLVILLE NJ 08332

12/00

BAKER & TAYLOR